Third War
Irregular Warfare on the Western Border 1861-1865

James B. Martin, Ph.D.

Foreword

In 1979, the Combat Studies Institute published the first of the Leavenworth Papers. The series afforded the CGSC Faculty the opportunity to present their scholarship to the professional military community seeking to learn about contemporary and doctrinal issues from historical events. After an eight year hiatus I am excited to bring back the Leavenworth Papers series to once again contribute to our Army's education and leader development.

That first publication of the Leavenworth Papers examined the evolution of US Army tactical doctrine since World War II. The research offered historical insights to senior leaders and doctrine writers charged with refocusing the Army toward a possible conventional conflict with Warsaw Pact military forces. In the 25 years that followed, the Leavenworth Papers series grew to include 22 studies that addressed historical cases that were likewise of tactical, doctrinal, and organizational interest to the Army. The subjects of these studies varied but the authors were intent on making history relevant to military professionals engaged in thinking about current and future challenges.

This latest publication of the Leavenworth Papers marks the continuation of this storied series. Third War offers a lucid and well-researched analysis of irregular warfare during the American Civil War. Dr. Martin's focus on insurgent operations in the western border region brings fresh insights to this area of study. Moreover, the history of insurgency in these western states offers a greater understanding of irregular warfare to those who may be tasked with mounting counterinsurgency operations in the not so distant future.

CSI – The Past is Prologue!

Roderick M. Cox
Colonel, Field Artillery
Director, Combat Studies Institute

The cover illustration is a drawing by an unknown artist titled, "Main Street While Morgan Was Expected," ca. 1864; obtained from the Kentucky Historical Society, Frankfort, KY, May 2012.

Contents

Page

Preface vii

Introduction 1

Chapter 1. Kentucky 17

Chapter 2. Kansas-Missouri 47

Chapter 3. Indian Territory-Arkansas 67

Chapter 4. Texas 85

Chapter 5. The Impact of Irregular Warfare 101

Chapter 6. Epilogue 121

Glossary 131

Bibliography 135

Appendix A. General Orders No. 100 .... A-1

Appendix B. General Orders No. 11 .... B-1

Appendix C. General Orders No. 59 .... C-1

Maps

Map 1. Regional Area of Operations..2

Map 2. Kentucky Area of Operations..18

Map 3. Kansas Area of Operations..48

Map 4. Missouri Area of Operations...51

Map 5. Oklahoma Area of Operations...68

Map 6. Arkansas Area of Operations..78

Map 7. Texas Area of Operations..86

Preface

Like many students of history in the United States, I have always been enthralled by the American Civil War. This short period in American History has captured the imagination of Americans and spurred them to consume the many volumes written about this brother-against-brother conflict. Most of these volumes have dealt with the important battles of the war, which pitted massive armies from the North and South against each other in a struggle to determine whether the country would separate or stay together. These battles, highlighted by Gettysburg, Antietam, Vicksburg, Fredericksburg, and others too numerous to mention, were the predecessors of similar grand conflicts that would rack Europe and the world in the decades to follow. Arguably, for the first time in history, an entire nation mobilized to conduct a war that would eventually spill over and affect most of the population. From the gentlemanly preparation for the First Battle of Bull Run to the consuming power of Sherman's march to the sea, the American Civil War involved far more of the American population than war in Europe historically had involved.

Least understood of the effects on this population, and least studied, is the personal war conducted in the Border States, where the North met the South. The number of titles written on this irregular warfare is dwarfed in the literature of the Civil War, with most of the early volumes being markedly partisan. Most of these focused on the violence at the Kansas and Missouri border which, while the most deadly, was by no means the only irregular violence along a border. Every state on the western border, from the gulf coast of Texas to the hills of Appalachia in Kentucky, was consumed by a violence that filled every street and town. This violence was not the type found on the battlefield at Gettysburg, where hoards of men in blue or gray shot at each other from considerable distance, finally moving to close quarters combat. This was a war that flowed into every barnyard or town square, pitting men with strong beliefs supporting one side against individuals they believed to be their enemy. One historian pointed out that "guerrilla war normally arises in impassioned circumstances" and the irregular war in the American Civil War was no exception.*

The hatreds and feuds that stayed below the surface in a civilized society were freed by the all-consuming violence of this war, allowing men to act in ways that would have been unacceptable at any other time. While the Union officials, notably Henry Halleck, tried to establish rules of war to control this personal violence, they were markedly unsuccessful. Union authorities attempted to use these rules to combat the southern irregulars, but often chose to abide by them only selectively themselves. Murder, arson, and robbery became common occurrences along the border and the only excuse necessary for such actions was a suspicion that the victim supported the wrong side. Men who had lived as neighbors for many years, some even related to one another, now took up a cause that made them violent enemies.

The border war would eventually degrade to such a level that death was not enough punishment for supporting the wrong side. Both sides would turn to dismemberment and mutilation as expressions of the total loss of control in border society. Actions previously reserved to savages and uncivilized people would now become common as a part of the border violence. This breakdown in society may be a major reason this part of the war has been given inadequate attention over the years. Many historians of the American Civil War have avoided this dirty, ugly war; preferring to continue the glorification of its heroes and grand battles. They, like the Union officers in this study, can't bring themselves to lend legitimacy to the irregular warriors of the border. Through the Second World War, combat was for the most part still a relatively conventional event, with the rules being followed by the belligerents under a common agreement. Since that time, more and more conflicts throughout the world have been fought unconventionally, with the rules of war either watered down or totally ignored. The more common occurrence of this type of conflict has given it more credibility as a viable form of warfare and, as a consequence, sparked a growth in the study of irregular warfare through history. While the reality is that larger military nations continue to question the validity of this type of warfare, it has become commonplace in the modern world and has to be understood.

This study is a product of that movement to further understand irregular warfare and examine its importance in history. The personal, no-quarter violence that existed on the border was by no means the determining event in the American Civil War, but it had effects on a large portion of the population and left wounds that would fester for many years. My hope is to clarify this portion of the greater conflict, portraying the social and psychological impacts on the population of the border, as well as the military effects generated by the irregular war. In addition, I attempt to show the parallels that exist between actions and reactions during this conflict and similar instances in the more modern irregular war fought in Iraq and Afghanistan. This is not meant to be a history of these more modern conflicts, but to point out the similarities that exist in the actions of regular and irregular warriors in these two periods. A discussion of lessons learned from this nineteenth century conflict concludes this study, which may offer instruction for modern military leaders.

This work has spanned parts of four decades and seen me continue it on four continents. As with any major project, I have many people that I must thank for their help and support. Professor Norman Brown has been my mentor for many years and without his continuing support, this study would never have been completed. Dr. James Klotter was the impetus for my original interest in guerrilla warfare during this period and continued to offer advice and support as I trudged along through the research and writing. My thanks to the many archives that opened their doors to me and gave me the latitude necessary to find the important papers. Particularly I would like to thank the staff of the Western Historical Collection in Norman, Oklahoma. Though they didn't know it, the missing papers of William E. Connelly were found there, providing me a resource that even Albert Castel thought was lost forever. Of course, I must thank the leadership and staff of the Combat Studies Institute, through whose auspices this project made its way into print. They provided me the opportunity every scholar searches for and I am very grateful.

Finally, I must express my gratitude to my family and friends. Colonel (retired) Ken Smith, who started my career as an historian, has always been a valuable supporter. Brigadier General (retired) Casey Brower supported me as an historian and gave me an academic role model to emulate. My parents have long wondered when I would give them a finished copy of this work, but have always done so in a supportive way. Now grown, Nathaniel and Benjamin grew tired in their youth of stories of guerrillas and never really understood why their father needed yet another book about the Civil War. Finally, Royce Ann has been my partner and intellectual mate throughout the end work of this study and is the reason why it is finally complete. I could not have done it without her and would not have wanted to try.

Ft. Leavenworth, KS

August 2012

---

* Anthony James Joes, *Guerrilla Conflict Before the Cold War* (Westport, CT: Praeger Publishers, 1996), p. xiv.

Introduction

Future years will never know the seething hell and the black infernal background of countless minor scenes and interiors (not the official surface-courteousness of the Generals, not the few great battles) of the Secession war, and it is best they should not — the real war will never get in the books.[1]

These are the words of one of America's greatest literary minds, Walt Whitman. He recognized that although the Civil War was composed of 60 or so major battles, the war went far beyond these battlefields. The scholarly community and the general reading public alike spend many hours in the study of this great conflict. Overwhelmingly, their focus is on the incredible carnage that characterized the regular combat during the most violent four years in American History. Yet, beyond these battlefields, in every town of every border state, the war raged on a daily basis. These towns experienced the irregular warfare that was imbedded within the greater conflict; a personal, low-intensity war that was brought into most of the streets and many of the homes along the border. Just to the west of the Appalachian Mountains, the citizens of Kentucky found themselves beset by guerrilla violence and living under martial law due to the effectiveness of these guerrilla bands. The violence here had profound effects, lasting well beyond the four-year duration of the war. The Kansas-Missouri border region became a scene of burning and burnt homes, the countryside dotted with the stone chimneys that marked the sites where farm houses once stood. The violence was so vicious that entire counties were forcibly depopulated to insure that no aid was available from the populace to support the Confederate guerrillas. This violence spilled over into the other two states in the four corners area, and Arkansas and present day Oklahoma (then the Indian Territory) were also caught up in the informal violence that permeated this part of the border. Confederate Texas, though not plagued by overt guerrilla violence as Kansas or Missouri, still saw this internecine conflict affect its communities and inflict pain that would be felt even after the war. This study is intended, to borrow a goal from historian Michael Dougan, to prove Whitman wrong and to insure that the "seething hell" is brought before Civil War historians.

Civil War historians have overwhelmingly been consumed with the need to provide every detail of the major battles which are the hallmark of this conflict. While there have been periods where authors like William Connelly, Virgil Carrington Jones, Albert Castel, and Michael Fellman have turned their attention to this topic, the vast majority of authors have either ignored these activities or argued that while they existed they were of little consequence.

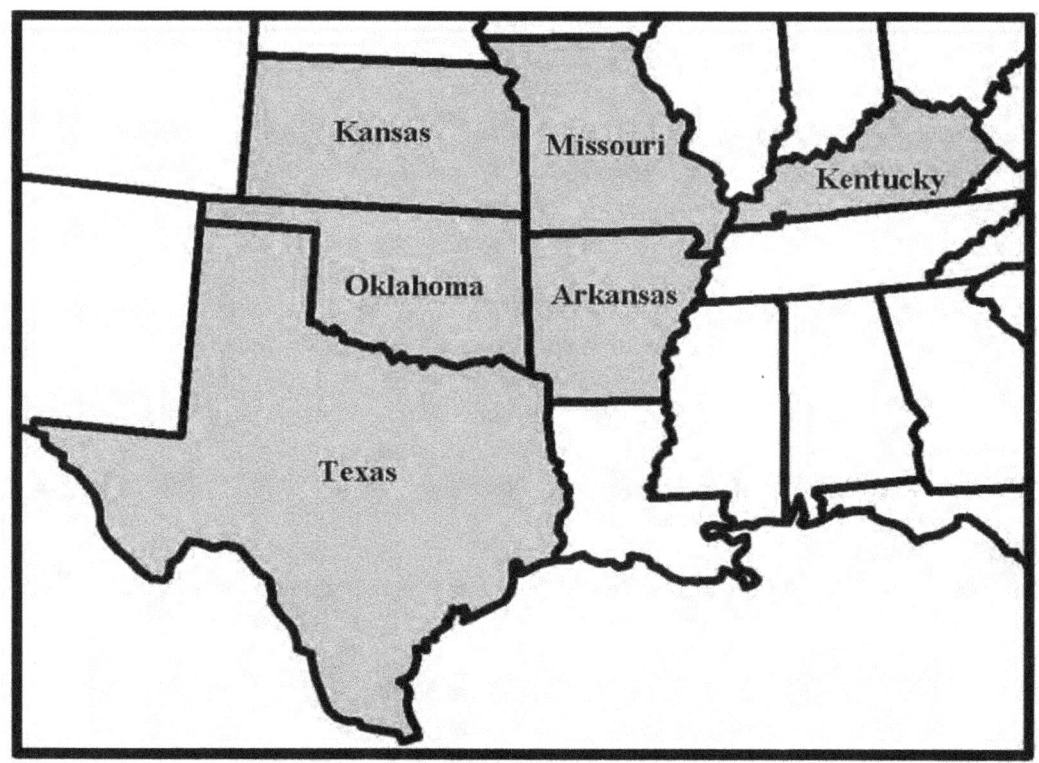

Map 1. Regional Area of Operations.

Since the turn of the century, however, a growing number of volumes have been dedicated to the study of this irregular warfare. Robert Mackey's The Uncivil War: Irregular Warfare in the Upper South, 1861-1865, delves into irregular warfare and its effects on the war through case studies of previously under-examined states, most notably Arkansas and Kentucky.[2] Clay Mountcastle's Punitive War: Confederate Guerrillas and Union Reprisals, examines the Union response to irregular warfare and the growth of what he terms "punitive war" through the course of the war. He represents well how Confederate irregular warfare and the Union response to it turned out to be the most brutal, personal violence ever seen in the United States.[3] A Savage Conflict: The Decisive Role of Guerrillas in the American Civil War, by Daniel Sutherland, is based on the premise that "it is impossible to understand the Civil War without appreciating the scope and impact of the guerrilla conflict…"[4] His study sets out to demonstrate how irregular warfare helped to determine the eventual outcome of the American Civil War.

These volumes represent a fresh look at irregular warfare during this period and helped shape this study. Each of these works, and those that preceded them, focused on the tactical and/or strategic military history of irregular warfare. It is not the goal of this study to examine this portion of the guerrilla war, though some of this will be necessary for background, but to examine how this very personal form of war affected the people of the border who had to live with it and through it. In almost every guerrilla conflict, the group that suffers the most is the population of the area under contention. Their story, and the effects of irregular conflict on them, is the focus of this study.

The initial, and certainly basic, cause of the guerrilla war that existed in the West was civil war. Few types of armed conflict are as violent as those which fall under the heading of revolutions, insurgencies, or civil wars. These wars are fought for the dismemberment of a state or the total overthrow of the existing government. They do not arise out of the differences between separate socio-economic systems or ideological structures, but are the culmination of social turmoil within a nation. People who once were of one mind and one country find themselves at a point where they can no longer live together as one entity in a peaceful environment. The American Civil War was fought for the dismemberment of the Union and represented a split in the populace of the United States along political and social lines. It pitted the North and the South against each other in violent struggle, with both believing that they were supporting the just side of the conflict. Avery Craven has written that "neither the North or the South could yield its position because slavery had come to symbolize values in each of their social-economic structures for which men fight and die, but which they do not give up or compromise."[5] The war in itself, apart from the slavery issue, was built along a similar mentality. Men from both sides were more than willing to die for what they believed to be right, and in many cases gave up everything they had in support of the cause.

The American image has long been represented as that of a peaceful nation, one which will fight only when wronged, a nation which prides itself in adhering to the laws of decency more than most other countries. A thorough examination of our historical record will, more accurately, portray a nation that longs for peace, but thrives on war. Most Americans would maintain that peace is our country's normal state and it is only occasionally interrupted by war. Numerous historians believe the opposite to be true and view the normal state of mankind as warlike and violent, with short periods of peace occasionally breaking out. In our military history, America has shown itself capable of behavior as violent as any other nation. This re-evaluation has revealed that the American nation was born as a direct result of violence, and has had a violent nature lurking below the surface of the national conscience for over two hundred years. During the Revolutionary War, Americans utilized whatever means were necessary to defeat the British Army. Similar adjustments were made during the American portion of the earlier Seven Year's War, when the standard European military mentality proved to be unable to deal with the guerrilla tactics of their Indian foes. The conquering of the interior of the American continent was accompanied by violence on a regular basis, as was the expansion into Texas and the American West. It should come as no surprise that the Civil War, which took the violent nature of the American character to new heights, spawned unparalleled violence at every level — not just on the battlefield.

Wars which pit portions of a single society against each other have always tended to be particularly bloody. Political and social cleavages, which are deep enough to bring about violence within a society, have always created conflicts that bear very personal traits. The Civil War did just that in the United States. Soldiers were not fighting for national honor in Mexico or against Indians on the frontier; they were fighting for the way of life in which they had been raised. No war in American history has ever approached the number of casualties on the battlefield that this mutually-destructive conflict produced. Along with that infamous record also must stand the level of personal violence that existed throughout the country. Beginning with the early border violence in the Kansas-Missouri area and continuing with the violent raid of John Brown on Harper's Ferry, the American people waged a war upon each other that did not restrict itself to the much-studied battlefields of Virginia and Tennessee. The war was felt anywhere that men and women of differing perspectives on the question of secession mixed together and could not be constrained to the pulpit or podium.

Even the conventional war, as fought by W. T. Sherman, Sterling Price, or others, was not the clean, gentlemanly war that professional soldiers had so long been used to waging. Total warfare grew out of the violence of this civil conflict, and men such as Sherman believed that the correct way to wage the war and win was to make the people of the South the enemy, not just their armies.[6] The burning and destruction which he and others practiced was symptomatic of the total nature of the war. With this great, violent war raging throughout the nation, it is little wonder that local violence raged just as strongly all along the border areas of the struggle. As one historian so aptly observed: "...civil war in the backwoods was hard to restrain like the immense national conflict of which it was a part (and to which it was giving certain characteristics). It was more easily started than controlled, and it could be extremely destructive."[7]

Since the American experience in Vietnam, we as a people, and the world as a whole, have become more aware of and receptive to the concept of guerrilla warfare. The guerrilla struggles in Iraq, Afghanistan, Vietnam, Central America, Africa, and other parts of the world have awakened the attention of scholars and non-scholars alike to the impact of this petite guerre on military actions, societies, economies, politics, and the national will of this country and others. The numerous studies of the momentous battles and important campaigns of our Civil War have focused, almost without exception, on the actions of major units and famous commanders. Countless volumes exist on Gettysburg or Antietam, but relatively few authors deal with the personal war that was fought everywhere along the border.

Before beginning to examine irregular warfare during the Civil War, a short history or background on this type of combat is appropriate. Though scholars have recently become more aware and accepting of irregular warfare, it must be remembered that it did not start with the Civil War, any more than it began in the jungles of Vietnam. The term "guerrilla" stems from the Peninsular War in Spain, is the diminutive of the Spanish word "guerra," or war, and is used to connote a small or petty war. "The dictionary of the Spanish academy gives, as the first meaning of the word guerrilla, *a party of light troops for reconnaissance, and opening the first skirmishes*."[8] In this context, the term referred to the bands of men, normally led by priests or lawyers, who came together to carry out a small, violent war against Napoleon's army during the Peninsular Campaigns. Napoleon himself never fully understood the strength of these small bands and was unable to deal with them effectively, though he commanded the finest army of his time. Though the term dates from the late eighteenth and earlier nineteenth centuries, the concept of irregular warfare can be traced much farther back than that. Robert Asprey, in his lengthy study of the guerrilla in history, War in the Shadows (1975), follows the roots of this conflict back to the days of Darius, Alexander the Great, and Hannibal. It was used against the Romans by Hannibal and again during the Roman attempt to conquer Spain. In America, this type of warfare was used effectively by the rebels who fought to free themselves from the King of England in the years 1775-1783. The fighting in the Carolinas against Lord Cornwallis and Banastre Tarleton was largely carried out by southern irregulars under the control of General Nathaniel Greene, who cared little for the niceties of British warfare. Their hit and run tactics helped to drive Cornwallis from North Carolina to Yorktown, Virginia, where he met defeat.

A common thread throughout this history of guerrilla activity is what Asprey calls an "arrogance of ignorance." Military commanders from the young British officer, who swore he could march through all of the Colonies with one hundred good troops, to the early commanders of the US Army in Vietnam, to the American leadership in Iraq and Afghanistan, have failed in their assessment of the abilities of guerrillas and the methods necessary to defeat them. This inability to adapt conventional tactics to meet the guerrilla threat has led to untold frustration, and such frustration has often led to a breakdown in military efficiency. The result of these breakdowns has often been an attempt to defeat the guerrillas by the use of organized cruelty. In the western border states, as in other places, local commanders misused power in an attempt to alleviate the pressure they felt from these irregular warriors. We will examine some of these actions, as the usual effect of such cruelty is renewed support of the guerrilla by the local populace and the general undermining of the military organization. Another common reaction to organized cruelty is a rededication of the guerrilla bands and a significant increase in their ability to recruit new partisans.

As in all historical inquiry, this study must be properly placed in the context of the period in which it occurred. The term guerrilla has a different meaning to us in the twenty-first century than it had for the men and women who lived in nineteenth century Kentucky or Missouri. To understand the actions and reactions of those who were participants in, or victims of, this type of conflict, it is important to understand these differences.

General Henry W. Halleck, later a pivotal figure in the Civil War, published a book in 1861, entitled, International Law or Rules Regulating the Intercourse of States in Peace and War.[9] In this book, Halleck included a section on guerrilla warfare and civil wars. His discourse on the definition of a guerrilla and the guerrilla's legal standing reflects a dominant legal theme of his day. He identified these groups of combatants as operating without authority of a legitimate state and their actions, therefore, created only a personal responsibility. He likened their taking of property to common robbery and their taking of life to murder, unprotected by the laws of warfare that allowed the same actions by regular soldiers. He denied that they were soldiers at all and indicated that they retained no rights to be treated as prisoners of war. He closed his comments by asserting that "…in modern warfare, partisans and guerrilla bands, such as we have here described, are regarded as outlaws, and, when captured, may be punished the same as free-booters and banditti."[10]

In this passage, Halleck laid the foundations for the definition and methodology which the Union forces and Federal government applied to the irregular warriors who plagued them throughout the border states. Similar response to irregular threats can be found in Texas, by the Confederate government that perceived a threat to their society and political structures. The term "guerrilla" became synonymous with bushwhacker, outlaw, and brigand. The words were used interchangeably and normally spoken with a distinct edge of derision by those whose political preferences were at odds with the raiders.

These irregular warriors were also viewed with disdain by most professional soldiers, even when they fought on the same side, who regarded their own form of warfare to be of a higher order than that of the partisan.

Normally, the opinions of a single legal scholar would not have had such far-reaching influence upon national policy, but Halleck was no average legal scholar. Not only did he serve as General-in-Chief of the Union Army for a time and Chief-of-Staff after that, but he was a former commander of the dominant general officers who contributed to the Union victory. Grant, Sherman, and Sheridan all served under Halleck when he was in command in the West, the theatre where the Union forces had their most consistent success. Not only did Halleck attain positions of considerable influence within the military establishment, but, as Lincoln's closest military adviser, he became directly involved in the war policy of the nation at the highest levels of government. With these credentials, his view on guerrillas and guerrilla warfare was seen throughout the policies that governed Union commanders in their attempts to deal with these shadowy figures. The views of many other Union officers echoed his instructions, as will be shown in later chapters.

Another scholar, Francis Lieber, also played an important role in the formulation of the Union policy towards the guerrilla question.[11] Lieber was the foremost legal scholar of his day, and when Halleck became General-in-Chief, he wrote to Lieber for his opinion on the legal question. Lieber answered the general in an essay, entitled "Guerrilla Parties Considered with Reference to the Laws and Usages of War," in which he set forth his definitions of pertinent terms and historical examples of each. He defined guerrillas as "an irregular band of armed men, carrying on an irregular war, not being able, according to their character as a guerrilla party, to carry on what the law terms a regular war."[12] Lieber's expertise was recognized by Halleck, who enrolled him to serve on a special commission set up to formulate the official policies for the Lincoln government. This commission's final product took the form of a military general order, dated April 24, 1863. This famous order carried the official designation of General Order No. 100 and contained 10 separate sections and 157 articles. These sections dealt with a wide spectrum of the problems involved in the law-of-land warfare, but most notable for this study is Section IV, in which the provisions for dealing with irregulars were laid down. This General Order and two others of specific importance are included in the appendices.

These articles made up the groundwork for the local ordinances that were used by commanders to regulate such irregular warfare in their unique area of operations. Lieber's influence was great in the writing of these articles, and evidence can be found in them that he disagreed on some points of law and definition with General Halleck. Halleck artificially placed any irregular into the category of guerrilla, not taking care to distinguish between what Lieber called partisans, war-rebels, or armed prowlers. This blurring of the legal categories in Halleck's model is reflected in the minds of most of the soldiers who were called upon to administer General Order No. 100. The General Order divided potential partisans into five categories, only one of which (Article 81) provided them the protection of prisoner of war status. All other categories called for summary punishment, which most often meant immediate death. As the administration of General Order No. 100 on the border emerged, the Union commanders chose to treat all irregulars under Article 82 (which allowed for summary execution of bandits and pirates), a perception that was echoed by the majority of the Unionist press and civilians in the Trans-Mississippi west and the Commonwealth of Kentucky. The question of whether these legal categories should have been considered by Union commanders is rarely addressed by historians. Few have even considered the distinctions laid out by Lieber, but one recent historian did offer an opinion.

Clay Mountcastle's book, Punitive War, focuses on the Union response to irregular warfare and does an excellent job of examining the progressively more violent reactions to Confederate guerrillas. Mountcastle takes the position that these distinctions are only important when "examining the Confederacy's use of guerrilla warfare"[13] and that they should not be used when examining the Union response to these Confederate actions. He maintains this because as Union soldiers and leaders did not recognize such distinctions, their responses were in no way dictated by those distinctions. Their universal treatment of all irregulars as guerrillas and bushwhackers was the common thread in their response to these shadowy warriors and because they were "Primarily occupied with the burden of defeating the Confederate Army in the field, the Federals had neither the time nor the inclination to analyze this guerrilla threat to any greater extent".[14] This study will disagree with Mountcastle, who in a way gives the Union a free pass for their actions, and the small group of historians who have considered the issue and determined that the vagaries of General Order No. 100 created a near "blank check" for the Union when dealing with irregulars. While this order did create legitimacy for the retaliatory violence on the border, it cannot excuse the executions of prisoners or the unwillingness to deal with partisan ranger units openly claimed by the Confederate government. The fact that Union forces ignored their own regulations is no reason to excuse actions that substantially violated General Order No. 100.

Thus, guerrilla warfare in the eyes of the Union leaders was totally separate from the regular warfare on battlefields such as Gettysburg, Antietam, and Chickamauga. One modern day analyst of the art of guerrilla warfare has expressed the opinion that "Union treatment of guerrillas seems to have been based on Old Testament thinking."[15] As reflected in this characterization, Halleck and the Union forces had a notably narrow outlook on the guerrilla and his place in war. They were admittedly not alone in their evaluation of the place of these irregular troops. A military intellect as sage as Napoleon had also failed to recognize the potential of this type of warfare in his Peninsular Campaign, and Carl von Clausewitz, one of the great military thinkers of the nineteenth century, characterized it as "a state of anarchy declared lawful, which is as dangerous as a foreign enemy to social order at home."[16] The other prominent military analyst of the period, Baron de Jomini, had a keener appreciation for the role and potential of this war within a war. Jomini wrote of the comparative benefits guerrilla warfare afforded the guerrilla, who had not only a fighting force, but also the support of the populace to provide supplies, shelter, and intelligence. His comments on the state of a commander facing such a force indicated the numerous problems when he wrote, "He holds scarcely any ground but that upon which he encamps; outside the limits of his camp everything is hostile and multiplies a thousand fold the difficulties he meets at every step." Jomini's experience in Spain appears to have given him a strong sense of the power of the guerrilla force's knowledge of the local terrain and their ability to gather intelligence on the army's actions.[17]

Jomini's description could have been taken directly from journal entries by Union military commanders in western Missouri or central Kentucky. As these regular soldiers attempted to find and eradicate the guerrilla organizations that roamed the countryside, they found both the terrain and the populace to be the ally of the irregular forces.

These two well known military analysts viewed guerrilla warfare as a force created by the people of a land rising up against an invading military or political force. In some ways they characterized it not only as a military phenomenon, but as a social force. It united the people of a given area or the elements of a social/political group and allowed them to participate in the war, either as combatants or as part of the support base for the combatants. The comment by Clausewitz reflects a general disdain for the guerrilla effort, a feeling similar to that of the Union general officers. Jomini, having served in Spain with the French Army, seems to be more of a realist. He neither applauds nor condemns this form of combat, but points out the difficulty that conventional forces have in coping with its irregular principles. Thus, in much of the nineteenth century, the subject of guerrilla warfare was treated as an afterthought. True to this form, most officers in the Union army had given very little thought to guerrilla warfare prior to 1861. Some had been exposed to it in Mexico (such as Halleck), a few in the various Indian conflicts in the early part of the nineteenth century, and others may have dealt with it in their own studies, but most had been concerned only with learning the tactical and strategic lessons which were taught at West Point and at such service schools that existed. They were unprepared to deal with guerrillas and unable to see them as soldiers, because guerrillas did not fit into the neat mold they had cast for their own soldiers.[18] After all, soldiers wore uniforms and faced their enemies in well-disciplined battle lines — they did not resort to ambush or the wanton destruction of property.

The study of guerrillas and guerrilla warfare has changed greatly in the past century. Even the term "guerrilla" carries with it a different popular definition than it did in the past century. To the Unionist living in central Kentucky during the war, the term denoted an outlaw, someone residing outside the law, with little or no respect for human life. Today the word is used with a greater legitimacy attached to it. One leading dictionary defines a guerrilla as "any member of a small defensive force of irregular soldiers, usually volunteers, making surprise raids, esp. behind the lines of an invading army."[19] This study adheres to this twentieth century definition. Having grown up as part of the "Vietnam generation," the author definitely views the guerrilla and his type of warfare as far more legitimate and far more important than did either the nineteenth century soldier or the pre-Vietnam historians.

Guerrilla warfare in today's context is far more than a form of military strategy or type of tactical maneuver. It is an all-encompassing world of total warfare in which almost anything goes, as long as it contributes to the accomplishment of the organization's goals. It is a brutal, no-holds barred combat that affects not only conventional soldiers, but anyone who comes in contact with it. The conflict in Southeast Asia laid the groundwork for a number of studies of this kind of war, and even more studies of previous guerrilla conflicts, creating extensive re-examinations of the importance of irregular warfare and its effects on the larger military or political conflict. The current conflict in Iraq has undoubtedly caused an explosion of analysis on the impact of such irregular warfare.

The terrorism that currently afflicts the modern world is an extension of the petty war beyond the visions of Clausewitz and Jomini. Just as people used different terms to refer to and define the irregular warriors who fought in the Civil War, the modern version of the irregular warrior may be termed a guerrilla or an insurgent or, more likely, a terrorist. This evolution of irregular warfare is now common in our world and is as likely to be motivated by religious ideals as by nationalism or ideology. Regular soldiers and politicians still disparage the warfare of the terrorist, just as they did the warfare of the guerrilla in the 1860s. Traditional military thinkers during the American Civil War underestimated the damage that guerrillas could do to Sherman's exposed lines of communication, just as American leadership underestimated the damage the insurgency in Iraq could do to US forces. Most historians have underestimated the damage guerrilla warfare on the western border did to the populace there, just as the damage that the campaign of terror would do to the Iraqi people and infrastructure, which was underestimated by most US leaders. History repeatedly shows us that the military attention paid to irregular combatants is less important in proportion than the impact they have on the population that has to suffer the pain of such personal violence. Because of this, a military force's unwillingness or inability to deal with insurgent violence in an efficient and timely manner can often lead to negative feelings from the local population and serve as a serious hindrance to localized stability.

The tactics of guerrilla warfare have changed little from the days of the American Revolution to the present. Small groups of men, operating independently or semi-independently, use their size and mobility to harass larger, better equipped, and more organized forces. Simply put, the guerrilla war can be used as the poor country's form of war, because it does not require large outlays in capital, manpower, or equipment. It is a war of stealth and shadows, mixed with intermittent and extremely violent combat. Without delving into the basic political issues, it is easy to see military organizations in recent history, from Vietnam to Somalia to Bosnia to the Sunni Triangle, that could not stand toe-to-toe with the conventional forces they faced. With smaller numbers and inferior equipment, they were forced to use tactics that made the larger numbers of their enemy work for the underdog. By utilizing the tactics of the petty war, they created untold problems for their adversaries. Thus, the face of guerrilla warfare has not changed substantially, only the weapons and the world's perceptions.

Guerrilla war has become a prevalent form of combat in the modern world. Since the end of the Korean War, few large scale conventional wars have been waged, with most occurring in the Middle East. During the same period, countless numbers of irregular wars or insurgencies have been fought in Central America, Southeast Asia, the Middle East, Africa, and other parts of the world. These small wars are easier to organize and finance, and can be used by other powers — regardless of political or religious ideologies — to support unrest in a desired area. The prevalence of this irregular warfare has contributed to its acceptance as a legitimate method of conducting war. It is within this framework that this study examines the Civil War on the border, to determine its origins, its personalities, and its effects.

Insurgent warfare occurred in every border state during the Civil War, from Maryland to Texas. In the pages that follow, this study will examine irregular conflict in the border area of the trans-Appalachian West. This theatre of war was treated much differently from that focused between Washington and Richmond, and the relative lack of attention in the West by both armies allowed irregular warfare to take center stage for much of the war. Six states or territories have been chosen for this examination, all of which were touched by the daily violence that guerrilla warfare in the West created. Their stories are at once similar and unique, shaped by their geographic location and their demographic makeup.

In 1860, Kentucky had almost equal parts of the North and South. While a slave state, most Kentuckians hoped that the Union could be maintained. Historically, Kentucky's roots were to Virginia and the other slave states, but the growth of the market economy had linked much of the border area strongly to the northern and eastern business interests. Unable to support the Republican Party because it was viewed as the party of abolition, the state also shied away from supporting its native son, John C. Breckenridge, who had been nominated by the radical southern wing of the Democratic Party. The Whig Party of Henry Clay had long been the dominant political organization in the state, and its death prior to the election of 1856 had left a serious void in Kentucky's political arena. The election of 1860 saw many Kentuckians support the Constitutional Union Party candidate, John Bell of Tennessee. As was the common practice in the antebellum period, this party avoided the sectional issues and sought only to arouse the patriotism of Americans and feed on their love of the national union. This party was most successful in the border states that stood to lose the most from civil strife. If the war came, it would obviously be fought in these states and they stood to lose no matter which side they chose to support.

Kentucky's attempt at neutrality in the spring and summer of 1861 proved unsuccessful. The secessionist sentiment in the state was insufficient to carry it out of the Union, but the government also rebelled at the thought of providing troops to Lincoln to force the Confederacy back into line. When, in the fall of 1861, both sides occupied portions of Kentucky, the battle line in the western theatre would stretch across the entire width of the Commonwealth.

From the beginning, Kentuckians who supported the Confederacy recruited soldiers behind Union lines and conducted a small-scale hit and run campaign against the Union forces. These minor skirmishes would be only a nagging sideshow to the Union authorities until the summer of 1863, when they would become the dominant form of warfare in the state. The reason for the elevation was the destruction of John Hunt Morgan's 2d Kentucky Cavalry during the Indiana-Ohio Raid of 1863. After the end of Morgan's raids, guerrilla forces seemingly sprang up from the barren ground and began a very effective war of harassment and terror that would occupy the state and federal officials consistently until after the end of the formal war. Most histories of the war in Kentucky concluded with Bragg's invasion and Morgan's demise. One of the best recent treatments of irregular warfare in Kentucky, by Robert Mackey, still brings this personal war in Kentucky to a close with Morgan's capture, indicating that "The summer of 1863 was the last real opportunity for organized raiding by conventional cavalry forces, the most acceptable form of irregular warfare to the Confederate army, to have a decisive role."[20] Morgan's demise did not end irregular war in Kentucky; it created an environment where former Morgan's raiders continued their fight against the Union in another form. One of the most prevalent of the partisans, Adam Rankin Johnson, is mentioned by name in Mackey's treatment of the 2d Kentucky Cavalry as the commander of the Morgan's Second Brigade.[21] In essence, the irregular war didn't stop; it merely morphed into something less controlled, but every bit as dangerous to the citizens of Kentucky. By moving on, once the large raids were over, historians have missed one of the most intriguing and important periods in Kentucky's history.

The original seeds of this irregular violence in the 1860's were planted in the soil of Kansas and Missouri in the mid-1850's, a period well-known as "Bleeding Kansas." This violence was sparked by the ongoing problem of the expansion of slavery, an issue which had become dominant on the national political scene. The people of the slave state of Missouri saw the Kansas Territory as the logical place into which they would expand the peculiar institution. Missourians took it for granted that their social and economic structure would be continued into what was to become their sister state. Anti-slave forces did not see this expansion as a foregone conclusion and organized the movement of Free State settlers into the Kansas Territory for the express purpose of winning this area for the anti-slavery cause by controlling the ballot box in the upcoming elections. The decision was to rest with voters, in keeping with the concept of "popular sovereignty," and organizations like the Emigrant Aid Society believed they could save Kansas from the institution of slavery by filling the Kansas plains with small farmers and merchants who would stand against the spread of the institution.

This race to fill Kansas with voters who would decide the issue of slavery created animosity and hatred so great, that it turned the eastern portion of the future state into a battleground upon which pro and anti-slave factions spilled blood at an alarming pace. Missourians crossed the border and voted in the eastern counties around Leavenworth and Lawrence with impunity, and groups of these pro-slavery forces, who were referred to as "border ruffians," roamed the countryside punishing those who were perceived to hinder their plans to dominate the future of Kansas. The support of the Buchanan Administration in Washington — support that was demonstrated by a total failure to curb this violence emanating from Missouri — contributed to a society in this border region that was filled with death, fear, and a growing hatred that would be carried over into the next decade when the rest of America was plunged into the Civil War. In this setting of rampant violence and crime, men and boys became desensitized to death and misery with the resulting growth of a class of men like James Lane, Charles Jennison, and the most noted name in American guerrilla violence, William Clarke Quantrill. These men, supporting different causes, came to know each other by reputation or personal contact. This familiarity that would breed hatred and even death lists when the violence surged east and west across the hills of Kansas and Missouri. The violence in Kansas and Missouri is best known along the border, with most of the volumes that have been written on the subject being centered here. This violence boiled over the geographical lines of these states, and the men mentioned above exported their violence south into the next tier of states.

As with most of the border states, there was considerable turmoil in Arkansas in late 1860 and early 1861. The question in many states was whether or not to secede and join the lower south, and so it was in Arkansas. The battle between the unionist and secessionist elements in the secession convention raged throughout the spring of 1861, with the secessionists winning limited victories.[22] It was not until the firing on Fort Sumter in April 1861 that the Unionist element was "overwhelmed by popular excitement" and the secession movement was given new life.[23] The debate between unionist and secessionist could have been carried on indefinitely in the absence of violence, but with the combat at Fort Sumter the people of every state were forced to make a decision. Straddling the fence was no longer a viable alternative, particularly for Arkansas, which lay between the Confederacy and the hopeful secessionists of Missouri. With renewed vigor, the secessionists pushed for the state's separation from the Union and on May 6, 1861, Arkansas finally voted to join the Confederacy.[24]

As with the rest of the Trans-Mississippi, Arkansas was not high on the list of strategic priorities for the Confederate officials in the early stages of the war. The question of how best to exploit the war on the border was relatively unimportant to Jefferson Davis and his advisors, whose focus rarely got further west than the Mississippi River. In the purely defensive strategy that marked the early part of the Confederate war effort, there was little or no role for a small frontier state that possessed nothing of worth beyond its manpower.[25]

The army, which was assigned the task of protecting the Trans-Mississippi Confederacy, first had its nose bloodied seriously in the Battle of Wilson's Creek, Missouri, on August 10, 1861. The war in Missouri and Arkansas surged back and forth across the border area. By late May 1862, after the Confederate defeat at Pea Ridge, Arkansas was in desperate straits. The Federal army was only thirty-five miles from Little Rock, the Confederate army had left the state entirely, the civil government was in a state of virtual collapse, food was short, and guerrilla depredations were occurring throughout the northwestern portion of the state. The state of affairs in Arkansas prompted one newspaper editor, who was obviously no supporter of the government, to ask if someone could inform the public of the state government's location and offer up that its last known location was "…aboard the steamer, Little Rock, about two weeks ago, stemming the current of the Arkansas River."[26]

In an effort to remedy the situation, General P.G.T. Beauregard issued orders, on May 31, 1862, assigning Brigadier General Thomas C. Hindman to command all Confederate forces in Arkansas. Though it may be questioned whether Beauregard had the authority to issue such orders, his action was the only one forthcoming and for lack of an alternative, Hindman proceeded to his native state to try to stem the Union tide.[27] Hindman recognized the role that could be played by partisans and issued his Order Number 17, which authorized the formation of irregular units to combat the Federals. Though his authority is suspect, it is obvious that to the populace of Arkansas he represented the Richmond Government, and that his action gave an air of legitimacy to the bands of Confederate soldiers or sympathizers who actively took the war to the federals and their supporters in northern Arkansas.[28] Hindman's actions and his acceptance of the guerrilla form of warfare did not go without notice from his adversaries of the Union side. In a letter in October 1862, Major General William T. Sherman cautioned Hindman that individuals on both sides of the war were committing acts that their leaders should not sanction, and that this tendency set a dangerous precedent. He closed by indicating that, "If we allow the passions of our men to get full command, then indeed will this war become a reproach to the names of liberty and civilization?"[29]

This comment on the propriety of certain types of warfare is interesting if for no other reason than its source. Not quite two years after this correspondence with Hindman, Sherman faced a similar situation with the guerrilla war in Kentucky and confided to an influential friend that "those side issues of niggers, State rights, conciliation, outrages, cruelty, barbarity, bankruptcy, subjugation, are all idle and nonsensical. The only principle in this war is which party can whip."[30] The years that intervened between these two letters appear to have significantly changed Sherman's outlook on the prosecution of the war.

To the west of Arkansas, in what is today known as Oklahoma, was the Indian Territory. The Five Civilized Tribes, having been forced to relocate from the Lower South decades before, were living in relative peace here. They had created their own tribal governments and societies that rivaled most of the white communities around them. The Cherokee Nation was governed by Chief John Ross, the elected principal chief. The Cherokees and most of the other tribes, Choctaws, Chickasaws, Creeks, and Seminoles reflected the southern society which they had been a part of previously. These tribal nations maintained the institution of black slavery in the Indian Territory, just as they had in Georgia and Mississippi. The geographical and social connections to the South cast a wide net over the emotions of the Indian people in Oklahoma. Decisions about allegiances had to be made, similar to those in Arkansas, and the situation in Oklahoma was far more complex than in any other area of the Trans-Mississippi. Old conflicts between those who wanted to fight the enforced movement to the Indian Territory and those who saw no other option boiled up again in the maelstrom which followed the beginning of the war. The conservative element of the Cherokee and Creek tribes cleaved to the Union, while the rest of the populace went with the Confederacy.

This split in the political and social fabric of Indian society created, as it did on the rest of the border, violence that would destroy the communities in the eastern portion of the Territory. Fed by the previous hatreds and quarrels, these elements would wage war on each other for the next few years. Added to these problems was the Territory's geographical position between the Kansas-Missouri theatre of war and the safety of Confederate Texas. The Texas Road was the highway in and out of the war in the west and the Indian communities along that route would suffer violence from names as notorious as William Clarke Quantrill himself. These depredations were not limited to the Confederate irregulars, as the Jayhawkers of Unionist Kansas were as prevalent in the personal literature penned by the inhabitants of Oklahoma as were the butternut ruffians.

At the southern end of the Texas Road was the Lone Star State, a horn of plenty in the burned up landscape of the Trans-Mississippi West. Cattle from Texas could be used to feed either army in the field, and it was viewed as a sanctuary by the Confederate troops, regular and irregular, who faced combat farther north. While the government of Texas was not in turmoil and its loyalty to the Confederacy was never in serious question, internecine warfare and the lawless activity that was prevalent above its northern border also existed here. The violent men who came south in the wintertime were initially sedate, but true to their nature they allowed their violent side to spill out into the southern community that had embraced them. This border area was also the haven for southern refugees from the internecine warfare in the Indian Territory, and the accumulation of temporarily homeless ex-patriots created a fertile environment for violence. Farther south, the German community in central Texas was the subject of considerable violence and suspicion, engendered by their anti-slave stand and perceived alliance with the Union cause. Much of the violent reaction created in the Unionist governments to the north was also to be found in the Confederate halls of government in Texas.

Gerald Linderman, in Embattled Courage, maintains that "every war begins as one war and becomes two, that watched by civilians and that fought by soldiers."[31] The violence on the western border represents a third war, outside of the boundaries of the violence about which Linderman writes. In this third war, civilians weren't simply observers, but unwilling participants on a daily basis. The opponents who fought it were not just regular soldiers, bound by conventional thinking, but a mixture of combatants who worried less about rules and more about how to most effectively inflict death on their enemies and further their own narrow goals. It was a dirty war, not of interest to most scholars and not falling into the neat categories so appealing to military historians. Even those historians who do write about the irregular war tend to shy away from the people who inhabited the border. One historian of this conflict wrote that "The civilians themselves are of little importance in an antiguerrilla campaign, except in how they supply and sustain the guerrillas."[32] While this may be accurate if the goal of the author's work is to focus on the pure military history of irregular warfare, it is inadequate to delve into dark corners of violence in which civilians and combatants had to live every day from 1861-1865.

Military history is part of the curriculum at the US Army Command and General Staff College for the express purpose of using historical context to inform military judgment in Army field grade officers. The most recent conflicts in America's history have clearly shown that the civilian residents of the operating theatres are of more than a "little importance" and an understanding of their role is critical to successful conduct of irregular warfare. This study is focused on the irregular warriors and how their lives intertwined with the inhabitants of the border states. These border states and territories were beset with irregular violence, some organized by the Confederate military and some born of the proximity of North and South. Many Americans died along the western border due to real or perceived allegiance to the wrong side on the wrong day. The importance of this violence and its pervasiveness is a story left to be told.

Notes

1. Walter Lowenfels, Walt Whitman's Civil War, (New York: Alfred A. Knopf, 1960), p. 293.

2. Robert R. Mackey, The Uncivil War: Irregular Warfare in the Upper South, 1861-1865, (Norman: University of Oklahoma Press, 2004).

3. Clay Mountcastle, Punitive War: Confederate Guerrillas and Union Reprisals, (Lawrence: University of Kansas Press, 2009). pp. 3-7.

4. Daniel E. Sutherland, A Savage Conflict: The Decisive Role of Guerrillas in the American Civil War, (Chapel Hill: The University of North Carolina Press, 2009), p. ix.

5. Avery Craven, The Growth of Southern Nationalism, 1848-1861, (Baton Rouge, La.: Louisiana State University Press, 1953), p. 397.

6. Herman Hattaway and Archer Jones, How the North Won: A Military History of the Civil War, (Urbana, IL: University of Illinois Press, 1983), p. 458.

7. Bruce Catton, Terrible Swift Sword, (Garden City, NY: Doubleday & Company, Inc., 1963), pp. 65-66.

8. Richard Shelly Hartigan, Lieber's Code and the Law of War, (Chicago: Precedent Publishers, 1983), p. 32.

9. For information on Halleck, see Stephen E. Ambrose, Halleck: Lincoln's Chief of Staff, (Baton Rouge: Louisiana State University Press, 1962.)

10. Henry W. Halleck, International Law or Rules Regulating the Intercourse of States in Peace and War, (New York: D. Van Nostrand, 1861), p. 386.

11. For information on Lieber, see Frank Friedel, Francis Lieber: Nineteenth Century Liberal, (Peter Smith, 1990).

12. Hartigan, pp. 9-10.

13. Mountcastle, p. 3.

14. Mountcastle, p. 4.

15. Robert B. Asprey, War in the Shadows: The Guerrilla in History, 2 vols. (Garden City, NY: Doubleday & Company, Inc., 1975), p. 165.

16. Carl von Clausewitz, On War, (London: Routledge & Kegan Paul, 1968), quoted in Asprey, War in the Shadows, p. 148.

17. Baron de Jomini, The Art of War, The West Point Military Library, (Westport, CT: Greenwood Press, 1971), pp. 27-28.

18. A parallel also can be drawn between the American Army's inability to initially recognize and respond to the insurgency in Iraq and the irregular warfare conducted in the Border States during the Civil War. The leadership went into the Iraq war with a mindset as to how it would proceed and what the enemy would look like. The denials concerning the importance of the insurgency by national leadership reflect the same "Arrogance of Ignorance" cited by Asprey and caused a slow and costly reorientation of the force.

19. David B. Guralink, ed., Webster's New World Dictionary of the American Language, 2d ed. (New York: Simon and Schuster, 1982), p. 621.

20. Mackey, p. 194.

21. Mackey, p. 178.

22. Guralink, pp. 47-59.

23. Guralink, pp. 59-60.

24. Guralink, p. 63.

25. Thomas A. Belser, Jr., Military Operations in Missouri and Arkansas, 1861-1865, (Ph.D. Thesis, Vanderbilt University, 1958), pp. 2-8; Michael B. Dougan, Confederate Arkansas: The People and Policies of a Frontier State in Wartime, (University, AL: The University of Alabama Press, 1976).

26. R.H. Johnson, quoted in Dougan, Confederate Arkansas, p. 88.

27. Dougan, p. 89.

28. Dougan, p. 89.

29. The War of Rebellion: A Compilation of the Official Records of the Union and Confederate Armies, 128 vols., (Washington: 1880-1902), Series 1, Volume 13, pp. 742-743.

30. Official Records, Series 1, Volume 39, Part 2, pp. 240-241.

31. Gerald F. Linderman, Embattled Courage: The Experience of Combat in the American Civil War, (New York: The Free Press, 1987), p. 1.

32. Mackey, p. 53.

Chapter 1

Kentucky

In the fall of 1864, newspaper reports began to identify a guerrilla leader who was operating against railroad lines in central Kentucky. The *Louisville Daily Journal* mentioned him in a short piece that said "…the Lebanon train did not arrive last night…the train was captured by guerillas and burned…we are informed by a railroad employee that the guerillas were fifteen in number, under the command of Billy McGruder, and…the engine was thrown from the track and baggage car burned."[1] The guerrilla leader was actually Henry C. Magruder, a former member of John Hunt Morgan's 2d Kentucky Cavalry who conducted operations against Union facilities and personnel in Kentucky after the fall of 1864. Magruder left an excellent record of his life after he was captured and tried as a common criminal. His closing statement at trial in Louisville was an eloquent account of how southern soldiers came to be active in Kentucky. He very pointedly indicated that he had never been involved in killing anyone who was not a Union soldier and that while he had killed soldiers in Kentucky, "they lost their lives in defense of their government, while we exposed ours in defense of what we were taught to regard as sacred and to which we had pledged our fortunes and lives." Magruder went through a chronological recitation of his time as a Confederate soldier, from his recruitment in the Confederate State Guard by General Simon Bolivar Buckner, his subsequent transfer to the cavalry unit of Lee Arnett at Fort Donelson, and eventual service as a bodyguard to General Albert Sidney Johnston at Shiloh. After Shiloh, he served with John Hunt Morgan's command and maintained in his statement that "to that command I belonged when I received the deadly wound from which I now suffer intensely." Magruder went on to ask for the same pardon that the leadership of the Confederacy had received and in closing asked that "surely you will not deny me the opportunity of again being, after the war, what I was before it. A peaceful, humble, unoffending citizen, and in coming years atone for any errors that in misguided, but honest zeal as a Southern soldier, I may have committed in defense of the interests of the South."[2]

Unfortunately for Magruder, the eloquence of his closing statement did not deter the military tribunal from sentencing him to die on the gallows. Though he had served in the regular Confederate army, he now fell outside of its protection and was hanged on October 29, 1865.[3] He had been captured in Union territory, in a small group of men who, though they often wore the Confederate uniform, were considered by the authorities to be marauders and murderers.

The type of border violence described above is best known by most historians as occurring in the Trans-Mississippi West. Predictably, this phenomena was not just a Trans-Mississippi problem, but very alive between the Mississippi River and the Appalachian Mountains. The border state of Kentucky was rife with guerrilla warfare and irregular violence for much of the Civil War.

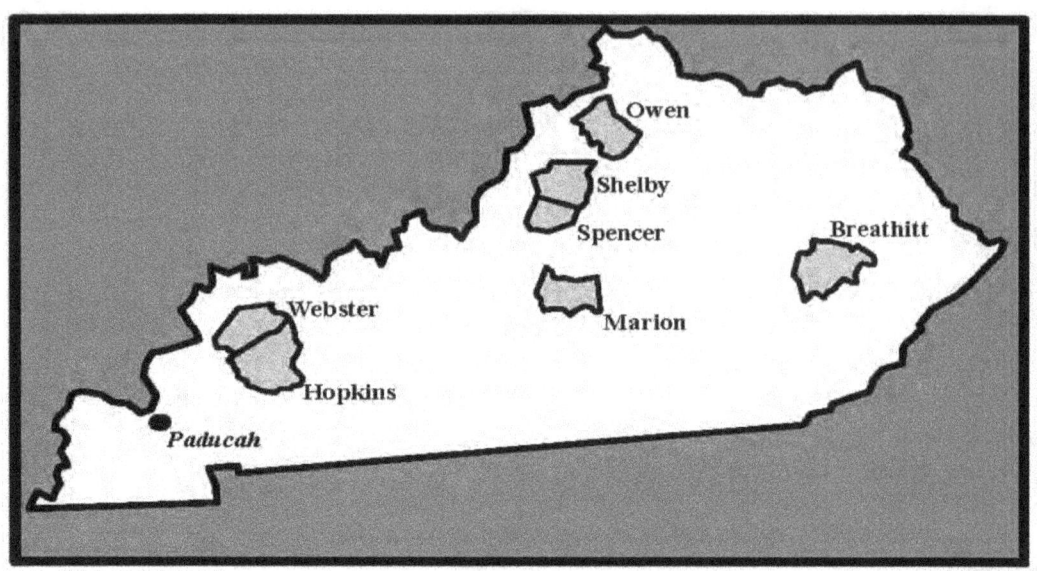

Map 2. Kentucky Area of Operations.

One notable difference in Kentucky was the presence of a partisan ranger unit directly commissioned by the authorities in Richmond to operate behind the lines in the Bluegrass State. While some debate is possible as to the legitimacy of most irregular warriors in the Trans-Mississippi, there is no debate concerning this unit – the 10th Kentucky Cavalry. Because of this distinction between Kentucky and the Trans-Mississippi, this chapter will pointedly address the differences between these partisan rangers and the other guerrillas in the Commonwealth. The model for this comparison will be the categories devised by Francis Lieber.

The letters and newspapers from this period are very clear as to the extent of the guerrilla activity in Kentucky during the last years of the war. The sheer weight of evidence reveals the incredible presence of these irregular warriors. Unfortunately, this literature seldom recognized any difference between the various groups that made up this wealth of terror. Colonel Thomas Campbell, the commander of the state militia in Hopkins County, Kentucky, responded to an order from the Adjutant General of the state to assemble his troops by indicating that regardless of when he might have received his orders, he was unable to complete them because of the level of guerrilla activity in the area of operations. He informed the Adjutant General that "we have never been clear of Guerrillas since the War commenced. We have now at this time not less than four hundred Guerrillas in Hopkins, Webster, & Marion Counties & they will remain here during the summer unless they are driven out of the county. The way matters are managed in this county it is perfect mockery."

Campbell continued to describe the ineffective actions of Federal forces in the area around Hopkins County, unhappily indicating that these forces would come in and make a show of force to drive the guerrillas away. Within a day or so, according to Campbell, the guerrillas would return and "commit more mischief than ever…robbing citizens of everything that is valuable… the time is coming when all the Union men will leave this part of the state…."[4]

Obviously, Colonel Campbell paid no attention to the subtle question of just who these men were, and what their true military affiliation could have been. This was the general attitude of almost everyone connected with the Union in Kentucky, when asked to deal with or discuss the irregular war that was raging all around them. It was far simpler to lump all irregular warriors together under a single label of "outlaw," than to attempt to deal with them on a more selective basis.

As in a comparison of William Clarke Quantrill in Missouri and John Mosby in Virginia, the guerrillas in Kentucky did not lend themselves to categorization under a single label. Some were just what they were called, outlaws, pure and simple. They were not engaged in a war against the Union, but in the pursuit of personal enrichment. Others were truly fighting the Union on behalf of the Confederate cause, but were not sanctioned by the Richmond government. Just as Quantrill was an embarrassment publicly, their warfare was professed by the Confederates to be out of their control. This may have been true, but these were, for the most part, ex-Confederate soldiers who had deserted the army or simply been separated from their units. They waged a war against the Union, not indiscriminately against all Kentuckians. Finally, there were in Kentucky, direct counterparts of John Mosby, authorized Confederate Partisan Rangers operating under orders from the Richmond government. Each of these groups requires examination, for each affected the war differently.

If one man can be considered the father of guerrilla warfare in Kentucky, it most certainly must be Brigadier General John Hunt Morgan. Morgan's brand of war was very much akin to that of Mosby. Though he spent more time operating as a conventional cavalry than did his Virginia counterpart, his personal preference was for the hit-and-run raid, operating against the enemy's communications and logistics installations. Morgan has been an extremely controversial figure in the study of the war. His detractors show him as unreliable, deserting Braxton Bragg when he was needed most, in order to lead a raid that went explicitly against his commander's wishes. Those who look at Morgan with a friendlier outlook, see him as the epitome of the Southern cavalier — a dashing, handsome young man riding a magnificent steed against the black-hearted Union beasts.

Robert Mackey focuses on John Hunt Morgan as a more conventional raider,[5] but biographers Howard Doll and James Ramage identify the guerrilla-side to John Hunt Morgan very explicitly, and reveal an awareness that it doesn't matter that Morgan wore a grey uniform and maintained a regular commission from the Confederacy — he was, at heart, a guerrilla. Morgan recognized his own penchant for the guerrilla at the same time that many of his contemporaries were chiding these irregulars. His division newspaper, *The Vidette*, printed the following excerpt:

> It is a pleasant assurance we have, from the Louisville papers, that the rebels of Kentucky are determined to resist the Federal Government. Guerrilla bands have been organized over the State, and several "outrages" committed on "peaceable Union citizens." Now, look here, Guerrillas – well, we won't scold you this time.[6]

General Morgan recognized the importance and potential of the small war, which he conducted against the Federal forces within Kentucky. Because of his strong affiliation with Kentucky, and the fact that his 2d Division was manned by nearly 90-percent Kentuckians, Morgan's raids normally were directed at Kentucky or passed through the Bluegrass State.[7]

While most contemporary newspaper men treated Morgan as a Confederate general who raided Kentucky, much the same way as Sheridan would later raid the Shenandoah, George Prentice, the influential editor of the *Louisville Daily Journal,* saw him in a different light. Prentice considered Morgan to be a guerrilla, and repeatedly referred to him as such in print. In March 1864, his newspaper commented that "we can appreciate John Morgan well enough...we detest him for having inaugurated in Kentucky the system of guerilla burnings, robberies, and general depredations."[8] In another short news story in the July 6th *Louisville Daily Journal,* Prentice reported that "the remaining three...were discovered to be Kentuckians, formerly belonging to the guerilla band of General Morgan."[9] Earlier, with reference to the proclamation by Morgan that he would cause the head of any Union officer he captured to be shaved, Prentice wrote: "We don't know if it is very cruel in John Morgan to shave off the hair of all the Federal officers he captures. If the officers have to associate long with him and his guerillas, they may escape a very revolting nuisance by being without hair."[10] As with any campaign that Prentice conducted, he may have stretched his references to Morgan as a guerrilla somewhat, but there was an underlying truth in his statements. Prentice reprinted a story from the *Indianapolis Journal,* which, while discussing the relative merits of the Indiana Legion, spoke of Morgan and the guerrillas in the same breath. After a discussion of how the guerrillas were swarming over the counties along the Ohio River, the article complained about the "Sons of Liberty, whose secret military organization is more damnable than the open operations of those who are butchering loyal men in Kentucky under authority of commissions from Jeff Davis."[11]

For over two years, John Morgan and his raiders consistently made raids into Kentucky, but not in an attempt to seize ground or conquer the Federal troops stationed there. They devoted their time to tearing up railroad tracks, burning railroad stations, destroying telegraph lines and offices, and confiscating any piece of the Federal Government's property that they could get their hands on. Morgan's Raiders had a very strong impact on Kentuckians and the men who had the job of garrisoning the state, but the personal impact of John Hunt Morgan was far more pervasive than just the exploits of his 2d Division. Morgan was a teacher and his organization spawned tens of smaller groups who sought to combat the Unionists in the same way as Morgan had earlier. Some of these groups were regular Confederate troops and their acts were sanctioned by law, while others were not under orders from Richmond, but plied the trade which they had learned so well under Morgan. A quick accounting of the names that occur in the literature of Kentucky in the latter years of the war will reveal the names of the guerrilla chieftains. It is amazing to find that many of these names, far more than half, can also be found connected with the name of John Hunt Morgan in some way.

Just as the tactics and strategy of Jomini dominated the thinking of the generals who planned the larger war, the teaching of Morgan, through example, dominated the conduct of the guerrilla war in Kentucky. Not only did his associates carry on the war on behalf of the

Confederacy, but when the Federal and State governments finally fell upon an effective means of combating the guerrillas – they called on a man who had formerly fought with Morgan and the 2d Division. As much of this chapter focuses on the latter war period in Kentucky, it is obvious that Morgan could not have been a major factor physically. He was either in prison in Columbus or in southwest Virginia during most of the time prior to his death. Even without his physical presence, John Hunt Morgan played a remarkable role in the history of Kentucky. He influenced the leaders of most of the guerrilla groups in the state and continued to plague the Federal Army through his lieutenants who carried the war to the "Yankees" until well after Appomattox.

Partisan Rangers

It is interesting to note the connection made by the Indiana newspaper between Morgan and the guerrilla forces in Kentucky, and between Morgan and the infamous "Sons of Liberty" organization that existed in Indiana and many other border states. Also of note in this story is the final line — the reference to operations in Kentucky of men who were under the authority of commissions from the President of the Confederacy. Perryville was long over, and the regular armies were caught up in battles to the south of Kentucky, so who were these soldiers carrying commissions from Jefferson Davis?

At least a portion of the soldiers to which the article refers were those of Colonel (later Brigadier General) Adam R. Johnson's 10th Kentucky Cavalry, a regularly constituted force of partisan rangers, assigned to an operational area inside the Union lines in Kentucky.

As was the case throughout Kentucky during this period, these partisan rangers were not viewed as legitimate Confederate soldiers, but placed in the general category of guerrillas, and as such, hunted down and treated as outlaws. Throughout the literature of the period, references can be found to members of the command, almost exclusively as guerrillas. Not that Adam Johnson and his men didn't act the part of guerrillas, they did, but they did so under the protection of the same act which protected John Mosby — the Partisan Ranger Act of 1862. By virtue of their status as partisan rangers, these men could carry the war to Union troops by the use of hit-and-run, guerrilla-type tactics and still be considered regular Confederate troops. This point of law was, unfortunately, not recognized or observed by the majority of Kentucky Unionists or military men in reference to Johnson's unit. To their contemporaries they were no more legitimate than any of the other guerrillas swarming over Kentucky.

Johnson had fought with John Hunt Morgan before the Indiana-Ohio Raid, and had narrowly escaped capture on that raid by swimming the Ohio River with a few hundred of Morgan's troops. His unit, as it operated in Kentucky in 1863 and 1864, consisted of many of these same troops and was led almost exclusively by officers from the old 2d Kentucky Cavalry. This cadre of ex-Morgan's raiders entered Kentucky to recruit from the Southern sympathizers and returned Confederate soldiers, in order to raise a regiment that could carry the petty war to the Union-occupied cities and counties of the Bluegrass State.

Even before riding with Morgan, Adam Johnson had been involved in activities behind the Union lines in Kentucky. Earlier in the war, he had been sent by General John C. Breckinridge into Kentucky on what was a two-fold mission. First, he was to deliver a message to a Southern sympathizer in Henderson, Kentucky, and second, he and his companion, Robert Martin, were to recruit among the secessionists in the vicinity and bring out as many troops as they could. They were reportedly offered command of any men they could succeed in bringing out.[12]

Having established that Johnson and a force of Confederates were in Kentucky, the historian must try to determine whether or not they had any effect upon the Commonwealth and its people. A short tour through the pages of the *Louisville Daily Journal* reveals a group that apparently had quite an impact. An editorial report published in the *Journal* demonstrated how widespread was the control of rebel authority, as represented by Johnson's command. The editor complained that much of Kentucky had been abandoned by Federal authorities, particularly that which bordered the Ohio River. While he may have exaggerated some when he opined that "It is true that our main army lines are now established on the border of the Keystone State of the Confederacy, Georgia; and it is equally true that armed men, claiming to be rebel soldiers, fighting under the rebel flag, hold undisputed possession of the largest portion of Kentucky..."[13]

The newspaper's contention that Confederate units held sway over a rather large portion of the state by the fall of 1864 is bolstered by the pleas of civilian and militia officials for help, such as Colonel Thomas Campbell's mentioned earlier. More importantly, the Confederate War Department issued Special Orders, Number 211, in September of 1864, affirming Johnson's authority to "inspect, muster in, and organize recruits and conscripts...organize new regiments of cavalry and infantry, and new companies of artillery." The order went even further than to just give Johnson this authority, but recognized his previous activities within his assigned area. It stated that the "action of Col. A. R. Johnson, heretofore had within the limits of the Department of Western Kentucky, is recognized as coming within the purview of his authority and duties, and is hereby confirmed and made the action of the War Department."[14] Though the Federal Government and the Unionist citizens of Kentucky had refused to recognize Johnson and his troops as anything but guerrillas, operating outside the law, the Confederate Government had officially sanctioned their actions.

This point may at first appear to be small, but it is central to the problem in studying guerrilla warfare during the Civil War and today. Other than one or two famous cavalrymen, guerrillas have been poured into a single mold by historians — as they were by the people of Civil War Kentucky. The actions of these irregular warriors are characterized as those of bandits or murderers who had little effect upon the outcome of the larger conflict. While it is difficult to show a direct correlation between the guerrilla activity in Kentucky and the outcome of Gettysburg or any other major battle of the war, that is not important. For Kentucky and Kentuckians, the war was fought at home by men who had opposing political ideals. While historians have portrayed the violence of the state as an aberration, separate from the war, it was actually an extension of the war into the homes of Unionist and Secessionist alike. This violence was not an aberration, but an example of the violence and tension that existed throughout the border areas of the South during the Civil War. It was, in fact, evidence of the Third War referred to in the opening chapter. The fact that a major portion of that violence was officially sanctioned by the Confederate Secretary of War displays the desire on the part of the Richmond Government to make the North feel the pain and fear of war firsthand, just as the people of the Confederacy had for years. The irregular warfare in Kentucky was not an accident of nature or a simple outbreak of social violence. It was a part of the war effort of the South, and had more impact on the populace of the Bluegrass State than any battle.

To visualize the forces that Johnson commanded as a single large group, occupying the western half of Kentucky, would be a mistake. His units were scattered widely over the central and western portions of the state in an effort to produce the illusion of a larger group. Johnson identified his method of creating this illusion when he wrote that "I sent men into the counties of Henderson, Daviess, and Union, with instructions to recruit men for the duty of picketing all the important roads and demanding passports from citizens; thereby producing the impression that there were various, large, well-organized bodies scattered over that part of the state."[15]

Johnson may have commanded as many as 1,500 men during the time he operated in Kentucky, but they were split into many small groups for operational purposes. Though the citizens of various towns may have expected Johnson at any moment to ride in with a large force, seldom did any of his groups exceed 100 men. The men who commanded his smaller elements, normally holding commissions as captains, were extremely active, as the newspapers of the time will attest. The names of Jacob Bennett, Tom Henry, and others constantly appeared in print for their escapades on the rivers and railroad lines of the Commonwealth.

To examine the background and contribution of each of these young officers would require a volume in itself, but the story of one of them, Captain Jacob Bennett, will serve as an example. Bennett is probably best known to Civil War scholars and enthusiasts as one of the Confederate soldiers who escaped from Columbus Prison with John Hunt Morgan in the fall of 1863.[16] To Adam Johnson and the men of the 10th Kentucky Cavalry he was a comrade in arms, noted for his bravery and loyalty to his men. He was the Captain of Company A, 10th Kentucky Cavalry, and participated in combat throughout the war as a part of this unit. He was with Johnson early in 1862, having been recruited during the trip into Kentucky under the auspices of John C. Breckinridge. Bennett rode with Johnson, in Morgan's Division, throughout 1863 and was captured during the Indiana-Ohio Raid in the summer of 1863. He was first sent to Johnson's Island Military Prison, but along with Morgan's other officers, he was transferred to the State Prison at Columbus to join General Morgan. It was from this prison that he and the others helped Morgan escape and return to the Confederate ranks.[17] Bennett returned to join Johnson's 10th Kentucky after his escape and was extremely active in Kentucky from the winter of 1863-1864 until the end of the war. There was, in Johnson's words, "no man in that regiment who was bolder or more fearless than Captain Bennett."[18] Bennett was the youngest officer in the regiment, but he could not have been accused of being anything less than a valiant fighting soldier.

Johnson's memoirs portray Bennett as a legitimate Confederate soldier, while other contemporary sources, particularly George Prentice, disagree. A comparison of the pages of the

Louisville Daily Journal and Johnson's memoirs shows a distinct difference in the perceptions of Bennett's valor, integrity, and legitimacy. For the same actions, Bennett is considered a hero by the one side, and a murderous horse-thief by the other. The first reference to him in the Louisville newspapers came on March 29, 1864, when the paper reported that the express train from Louisville had been captured by guerrillas at the small way station of Newport and that "the guerillas at the train were...under the command of a villainous character known by the name of Bennette..." The depredation in this case was the stopping of the train, but no one was harmed, as the paper reported, that after burning the passenger cars, Bennett allowed the engine, tender, baggage car, and express car to proceed to their destination.[19] Bennett's entry onto the guerrilla scene in Kentucky was not seen as the triumphant return of a valiant warrior by the Unionists by any means, and through the next fourteen months he would become one of the most feared and wanted men in the Bluegrass State.

Bennett's chief targets seem to have been those that one should expect a regular soldier to attack in the enemy's rear area. He was particularly active along the railroad lines and the rivers of Kentucky, which provided the supplies and communication for the Union armies that were taking the war to the Confederate armies farther south. One month after the first entry in the *Daily Journal*, Bennett was again in the news when it was reported that a steamer on the Green River, the R.B. Speed, was attacked by guerrillas and "Bennett and his gang made the Speed their boarding house until the Dunkerson came up, when the rebels took possession of her, and proceeded to rifle the boat and passengers."[20]

Jacob Bennett continued to be a news item on a very regular basis throughout the remainder of the war. He was normally cast as a notorious horse-thief and murderer, as most of the Confederate guerrillas were, but his actions were entirely consistent with the objectives of a legitimate Confederate cavalry officer, engaged in a war of shadows against an occupying Federal army. Another example of Bennett's actions, this time with no connection to the railroads or communications, continues this thread of action against the government. On May 2, 1864, the *Journal* reported that he and his band were in Morganfield for the session of the Circuit Court. No one was murdered and, as far as can be determined nothing was stolen. Bennett came after a specific officer of the Kentucky State Militia, named Fombell, and when the judge protested, Bennett arrested him. When Fombell finally came forward he was required to give an oath and bond, upon which Bennett released both Fombell and the judge and left.[21]

As stated earlier, Captain Jacob Bennett was not the only partisan ranger who was active along the waterways of Kentucky. A news item in the *Journal* on July 12, 1864, details the account of another band working in this fertile field. In this case it was a group commanded by a guerrilla named Tom Henry, upon whom the newspaper conferred the rank of captain. A small group of six guerrillas, apparently from a larger command of about 50 former Morgan raiders, had taken control of a steamer on the Ohio River named the Tarascon. They had appeared very comfortable in their situation and, upon finding a Federal soldier on board, "they at once insisted that he should accompany them to the bar and join them in a social drink...when the glasses were filled, one of the scoundrels proposed a toast to 'the health of Jeff Davis.'"[22]

This story illuminates some interesting aspects in the activities of the partisan rangers in Kentucky during the latter stages of the war. The extent to which guerrillas, whether partisans or not, were effective in creating problems along the Ohio River and other waterways is well documented. Attacks on river steamers were not unique occurrences, but almost every-day events. Only by stationing gunboats off of the major landings or at strategic points along the rivers could the Union forces slow down the rebel work against this avenue of commerce. Even then, only the locations at which there were gunboats were safe, and the banks of the Ohio stretched over a great many miles. Captain Tom Henry was another partisan ranger belonging to Johnson's command. Formerly of the Eleventh Kentucky Cavalry, Henry was placed under the 10th Kentucky after the reorganization of the Eleventh in June of 1863.[23] His band of 50 men was representative of the size of the companies of the 10th Kentucky that operated under Johnson's direction. The fact that the guerrillas did not harm the steamer or its crew because it was not "connected with the Government" gives an indication that they were more than just highwaymen. It wasn't consistent with the image of a mere robber to allow possible booty to slip through their fingers. Robbers would have plundered a private vessel just as quickly as one which was under contract to the Federal Government. Lastly, and possibly most interesting, is the air of calm that the article accorded to the six guerrillas. Their relative lack of urgency indicated the freedom that Confederate guerrillas were accustomed to in these months. They were comfortable enough to pause for a cool drink to Jeff Davis' health, and to invite a Federal soldier to join them.

To an outside observer, it would appear that these actions are more in line with those of a soldier than those of a common thief. Bennett is a perfect example of the question of legitimacy that was raised earlier. He was a commissioned officer in the Provisional Army of the Confederate States of America and had been accorded the privileges of a prisoner of war after his capture in Ohio. He was still a member of the same unit that he had been in during that raid, and was, in fact, still serving under the same commander as he had been in the summer of 1863. His actions were consistent with the tactics of John Hunt Morgan's 2d Division and he was considered to be on a valid mission under the rules of warfare by the Richmond Government. With all of this going for him, Bennett was still viewed as a mere outlaw by the people of Kentucky and the Federal authorities.

By August of 1864, Bennett and the other members of Johnson's command had become such a thorn in the side of the Union element in the state that Brigadier General Hugh Ewing felt justified to instruct General E. H. Hobson in Evansville that "if Johnson is taken, he should be shot on the spot. I will be responsible for the killing of the entire command," Johnson included. "This is law; I hope you will execute it."[24] The law to which Ewing refers is obviously General Order No. 100, but that law refers to bands of men who are not regularly constituted and do not continue the war on a permanent basis. To apply this to Johnson's men appears to be a misperception, for they were a recognized unit of the Confederate Army. In an October 6, 1864, letter to his Union counterpart, Robert Ould, the Confederate representative concerning prisoner exchanges, wrote that:

> It is represented to me by very reliable authority that 100 of Col. Adam R. Johnson's men and twenty-five or thirty of General Morgan's men, embracing

three or four officers, are at Louisville and not held or treated as prisoners of war. How is this? All these men are regularly enlisted soldiers.[25]

It appears obvious that the Union authorities chose to deal with Johnson's command under Article 82 of Order No. 100 (see Appendix A), which placed them in the context of highway robbers and pirates. With the overt reference to these men as Confederate soldiers, Robert Ould placed them in a different category — that covered by Article 81 — which delineated those actions required towards partisans. As partisans, Johnson's men were entitled to be accorded all the privileges of prisoners of war.

Obviously, Adam Johnson's men had a great deal of effect in Kentucky, but they were not the only regular Confederate troops who were active in the Bluegrass State during this period. Other units, acting under authority from General Nathan Bedford Forrest or General Joseph Wheeler, found their way into Kentucky with various objectives and missions. Kentucky was nominally under Union control, but its populace was filled with Secessionists and returned Confederate soldiers, who were either on parole or had deserted. As the war became one of attrition, this pool of possible recruits became more and more important to the Confederate war effort. Forrest, though publicly espousing a dislike for guerrilla warfare, was responsible for sending groups into the Bluegrass State in an attempt to tap this important personnel resource.

A letter from an anonymous Union soldier details the status of his section of the state and the activities of one such recruiting mission. He complained to his correspondent about conditions in the local area, indicating significant problems with horse thieves and guerrillas. He openly accused them of murder and indicated that "what Union men they do not murder, are fleeing as chaff before the wind to escape their foul hands and death." The soldier expressed his concerns that Federal authorities had not been able to deal with guerrillas and concluded "that portion of the district west of the Nashville Railroad and south of the Salt River, thence to the Ohio and Cumberland Rivers, is subject to these outlaws and controlled by them." Interestingly, though he referred to them as outlaws, he went on to indicate that they were recruiting for the Confederacy and shared an oath of allegiance that was found on one of their number who was captured. In the end, he indicated the long term problem the group posed for the Union, when he surmised that "If we are to keep Gen. Sherman's communications open, and prevent his supplies from being cut off, this insolent recruiting must be stopped."[26]

The prevalence of the guerrilla menace is again underlined by this plea from a Kentuckian who had experienced the problem firsthand. The oath that the recruiting team carried is particularly interesting in light of the legitimacy question. There would be little reason for outlaws to require an oath of allegiance to Jefferson Davis and the Confederacy, as they would owe no allegiance to anyone but themselves. How many of the recruits secured by the Confederates stayed in Kentucky to operate as guerrillas and how many journeyed south to join Forrest or another Confederate unit cannot be measured, but it is obvious that the Richmond Government or its military emissaries attempted to secure men from the heart of Union-occupied territory.

Another reason for Confederate incursions into Kentucky was to secure needed supplies and deny such supplies to the Union armies. This subject will be dealt with at length later, but a short news item from the *Journal* serves to outline the intent of the Confederates and the involvement of Nathan Bedford Forrest. It outlined the capture of a group of guerrillas who indicated they had been sent into Kentucky by General Forrest specifically to recruit, as was the group previously mentioned, but also to prevent the harvest of the bountiful crops that could be used to feed Union armies. Predictably, this pursuit was not well received by the editor of the *Journal*, as he complained that "if lawless characters can be instigated to band together and rob the farmers of their horses, pillage the country, interrupt civil pursuits, carry terror to the hearts of the people, they will gloat over the successful scheme and applaud the fiendish warfare."[27]

These people and events do not represent the total picture of the partisan ranger activity in Kentucky in 1864 and 1865, but are intended to serve as an outline of the operations in which they were involved and the effects that these operations had upon the state.

The second category in this scheme of guerrilla warfare is that of the war-rebels. This category represents returned Confederate soldiers or Secessionists who chose to take the war to the Union authorities and citizens in their own unique way. They represent the gray area in the question of legitimacy, and are the most intriguing of the three categories of guerrillas.

War-Rebels

This second group of Confederate guerrillas is a much looser entity than the partisan rangers as represented by Adam Johnson's command. These small groups of ten to fifty men were normally not connected with any larger organization, although one of these groups — commanded by Colonel George Jessee — at times numbered in the hundreds. These groups included the guerrillas who got the most press in Kentucky, and this contributed to the misperception of the role of partisans who operated during the same period.

These groups were not specifically authorized to operate in Kentucky, as were Johnson and others, but were in some cases recognized by the Richmond Government as serving their purpose quite well. They were treated by the Unionists under Article 82, which provided much less legitimacy, and within the strict legal limits of the period, they probably did fall under the power of this article.

Regardless of their status as guerrillas, these men believed themselves to be soldiers, dedicated to the Confederate cause. They were normally ex-Confederate soldiers, often having served with Morgan, and continued to carry the war to their sworn enemies from the North. It should not come as a surprise to anyone that these men acted as they did. They had been active in the battle against the invading Federal armies on many battlefields and could hardly be expected to lay down their arms simply because they were no longer under the direct command of the rebel authorities.

Kentucky provided an environment that allowed these war-rebels to flourish and complicate the Union war effort. Though under Federal martial law, the state was replete with men who had Southern sympathies and these people provided a support base for not only the partisan rangers, but also the war-rebels who fought throughout the state. As with the partisan rangers, a look at the men that are categorized as war-rebels explains their reasons and importance.

Without a doubt, the most infamous guerrilla in the Civil War was William Clarke Quantrill. Though his name surfaced in every border state of the Trans-Mississippi, Quantrill closed out his career in the Bluegrass State and was buried there after his violent demise. An interesting little book on Quantrill's time in Kentucky was published by Thomas Watson in 1971. Entitled *The Silent Riders*, the small volume was originally written as a radio documentary for a Louisville radio station, and later published in paperback. According to Watson, Quantrill and his band entered Kentucky between the first and fifth of January 1865, entering the state in the southwestern corner. For the next four months, Quantrill brought the violent brand of warfare that he had practiced in Missouri to bear upon the Unionists of Kentucky. He opened his stay in Kentucky with the murder of fourteen Union soldiers whom he had convinced that he was a Union officer.[28]

While the Richmond Government chose not to emphasize its relationship with Quantrill, he held a valid commission as a Captain in the partisan rangers, and had seen regular service with General Sterling Price and others.[29] Because he and his followers followed the "black flag" and had perfected the art of fighting on a no-quarter basis, he was at times an embarrassment to the Confederates.[30] Nevertheless, they did not hesitate to utilize his unique skills when it suited their purpose. As he had in Missouri, Quantrill struck terror in hearts of Kentuckians and was perceived as an arm of the rebel cause. This is not to say that he was accorded the protection of the laws of warfare, for he was not. He was considered to be an outlaw, possibly the most notorious to ever walk on Kentucky soil, and had he survived his wounds, would most certainly have been tried as a criminal, as were many of his Southern counterparts.

Though Quantrill was the most celebrated of the men who fall into this second category, he was by no means the most important. He spent a relatively short period of time in the Commonwealth and did not have the long-term effects of a few other war-rebels who spent much longer combating the Unionists of Kentucky.

The most celebrated Kentucky war-rebels were all products of the John Hunt Morgan "school of guerrilla warfare." With colorful names such as One-Armed Berry and Sue Mundy, a number of these individuals stand out among the rest. Berry and Mundy were first introduced in the literature of Kentucky in a *Louisville Daily Journal* news item in October 1864. The article identified the leaders of the guerrilla band to be "a man with but one arm named Berry, formerly of Morgan's command" and "the officer second in command, recognized by the men as Lieutenant Flowers." After this standard identification, the article goes on to indicate the uniqueness of this particular second-in-command, in that "the officer in question is a young woman, and her right name is Sue Mundy. She dresses in male attire, generally sporting a full Confederate uniform. Upon her head she wears a jaunty plumed hat, beneath which escapes a wealth of dark brown hair..." The newspaper, in this article, connected this group to John Hunt Morgan and at least hinted at their previous service in the Confederate army. With this group now operating in Kentucky without Morgan, they have assumed a status different from the Partisan Rangers. This group was a favorite target for George Prentice and he closed the article with a further description of Sue Mundy, indicating that "prior to connecting herself with Berry's gang of outlaws, she was associated with the gang commanded by the notorious scoundrel Captain Alexander."[31]

In reality, Sue Mundy was not a young lady or Lieutenant Flowers, but an ex-Confederate artillery captain named Marcellus Jerome Clarke who had served with Morgan on his last raid into Kentucky. His father had been a storekeeper in Bloomfield, Kentucky, and Mundy was active in that area until March of 1865.[32] Mundy represents the epitome of the war-rebel category in Kentucky. Entering Kentucky with Morgan on his last raid, he remained with his division until Morgan's death and then returned to the Bluegrass State. The earlier reference to his being part of a group led by Captain Alexander puts Mundy in the command of Colonel George Jessee, who will be discussed later in this section. Being in his home state, no longer connected to the main Confederate army, Mundy took the war to the people he considered the enemies of his country and state in the same way as John Morgan had in earlier years. During the rest of 1864 and the spring of 1865, many of the exploits of Confederate irregulars were attributed to Sue Mundy. The many reports of his activities, when compared, indicate that he could not have been in all the places that were claimed. As with other notorious guerrillas he was credited with many actions in which he could not possibly have taken part. His name brought forth the same kind of terror that Quantrill's did and they were reputed to have joined forces for a period of time.[33] When finally captured in March of 1865, Mundy was given the semblance of a trial and sentenced to be executed for murder. He claimed that he was a Confederate soldier and had carried out the killings that he was accused of in that role. He claimed his Confederate commission and, as Henry C. Magruder in the opening lines of this chapter, he maintained that he was acting on behalf of the Confederacy throughout his time in Kentucky. In the end, just before his death, he proclaimed: "I hope in and die for the Confederate cause."[34]

Mundy's continued emphasis on his Confederate commission and his relationship with Morgan and Buckner were calculated to align him with more regular soldiers. His detractors have maintained that he would have said anything to have escaped the noose and this would seem reasonable, but could he have really believed that he could have saved himself at such a late hour upon the gallows? It is completely possible that his statement from the platform represented his own perception of his deeds and was an honest attempt to represent his life and actions. His life, and death, comes down to a difference in perception between Mundy and the Union authorities who held the power of life and death over him. It should come as no surprise that he was hanged when one remembers the orders of General Ewing earlier in regards to a force that possessed a far greater claim to legitimacy.

A third individual, beyond Clarke and Magruder, who has been placed in the category of war-rebel is Colonel George Jessee. Jessee was a regimental commander with John Morgan on his final raid into the Commonwealth, apparently cut off from the command after the defeat at Cynthiana. In a report to the Confederate Congress, Jessee detailed that "he had remained in this [Owen] and one or two adjoining counties, with his men not held together in compact form, here in the very heart of Kentucky, for many months, almost undisturbed by the Federal troops immediately in his vicinity."[35] Jessee and his troops, including the unit referenced earlier under Captain Alexander,[36] had been separated after the disastrous fight at Cynthiana and had found it to be much safer to stay in the area of Owen County than to attempt to return to Confederate lines. Though now behind the lines of the main armies, Jessee's fervor for the war appears to have lost none of its edge. He repeatedly, until after the surrender at Appomattox, continued the war in that section of Kentucky with a unit that he claimed to be over 1,000 strong.[37]

The case of Jessee and his soldiers accentuates the problem in dividing the guerrillas into separate categories. He was, by the admission of Confederate representatives, a regularly enrolled member of the Confederate Army and so were his soldiers. They could hardly be accused of not believing in the Confederate cause, after following Morgan into Union-held Kentucky. These were soldiers, but unlike the rangers they were without specific orders authorizing their activities and failed to return to the main Confederate armies. Though not considered deserters by the Richmond Government, they were considered as outlaws by Union officers. General John Palmer, then commanding the Union forces in Kentucky, in responding to a proposal of surrender from Jessee and another guerrilla leader, Moses Webster, informed Brigadier General Stephen Burbridge that "I do not recognize Colonel Jessee or any other pretended military officer as having authority to speak for any other person."[38] Though a regular army officer in the service of the Confederacy, Jessee's form of warfare earned him the name of outlaw and the treatment that went with it.

These men represent the category of war-rebels well, but it must be remembered that there were many more than just these few. War-rebels made up the majority of the guerrillas studied during the research for this project, for they received the most press coverage and built reputations that struck terror in the minds of the Union citizens. Other names, such as the notorious Champ Ferguson, also evoked the same fear that Mundy or Magruder did and these represent only the more famous of the Kentucky war-rebels. Each area of the state had their own hero or villain, as much of the guerrilla warfare was carried on by local men against other local men. The difference between these men and the partisan rangers discussed earlier should now be apparent. Though both professed to fight for the Confederate cause, the rangers had the benefit of specific authorization from Richmond while the war-rebels carried the war to the Federal authorities on their own account without authorization beyond the ties they held with the regular Confederate army and its cause.

Outlaws

The third and final category of guerrillas is the outlaw. The editors of the *Journal* and the Federal authorities wrote and spoke constantly of the outlaws, brigands, murderers, and bushwhackers who roamed the hills of Kentucky. As has been shown in the preceding pages, some of the guerrillas that were active in Kentucky were actually Confederate soldiers and others were war-rebels who, at least in their own perceptions, fought for the Confederate cause and not simply the personal aggrandizement for which an outlaw strives.

A portion of the guerrillas reported in the Bluegrass State were simply what the authorities said they were — outlaws. Towns were sacked and people murdered without any consideration as to their political allegiance or geographical sympathies. As in any violent society, a faction arose that held no concern for human life and used the war as an excuse to either settle old debts or seek personal gain. These men were similar to other groups found throughout the border states during the war, but in Kentucky they were particularly evident in the months and years that followed the war. As the war closed, the partisans and war-rebels surrendered and sought the protection of the amnesty oath. This third category of men, not constrained by the failure of the Confederate effort, continued their depredations upon the people of Kentucky. A letter written to General D. W. Lindsey, the State Adjutant General, in October 1865 indicates the extent of the problem in Breathitt County. In it, two prominent citizens request the presence of state troops to "preserve law and order and assist the Civil Officers of said county in the execution of the laws." These men exhibit significant dismay with the state of Breathitt County and close the letter by indicating that "there are still lawless bands and ill disposed men in said county who resist the arrest of men indicted for various crimes and the Civil Officers are unable to make the necessary arrests and do their official duties generally..."[39]

Though it is impossible to identify the individuals to whom the Breathitt County citizens refer, it would be hard to justify their actions under the auspices of support for the Confederate cause. It is possible that some of the men who are here classified as war-rebels crossed the line after the war's end and deserve the label of outlaws. The categorization of these men has been done arbitrarily and as such is imperfect. Clear-cut lines of demarcation between the second and third groups are hard to find, and even harder to support.

The final goal of this portion of the study must be a discussion of the legitimacy of each of these groups in respect to their connection to the Confederate Government. The first and third groups are easily dealt with on this subject. The rangers were, by the admission of the Confederate authorities, regularly enlisted soldiers in the Provisional Army of the Confederate States of America. Their leaders carried valid commissions from the Confederate Congress and had been assigned the specific mission in which they were involved. There can be little argument as to the legitimacy of their claim and their entitlement to be treated as prisoners of war. The Union authorities, who at first treated them as outlaws, later admitted their actual status and accorded them those rights and privileges.[40] The outlaws who made up the final group obviously fall outside the purview of any legitimacy from the Confederacy and were rightfully treated under the rules set down in Article 82 of General Orders No. 100.

The category that allows bountiful room for discussion and disagreement is that of the war-rebels. These men were perceived as outlaws by the Union authorities and hanged as such when they were captured. They were ignored in their pleas that they were Confederate soldiers and should have received the same privileges as the partisan rangers. They perceived themselves, or maintained that they did, as serving the Confederacy against its enemies and in large part were former soldiers of the Confederate army who had, for one reason or another, found themselves in Kentucky during the latter stages of the war. Could they have been expected to remain idle while surrounded by Federal soldiers and martial law? In a time in our history when violence was not an aberration, but the normal condition of society, who could be surprised that these fighting men chose to continue their fight against the North? After all, had not the fire brands of the secession movement painted a picture of military rule and the terror of black soldiers policing the South? In Kentucky, this was exactly the situation that the returned Confederate soldiers found. Martial law was in effect and though the Emancipation Proclamation did not apply to slaves in Kentucky, blacks were being enlisted into the Federal service to police the state. It would be hard to imagine a harder pill to swallow for men who clung to the Southern mentality, and believed in the institutions that characterized the South prior to the war.

Whether or not these men were legitimately fighting for the Confederate cause or simply blood-thirsty outlaws is totally a matter of perceptions. The Union authorities perceived them as bearing no legitimacy and thus treated them as outlaws. They professed to be soldiers and apparently perceived themselves as more than outlaws, but patriots of the Confederacy. To the historian it is a hard decision to make as to how they should be classified. As this study has chosen to deal with these individuals as a separate category, it should be easy for the reader to identify the bias of the author. Relying on the more modern definition of the guerrilla and the legitimate role of guerrilla warfare in society, the author believes these men to have been Confederate soldiers by the spirit of General Orders No. 100, if not by the letter of it. The historical evidence indicates that their actions were, for the most part, directed at the Federal authorities and Union sympathizers who they believed to be their enemies. Their burning of crops, destruction of trains, interruption of commerce, and killing of soldiers bears a remarkable similarity to the actions of Sherman in his march to the sea or Sheridan's campaign of destruction in the Shenandoah Valley. Though not a proponent of counter-factual history, the author found himself constantly wondering how these men would have been treated if the South had emerged intact after the war. Would they have been treated as criminals, as they were by the Union authorities, or would they have been hailed as heroes by the people for whom they professed to be fighting?

As with any story, the guerrilla war in Kentucky had more than one side. In the preceding pages we have categorized the Confederate guerrillas, identified some of the more important leaders, and examined the causes and impacts of guerrilla war in the Commonwealth. Now we must turn our attention to the Union side of the conflict. The subject has been broached in broad terms during the discussion of the petty war's impact upon the politics of the state, but there is much more that must be said.

The old saying that "violence breeds violence," is borne out very clearly in the response of the Union officials in Kentucky to the continual crisis in which the state found itself from 1863-1865. The larger war had been in the Bluegrass State and left the state in a disorganized condition. A Confederate government had been installed in Frankfort and then forced to flee at the double-quick. The joy of secessionist sympathizers was short-lived, for the Federal Government was quick to return the state to the status quo. State officials such as Governor Bramlette must have breathed a sigh of relief when the invaders left, anticipating a much calmer time with the war gone from the Commonwealth's borders. But this calmer time was not to be for the people of Kentucky.

While it was true that the grand armies had left the state and would not return in earnest for the remainder of the war, Kentucky was far from peaceful. The guerrilla bands identified earlier were, in many cases, just beginning to hit their stride in damaging the Union war effort. It was in the latter part of 1863, after the disastrous raid by Morgan into Indiana and Ohio, that the number of guerrillas in the state began to increase dramatically. Adam Johnson brought his cadre to the Bluegrass State and began recruiting, and soon Jacob Bennett and his contemporaries were hard at work on the state's rivers and railroads. The State officials, particularly Governor Bramlette, were confident that the State and Federal forces would be able to handle the guerrilla challenge without problem. He and the other Union authorities were overcome by the "arrogance of ignorance," mentioned earlier. Possessing superior numbers and firepower they saw the defeat of these small bands as a simple numerical equation — something which it was not.

Though the guerrillas were relatively few in number, they were at home in the territory where they operated. The units sent to deal with them lacked the leeway to chase them wherever necessary and if they were Federal troops, rarely knew the country. A newspaper's complaint that "Federal cavalry, unacquainted with the country, lose all of their effectiveness when sent in pursuit of these bold marauders,"[41] was representative of problems that regular cavalry had in dealing with the elusive irregulars. An additional problem, possibly more significant to the Governor, was the infrastructure of supporters that the guerrillas had throughout the state.

With a large group of supporters, guerrillas could obtain shelter, food, and information whenever they needed. The guerrillas were viewed by most of the state as fighting the Confederate fight, a perception that led many a Kentucky family to harbor or feed the irregulars. The problem was emphasized in many newspaper accounts throughout the state and editors like Prentice complained that "the guerrillas are shielded by many of the citizens, and it is next to impossible to surprise and capture them, as they are informed of all of our movements by their sympathizing friends."[42]

These problems, the guerrilla's knowledge of the ground he selects to haunt, and the existence of a support structure within society, are trademarks of the guerrilla war that exist to this day.[43] Bramlette grew frustrated by his inability to stop the depredations of these irregulars through normal military means. Feeling the need for more drastic action, the Governor determined to strike at that portion of the guerrilla menace most available to them — their support structure. On January 4, 1864, he published a proclamation that began an escalation of the guerrilla war that would not end until many men had been hanged without benefit of trial and many families had been deprived of their possessions and homes. The Governor's purpose, and his target, is clear from the text of the statement. He identified the level of guerrilla depredations that he perceived in the Commonwealth and complained that much of it "can, in a large degree, be traced to the active aid of rebel sympathizers in our midst..." He believed these sympathizers to be guilty of providing aid and intelligence to Southern guerrillas and maintained that by "giving them information, affording them shelter, supplying them with provisions, and otherwise encouraging and fomenting private raids are in criminal complicity with all the outrages perpetrated by the marauders whom they secretly countenance." His answer to dealing with that portion of the population that he perceived to be disloyal was simple, he instructed state and local officials that "in every instance where a loyal citizen is taken off by bands of guerrillas, immediately arrest at least five of the most prominent and active rebel sympathizers in the vicinity of such outrage for every loyal man taken by guerrillas." He particularly instructed the officials to concentrate on relatives of known guerrillas, commenting that if the disloyal citizens of Kentucky chose not to aid authorities in policing these guerrilla bands then "they must expect to reap the just fruits of their complicity with the enemies of our State and people."[44]

The Governor's attempt to eliminate the support structure aiding the guerrillas opened up a number of touchy questions concerning the legitimacy of the guerrillas and the means of identifying rebel sympathizers. Bramlette's methods, while not as radical as General Ewing's Order No. 11 (see Appendix B) in Missouri, begged for retaliation from the irregular warriors.

Repeatedly, the Governor and others referred to those who aided these irregular soldiers as "rebel sympathizers" and supporters of the rebellion. Though these people were hard to identify, what would this mean if he was correct? By recognizing the supporters of the guerrilla war as true believers in the Confederate cause, the Governor by inference aligned the guerrillas themselves with the Confederacy. Though inferring this through his identification of their supporters, he and the Federal officials later maintained that the guerrillas were not supporters of the rebellion — a position which might elevate their actions in the eyes of many — but simply outlaws, devoid of political conviction or passionate beliefs. The dichotomy represented by the Governor's actions is readily apparent. Though convinced that the support structure was firmly based on a belief in the rebellion, he was unable to admit that the guerrillas whom these citizens supported were fighting based on that same belief. If, in fact, these guerrillas were simply outlaws with no political or social goals, they would hardly have spared the Confederate sympathizers while depredating against the Unionists. Some of the wealthiest families of the Bluegrass State were supporters of the rebellion and they would have made tempting targets for these shadowy warriors. An objective look at the situation, a perspective that one could hardly expect the Governor to have had, would reveal that the authorities could not have it both ways. If the method of identifying the guerrilla's supporters was their loyalty to the Confederate cause, then it must follow that the guerrillas were in general tied to the same belief. If the guerrillas were not true believers, but the unprincipled outlaws of whom Prentice wrote, then it was unjust to lay the whole blame for their support upon the heads of those perceived to be rebel sympathizers. By identifying the guerrilla's supporters with the rebellion, the officials of Kentucky gave these irregulars a form of legitimacy, which cannot be denied. Though whether or not many of them were Confederate soldiers can be debated, the Governor's actions moved them up the ladder to a point where they were, at the least, considered to be patriots of the Confederacy.

Additionally, another outcome of the proclamation was possible. By identifying those of southern sympathies with the guerrillas, Governor Bramlette greatly enlarged the support network that was available to these bands. It would be hard to measure the number of families identified as supporters, but what was the reaction of sympathizers, who in no way supported the guerrillas, after they were punished for something they had not done? The State authorities ran a very high risk of turning many rebel sympathizers, who looked upon the guerrillas as outlaws, into their supporters because of this alignment of the two groups.[45]

Another problem area that the proclamation posed was how the Government went about identifying these citizens who possessed sympathies for the Confederacy. It would have been easy if all of those who believed in the "cause" had worn a badge or lived together in one community, but that was not the case. Every town was inhabited by supporters of both sides and even families were split by the question of secession, which underlies the rebellion. George Prentice could hardly have been considered to be a sympathizer with the rebellion, but his wife was a known secessionist and his sons served in the Confederate Army. With this intermingling of politics and personalities, it would have been difficult at best to identify rebel sympathizers. Unfortunately, the question came down to the perceptions of loyalty, as it did all along the border. In Texas, men were hanged for being thought to support the Union and jailed for refusing to accept southern currency. Any possible inkling that a man was not "right" was enough to place him under suspicion and thus in danger.[46] In Kentucky, things were not much better. When a guerrilla raid occurred, and they occurred regularly, the area was scoured for perceived sympathizers, regardless of their actual complicity or innocence. The fact that a man had a son in the Confederate Army or supported George B. McClellan for president was ample proof that he was guilty of supporting the rebellion and thus the guerrillas. The old adage, "if you're not with us, you're against us," came into play time and time again, as State and Federal officials made the determination of who was loyal and who was not, in line with their information and feelings. How many people were wrongly denied their civil rights (even though martial law was not declared until July 1864) cannot be measured, but it would appear to be significant. An additional complication, which will be discussed later, was the questionable caliber of a few of the military men who were given the authority to determine who was loyal and who was a sympathizer.

Governor Bramlette's proclamation failed to slow the tide of guerrilla violence, though it is hard to determine whether it was because of ineffective enforcement or targeting the wrong segment of the population. The year that followed his decree included the worst guerrilla depredations of the war and led the Federal authorities to take matters into their own hands by the summer of 1864.[47] The Union army officers who were given the power to police the state by Lincoln's proclamation of martial law were operating under the legal framework of General Order No. 100. The order severely limited the possibility of legitimacy being accorded to any irregular fighter, regardless of his background and circumstances. The men who were placed in power to carry out the order gave the guerrillas even less opportunity to be recognized as soldiers. Beginning with General W. T. Sherman, the Union commanders in the West took the view that the only way to deal with guerrillas was swift and violent action. This action was not to be limited to locating guerrillas and killing them on the field of battle, but would extend to the depopulation of their perceived supporters and summary executions in reprisal for raids.

In a letter to General Leslie Coombs shortly after the declaration of martial law, General Sherman confided that he knew "that families of hitherto great respectability in Lexington and Frankfort, blind to the interests of the industrious classes of your State, have and do continue to encourage the public enemy in every way in their power."[48] Recognizing the need for someone to subdue the guerrilla forces in Kentucky and believing that Governor Bramlette's actions were inadequate, General Sherman was prepared to act.

Sherman's determination to solve this problem and get on with the business he deemed necessary is evident throughout his correspondence. His representative in Kentucky, Brig. Gen. Burbridge, was given great leeway in dealing with the guerrilla menace; so much leeway that he was repeatedly accused of abusing his power and the people of Kentucky. It is hard to imagine how General Burbridge could have overstepped the bounds of his authority when one reads the instructions sent to him by General Sherman in June of 1864. Sherman begins by providing explicit guidance on the legitimacy of guerrillas in Kentucky, indicating that they are "are not soldiers but wild beasts unknown to the usages of war." His description of what constitutes a soldier, rather than a guerrilla, is standard for the time and involves the need for a soldier to be "enlisted, enrolled, officered, uniformed, armed, and equipped by some recognized belligerent power, and must, if detached from a main army, be of sufficient strength, with written orders from some army commander, to do some military thing..." It is interesting that Adam Rankin Johnson's Partisan Rangers meet this description, but Sherman never bothered to make a distinction amongst any irregular warriors in Kentucky. After his instructions to Burbridge concerning the legitimacy of guerrilla warriors in Kentucky, Sherman goes on to deal with the issue of sympathizers by ordering his subordinate to "arrest all males and females who have encouraged or harbored guerrillas and robbers...and when you have enough, say 300 or 400, I will cause them to be sent down the Mississippi through their guerrilla gauntlet, and by a sailing ship send them to a land where they may take their negroes and make a colony with laws and a future of their own."[49]

Seldom in the history of our country has a military officer been given such official leeway to deal with armed men and noncombatants alike. Burbridge was authorized to take whatever actions were necessary to rid Kentucky of these "wild beasts," an authority he did not hesitate to use. Of just as much interest is General Sherman's reference to sending southern supporters down the Mississippi. As stated before, one of the important characteristics of guerrilla warfare is the existence of a support infrastructure. Governor Bramlette had recognized this and attempted to deal with it in his January 1864 proclamation. General Sherman chose to take the idea one step farther, determining that the best way to break-up the support network that made the guerrillas so hard to deal with was to depopulate the areas where these supporters lived. As in the Missouri counties affected by Order No. 11, by simply removing the populace the Union army hoped to destroy the irregulars' ability to hide, refurbish, and gather information. It is interesting, in light of General Sherman's concept, to observe the guerrilla war that once raged against Soviet forces in Afghanistan. In the latter part of 1985, the American news media reported that the Soviet army was carrying out a forced depopulation of those areas under the nominal control of the guerrilla forces. The villagers were being forced to move out of the country, into neighboring Pakistan. Apparently, the Soviet army also believed that the lessons of history showed depopulation to be an extremely effective means of delivering a blow to irregular fighters, regardless of country or century.

General Burbridge took the instructions from his commander seriously, and on July 16, 1864, issued his edict to the people of Kentucky. This edict took the form of General

Orders No. 59 (see Appendix C), which was directed at the guerrilla problem point blank and contained some extremely drastic measures to combat these irregulars. His orders directed that sympathizers "living within five miles of any scene of outrage committed by armed men...will be arrested and sent beyond the limits of the United States..." Not only were individuals perceived to be of Southern loyalties deported from Kentucky if they lived too close to a guerrilla raid, but his order also caused their property to be seized and used to pay the government or citizens who had incurred damage. His order did not stop at deportation or economic penalty, but also contained a final provision requiring that "whenever an unarmed Union citizen is murdered, four guerrillas will be selected from the prisoners in the hands of the military authorities and publicly shot to death in the most convenient place near the scene of the outrage."[50]

The first two passages of the General Order are simply restatements of the directions of General Sherman on June 21st, with all of the attendant problems of identification of sympathizers and alienation of the populace. The last passage, that dealing with the summary execution of four "guerrillas" for every Union man murdered by the irregular soldiers, must be credited to Burbridge himself. Nowhere in his orders was he instructed to take such action, and it can be argued that the summary execution of men in such a manner went well beyond the "discretion" with which General Sherman had called upon him to utilize.[51]

Some discussion on the administration of the first two passages will follow later, but for now we must examine the requirement for reprisal killings. Two possible problems existed in following this course of action; how to identify guerrillas and what would be the reaction of the people of Kentucky. The first problem was very easy to solve if one chose not to worry about executing men whose status as guerrillas was questionable. Confederates captured in the Commonwealth of Kentucky during the summer and fall of 1864 could count on being incarcerated under the charge of conducting guerrilla operations. Written authorization from the Richmond Government (the recognized belligerent of Sherman's letter), the wearing of a Confederate uniform, or the size of the unit had no bearing on Burbridge's determination of who was a soldier and who was a guerrilla. Union authorities took the easiest way out at the time, they simply designated everyone suspected of armed conflict with the Federal Government in Kentucky to be a guerrilla and dealt with them accordingly. Though the number of men actually executed under Burbridge's decree is hard to pin down, it undoubtedly exceeded 30 in the months that followed. The newspapers consistently carried references to the executions conducted under this order. In one, a Union lieutenant was ordered to select four guerrillas under his control and have them executed in retaliation for the murder of a local Unionist. In carrying out this order, he selected four prisoners at random from the military prison and executed them, including John Brooks, Robert Brooks, and J. Bradis. At this point, the newspaper finished the article by indicating that "Bradis claimed to be a soldier of the 2d Kentucky rebel cavalry, a member of Company L..."[52]

Bradis' contention that he was a soldier in the 2d Kentucky cannot be verified, a contention, which if true, would place him squarely in the category of war-rebel. Though Bradis may have been the outlaw he was made out to be, two of the men cited in the newspaper article can be positively identified as members of the partisan ranger organization under the overall command of Adam Johnson. Robert Brooks appears on the roster of Jacob Bennett's unit, Company A, 10th Kentucky Cavalry,[53] and John Brooks is listed as a First Lieutenant in Company C of the 10th Kentucky.[54] The latter Brooks is eulogized in *Partisan Rangers* as "John Brooks, of Hopkins county. Murdered by General Steve Burbridge's order at Louisville, 1864."[55] Other evidence of the execution of Confederate soldiers without trial can be found throughout the newspapers of Louisville. In November 1864, after Johnson's men were finally recognized as soldiers and accorded the benefits allotted to prisoners of war, the *Journal* noted that "they established to the satisfaction of the authorities that they were Confederate soldiers, and not outlaws, and had a right to demand that they no longer be treated as guerillas...Capt. L. D. Buckner, of the same command, was executed some weeks since, by order of General Burbridge, as a guerilla..."[56]

While it is true that the perceptions of the Union officials entered into the determination of who was executed, it is incumbent upon any military officer, regardless of time and circumstances, to safeguard legitimate prisoners of war. Similar incidents in Texas and Missouri have long been considered to be massacres, incidents that bear remarkable similarities to those in Kentucky. They were carried out under martial law authority, without the benefit of trial, and with little concern for the guilt or innocence of the people executed.[57] In this matter, the author is dangerously close to criticizing General Burbridge, who is obviously unable to defend himself. The decisions of historical figures must be studied in the context of the environment in which they were made, and it is extremely difficult for the historian to fully understand the pressures under which an official such as Burbridge had to act. In this case, however, Burbridge must be brought to task for errors made by his command. It was at his express order that guerrillas, or suspected guerrillas, were executed. He was, in essence, the judge and jury for these individuals, but no personal guilt was established prior to execution. The execution of Sue Mundy can be understood, as he was specifically charged with certain crimes, but Burbridge's orders to his subordinates contained no specific names of guilty parties, he simply instructed them to "take four guerrillas from the prisoners in your hands," and execute them in the streets.[58]

The names of men executed publicly can be derived from the newspapers and secondary accounts of Kentucky history. It is reasonable to believe, however, that these were not the only executions carried out under the orders of General Burbridge. In his report to the Confederate Senate in March 1865, Colonel J. D. Morris, C.S.A., detailed his capture and subsequent detention in the prison at Lexington. Morris had been sent into Kentucky to gather information and had been captured by Union soldiers. His report indicated that other prisoners, not just those publicized by the media, were executed during Burbridge's command. He detailed the process whereby the officer-in-charge came into the confinement facility and "looking over the men picked out fifteen. They were carried downstairs. In a short time five of them returned. They had drawn lots for their lives and escaped; the other ten were taken out and shot." The depiction of this incident illustrates the random nature of the executions carried out under Burbridge's orders. It appears to have been a common occurrence and, while the exact number of Confederate soldiers who were wrongfully executed will never be known, Colonel Morris' report goes on to give a rough accounting in his experience when he closed by indicating that "three men who were brought in and belonged to Jessee's command, within four hours after their arrival were carried from the prison and hung, and this thing went on until twenty-eight of our number, almost invariably Confederate soldiers, had fallen victim to this unheard of barbarity."[59]

While there is considerable leeway for argument concerning the validity of Burbridge's action, it is difficult not to condemn him. Later in the fall of 1864 he gave orders to take no guerrilla prisoners, officially sanctioning the no-quarter technique that had been used in Missouri for a number of years. Though equally violent, the practice of giving no quarter appears to the author to be far more humane and much closer to the letter of General Orders No. 100. Based on the General Order, the military had the right to summarily execute guerrillas, but upon capturing suspected guerrillas and imprisoning them, it would appear that greater care in the determination of their guilt was incumbent prior to their execution. No requirement of time clamored for their death, and the Federal authorities could have looked into individual guilt at their leisure.

The reaction of Kentuckians to Burbridge's General Orders No. 59 was, as could have been anticipated, dissatisfaction and elevated violence. Shaler wrote that the interference with the people took the form of "taxing of so-called rebel sympathizers for the damage done by the guerrillas...the outrages which the so-called Confederate sympathizers were forced to make good were utterly beyond their control."[60] Federal officials required payments from communities based on their belief that the inhabitants were supporters of the rebellion, without specific evidence.[61] These drastic economic reprisals did little to stop the guerrilla escapades of the numerous bands in Kentucky. Unfortunately, it provided a vehicle to drive the wedge in Kentucky society even deeper. Federal officials were advised by the good Union men of the area, and the advice of these men was constantly colored by vindictive feelings and avarice. The question of loyalty was utilized as an economic weapon by many, as one had only to cast dispersions upon the competition's politics to ruin his business entirely.

The reprisal killings were characterized by a familiar lack of effectiveness. Rather than discouraging the irregulars from their activities, the order simply prompted a renewal of guerrilla violence at an even higher level. It was in the fall of 1864 and spring of 1865 that Mundy, Magruder, and Colonel Jessee were the most active, indicating that the edict had little effect. Published accounts show that the guerrillas specifically threatened to match execution with execution, as in a September newspaper article which indicated that "the guerillas say all deserters are their friends, and they took an oath that they would kill four Union men for him (one of the partisan rangers killed on September 6th); and also say they will kill four for every rebel shot by the Federals, or Yanks, as they call them."[62]

As with most of the measures used by the Federals in their attempt to deal with the guerrillas, General Orders No. 59 probably did more harm than good. The edict, and the manner in which it was carried out, produced little relief from the petty war, while creating further animosity between the military and the populace. One commander, General E. A. Paine, did particular damage in his application of the order.

Paine took command of Paducah in July 1864 at the request of the Union League of America, a request based on the belief by Unionist residents that "rebels are doing all the business, and they are reaping all the advantages of trade."⁶³ Paine's command was short-lived, a total of fifty-one days, but he made the most of the time that he had in punishing anyone who he deemed to be of Confederate sympathies. He levied taxes, seized rents, and confiscated the wealth of many citizens whom he decided were not "loyal." In addition to his economic depredations, Paine jailed a great number of people and carried out the execution of nearly forty.⁶⁴ Coulter describes Paine's tenure as a "military extortion" and characterizes his actions as an "insane course." Complaints of Paine's conduct were so widespread that Governor Bramlette called upon President Lincoln for relief,⁶⁵ and General Ulysses S. Grant was moved to write General Halleck that "he will do to put in an entirely disloyal district to scourge the people, but even then it is doubtful whether it comes within the bounds of civilized warfare to use him."⁶⁶

General Grant's opinion was shared by many, both in and out of the military, and Paine was removed from command, a removal punctuated by his flight to Illinois to avoid the military investigators. Considerable disgust was evident in Kentucky when, in January 1865, a court-martial hearing on the charges resulted in no more than a reprimand for the inept and unprincipled general officer.⁶⁷

Actions such as Paine's and the ill-advised violence that Burbridge's order condoned were of no help to the Union cause in Kentucky. They had little negative effect upon the actions of the guerrillas they were intended to combat, and had serious impact upon the attitude of the people of Kentucky towards the Federal Government.⁶⁸ As 1864 came to a close and 1865 opened, relations between Governor Bramlette and General Burbridge reached an impasse that threatened violence between State and Federal troops. Faced with these circumstances, President Lincoln decided to remove Burbridge from command. On February 10, 1865, the *Louisville Daily Journal* printed an announcement reveling in the fact that, "Maj. Gen. John M. Palmer of Illinois has been appointed to command in Kentucky. Thank God and President Lincoln."⁶⁹ It was now left to General Palmer to deal with the guerrilla problem his predecessor had been unable to solve.

For nearly two years, the State and Federal troops had tried, without much luck, to run down and capture the numerous guerrilla bands roaming the State. The infantry units assigned to the mission had proved to be utterly worthless because the guerrillas were invariably mounted. The conventional cavalry units had experienced a bit more success, but the continued rise of guerrilla raids and violence proved the limits of these troops. As noted earlier by George Prentice, the Federal troops were often from outside of the state or from another county and they seldom had adequate knowledge of the countryside for their mission. The guerrilla bands knew every trail and hiding place, and combined with the possibility of help from their supporters, they were nearly impossible to find.

To combat these disadvantages, General Palmer authorized a new technique against the irregulars. He recognized that the only way to beat the guerrilla was to defeat him at his own game. Regular units had too many restrictions on their actions and were tied down to supply bases and communications lines. Palmer sought to overcome these shortcomings by organizing small units of state troops and civilians (who would have better knowledge of the area) along the same organizational lines as the guerrillas that they would chase. They were given the leeway to stay with a guerrilla band wherever they went, not restricted by artificial lines of jurisdiction or logistics. They were empowered to impress horses and supplies from citizens when necessary, enabling them to stay with the guerrillas and literally run them to ground.

Many of these Union anti-guerrilla units were formed, but the most successful seem to have been those commanded by Captain Ed Terrell and Captain James Bridgewater. These two men became the scourge of the guerrilla units in central Kentucky, establishing a considerable reputation among the people of the State. Their methods worked, and they did much to slow the guerrilla violence, but their violent means and impressments of horses alienated many of the citizens, Unionist and Secessionist alike.

Ed Terrell was a native Kentuckian and had recruited his scouts from the Shelby and Spencer County areas. He was twenty-years old when he signed on as a Union guerrilla-fighter and had already had considerable experience in the war. Terrell had enlisted in the Union army earlier and upon his return to the state, he had joined the militia. Terrell's early career is marked with shadows and violence, but it appears that he deserted the Union army at least once, and may have served in the Confederate service prior to that.[70] Terrell was a violent young man and eventually died a violent death after the war. He was accused of murder numerous times during the war, but his orders from the Government were virtually a "license to kill" and that is exactly how he used them. Terrell's fame was mainly derived from his capture of the Civil War's most hated and feared guerrilla — William Clarke Quantrill.

When news of a guerrilla column came to Terrell, he followed the trail until he found guerrillas or the trail ended, nothing else could draw him off. In May 1865, Terrell picked up the trail of a party of guerrillas near Bloomfield and began to track them. Though the Civil War was virtually over, General Lee having surrendered over a month earlier, Kentucky's petty war was not finished. Terrell and his men found the band of guerrillas in a barn near Wakefield Station and attacked. In the barn were Quantrill and his band of irregulars. Quantrill was wounded in the exchange and captured. Those men of his band who escaped from Wakefield surrendered to authorities in late July 1865.[71]

The other man who epitomized the Union guerrilla-fighters was Captain James Bridgewater. Bridgewater had been active in the State service well before Palmer's assumption of command, and had already established himself as a fighter. A prominent resident of Bloomfield, Kentucky, wrote to Bramlette requesting protection. Her request went on to say that "a threat... would be all sufficient, I presume, it would probably never require to be executed, especially if Bridgewater should be named as executioner-for his *name* is a terror through this community."[72] A review of the Quartermaster and Adjutant General's Papers at the Kentucky Military History Museum reveals that Bridgewater was extremely active in the spring of 1865. From the number of horses that he and his men impressed during the performance of their missions, they could rarely have had time to sleep. Months after the end of hostilities, citizens of Kentucky were still complaining to the Adjutant General that their horses had been wrongfully impressed and desiring their return.[73]

Terrell and Bridgewater are representative of the men who Palmer used successfully to combat the guerrilla menace. Though it is hard to ascertain whether they would have been as effective if the war had not ended in the spring of 1865, it appears that the Union authorities had finally stumbled onto the only method that would work against the guerrillas. They had unsuccessfully tried to eliminate the base of support from which the guerrillas received sustenance and had been unable to deal with these bands using regular infantry and cavalry. The Union guerrilla-fighters were given a blank check in their effort to deal with the irregulars. They utilized the same tactics of terror, speed, and violence that were the trademarks of their adversaries. It was only by becoming guerrillas, with all the attendant rough edges, that the Union soldiers were able to meet the guerrillas on even terms. Reports of outrages by State troops can be found throughout the literature of the period, but these appear to have been isolated instances of lawless violence. The guerrilla-fighters that were used in 1865 were violent and their methods unusual, but they operated under orders, which had only one important clause — stop the guerrilla outrages — and this they did well.

If the earlier contention that one of the objectives of the guerrilla war in Kentucky was to affect the civilian administration of the state, then the guerrillas who worked the Commonwealth must be given great credit for accomplishing that mission. It is obvious that they dictated the Union response to their violence, and forced the Government to consider acts that were drastic and at times detrimental to their own political well-being. The Union response was repeatedly over-zealous and aimed at the wrong part of the populace. It was not until the military recognized that conventional tactics would not eliminate the menace that an adequate plan emerged from the State and Federal authorities.

Notes

1. *Louisville Daily Journal*, September 2, 1864.

2. *Louisville Daily Journal*, September 29, 1865.

3. Thomas Shelby Watson, *The Silent Riders*, (Louisville, Ky.: Beechmont Press, 1971), p 43.

4. Col. Thomas Campbell to General D. W. Lindsey. July 8, 1865. The Quartermaster and Adjutant General's Papers, Kentucky Military History Museum, Frankfort, Kentucky.

5. Robert R. Mackey, *The Uncivil War: Irregular Warfare in the Upper South, 1861-1865*, pp. 123-154.

6. Mackey, p. 46.

7. Bennett H. Yount, *Confederate Wizards of the Saddle: Being Reminiscences and Observations of One Who Rode with Morgan*, (Boston: Chapple Publishing Company, 1914; Reprinted., Dayton, OH.: Morningside Bookshop, 1979), p. 369.

8. *Louisville Daily Journal*, March 19, 1864.

9. *Louisville Daily Journal*, July 6, 1864.

10. *Louisville Daily Journal*, March 8, 1864.

11. *Louisville Daily Journal*, July 1, 1864.

12. William J. Davis, ed., *The Partisan Rangers of the Confederate States Army*, (Louisville, Ky.: George G. Fetter Company, 1904; Reprinted., Hartford, Ky.: Cook & McDowell Publications, 1979), Chapter XI. This appears in Johnson's memoir, and as such is embellished. It is, however, believable in light of other officers who were sent into Kentucky during the war with the same mission.

13. *Louisville Daily Journal*, October 29, 1864.

14. *The War of Rebellion: Official Records of the Union and Confederate Armies*, 128 vols., (Washington: 1880-1901), Series 1, Volume 39, Part 2, P. 817.

15. Davis, p. 100.

16. Davis, pp. 363-384.

17. Davis, pp. 277-279.

18. Davis, p. 278.

19. *Louisville Daily Journal*, March 29, 1864.

20. *Louisville Daily Journal*, April 29, 1864.

21. *Louisville Daily Journal*, May 2, 1864.

22. *Louisville Daily Journal*, July 12, 1864.

23. Davis, p. 341.

24. *Official Records*, Series 1, Volume 39, Part 2, p. 263.

25. *Official Records*, Series 2, Volume 7, pp. 926-927.

26. *Louisville Daily Journal*, July 15, 1864.

27. *Louisville Daily Journal*, April 30, 1864.

28. Watson, pp. 21-23.

29. Richard S. Brownlee, *Gray Ghosts of the Confederacy: Guerrilla Warfare in the West, 1861-1865*. Baton Rouge, LA; Louisiana State University Press, 1958, Louisiana Paperback Edition, 1984, p. 99.

30. The reference to no-quarter indicates that the combatants did not recognize the more subtle rules of war in respect to each other, but were inclined to whatever form of violence that suited them should they be captured. Summary execution was the common result of capture in a no-quarter environment.

31. *Louisville Daily Journal*, October 11, 1864.

32. Watson, pp. 26-27.

33. Watson, pp. 36-37.

34. *Louisville Daily Journal*, March 16, 1865.

35. *Official Records*, Series 2, Volume 8, p. 384.

36. *Louisville Daily Journal*, September 2, 1864.

37. *Louisville Daily Journal*, July 15, 1864.

38. *Official Records*, Series 1, Volume 49, Part 2, pp. 355-356.

39. D. K. Butter and James Lyndon to General John W. Finnell. October 4, 1865. The Quartermaster and Adjutant General's Papers, Kentucky Military History Museum, Frankfort, Kentucky.

40. *Louisville Daily Journal*, November 24, 1864.

41. *Louisville Daily Journal*, July 11, 1864.

42. *Louisville Daily Journal*, August 23, 1865.

43. Examples of this issue are evident in any examination of recent wars in Iraq or Afghanistan. Particularly along the border between Afghanistan and Pakistan (artificially drawn by the British years ago) the Taliban retains a great advantage in their knowledge of the mountains and the support of different Pashtun tribes which occupy these areas. Their tribal affiliations provide them access to aid and intelligence which is difficult for NATO troops to overcome. To make this problem worse, most Western nations are rotating troops in and out of country on tours which are six months to one year in length. This makes it incredibly difficult to create relationships or gain intimate knowledge of terrain in such a short period of time.

44. This policy of making hostages out of family members of suspected insurgents continues today, as units of the US Army used this same tactic in operations in Iraq. It would appear that the tactic is no more successful today than it was in the 1860s.

45. This problem also still exists in the military's operations in the Iraq and Afghanistan. When units punish community members for things they did not do, rather than stemming the flow of the insurgency, they merely add recruits to the enemy force.

46. Alwyn Barr, "Records of Confederate Military Commission in San Antonio, July 2 – October 10, 1862," *Southwestern Historical Quarterly* 70 (July 1966): p. 95.

47. Barr, pp. 345-346.

48. *Official Records*, Series 1, Volume 39, Part 2, pp. 240-241.

49. *Official Records*, pp. 135-136.

50. *Official Records*, p. 174.

51. *Official Records*, pp. 144-145.

52. *Louisville Daily Journal*, September 1864.

53. Davis, p. 309.

54. Davis, p. 315.

55. Davis, p. 341.

56. *Louisville Daily Journal*, November 24, 1864.

57. R.H. Williams and John W. Sansom, *The Massacre on the Nueces River: The Story of a Civil War Tragedy*, (Grand Prairie, TX.: Frontier Times Publishing Company, ca. 1911), pp. 11-23.

58. *Official Records*, Series 1, Volume 39, Part 2, p. 172.

59. *Official Records*, Series 2, Volume 8, pp. 383-389.

60. Nathaniel S. Shaler, *Kentucky: A Pioneer Commonwealth*, Boston, Houghton, Mifflin and Company, 1897, pp. 333-334.

61. E. Merton Coulter, *The Civil War and Readjustment in Kentucky*, Chapel Hill, NC: The University of North Carolina Press, 1926; reprint ed., Gloucester, MA: Peter Smith, 1966, pp. 221-222.

62. *Louisville Daily Journal*, September 7, 1864.

63. *Official Records*, Series 1, Volume 39, Part 2, p. 171.

64. Coulter, *Civil War*, pp. 220-222.

65. Coulter, p. 222.

66. *Official Records*, Series 1, Volume 39, Part 2, p. 342.

67. Coulter, p. 222.

68. Organized cruelty rarely has a positive long-term effect unless the society that supports the military force is openly willing to support it. In most democracies, this tactic works as long as it is not common knowledge in the public sphere, but rarely meets with general approval. Beginning the use of this tactic is rarely useful, unless the military is willing to utilize it to the final conclusion of extermination. If not, eventually the society will be repulsed by its use and the military will be held accountable for its actions.

69. *Louisville Daily Journal*, February 10, 1865.

70. Watson, pp. 45-47.

71. Watson, pp. 45-66.

72. Mrs. Glasscocke to Governor Bramlette, January 2, 1865, The Quartermaster and Adjutant General's Papers, Kentucky Military History Museum, Frankfort, Kentucky.

73. Mrs. Glasscocke to Governor Bramlette, January 2, 1865; John Davis to General Lindsey, August 10, 1865.

Chapter 2

Kansas-Missouri

On August 21, 1863, William Clarke Quantrill led approximately 450 irregular warriors into the streets of Lawrence, Kansas, in what has been the most publicized event in the history of the border warfare. Unexpectedly, he and his guerrilla followers struck this town of nearly two thousand in search of plunder, revenge, and blood. The story of Lawrence is well documented in the literature of the border and won't be retold in detail here. The guerrillas came to town with a death list, drawn up to insure that none of their intended targets were forgotten in the excitement. They eventually killed nearly 200 people, most were innocent male residents of Lawrence who happened to be living in the wrong town on the wrong day. The mixture of revenge, grief, and alcohol became a violent brew that turned the raid into a massacre, shocking the entire nation. Even many Confederate sympathizers found it hard to justify the actions of these Missouri raiders, as the raid was too violent even for the population of the border-lying states, which was used daily to exact death and destruction. With this act of barbarism, the guerrillas stepped over a line that they had been close to for some time. It galvanized the Union populace and leadership along the border and prompted a response that nearly ended the career of Quantrill and his band. As the smoke was still billowing from homes in Lawrence, the guerrillas came under pursuit from troops and civilians alike, determined to ride down the animals that had attacked the fair city and take so many lives. Much of this was accomplished, as many of the men who rode in the raid never lived to enjoy the plunder they took. The countryside between Lawrence and the Missouri border swarmed with armed Unionists and only a skillful rearguard fight by the guerrilla forces prevented the total destruction of the raiders. Making the Missouri line, the group split up and the men went to ground to hide from their pursuers.[1]

The raid on Lawrence, Kansas, by Confederate irregulars epitomizes the violence that was pervasive throughout the border counties of western Missouri and eastern Kansas. In this small geographical area, a guerrilla war raged for nearly 10 years. The violence along this part of the border is probably better known by Civil War historians than any other portion of the border conflict. The bulk of volumes written on this subject center in the counties around Kansas City and examine the conflict between Missouri southerners and Kansas unionists. This is not merely a story of the Civil War though, for the violent roots reach deeper into the historical soil of the area. The guerrilla violence of the Civil War period did not just rise up in 1861, but was marked by an evolutionary process that began in "Bleeding Kansas" in the 1850s. To lay the proper groundwork this story must begin in the pre-Civil War era.

Bleeding Kansas

The conflict that eventually led to the beginnings of the Civil War had its roots in the soil of Kansas. Compromise after compromise had been reached on issues such as slavery at the national political level for many years. With the passage of the Kansas-Nebraska Act of 1854, the stage was set in Kansas for a contest that would lead to intrigue, violence, and murder. Missouri was by every test a southern state. It had been settled by southerners and was fully inculcated with the cultural heritage of the lower south. While it was not a largely slave-owning population, slaves were common and bondage was an accepted practice for the white population. The burning desire to control the popular election in Kansas rested on the dread of an anti-southern state on the western border of Missouri. Though the central and western portions of Kansas were not well suited for the small farming endeavors that were common in Missouri, many vocal members of the Missouri electorate believed that Kansas had to be a slave state to protect their culture.

Map 3. Kansas Area of Operations.

On the other side of the state line, in Kansas Territory, was a mixture of New Englanders, New Yorkers, and settlers from the middle states in the Ohio, Indiana, and Illinois area. Though the contemporary press painted Kansans to be ardent abolitionists, the average farmer or store owner was probably anti-Negro, but not particularly anti-slave. The most vocal political leaders of the Territory were against the institution of slavery and used this as a political club as often as possible to further their ambitions.

As the vote approached to determine the future of Kansas as a state, groups of men from western Missouri (derisively known as *Border Ruffians*) crossed the border into Kansas Territory and voted in many of the border towns, skewing the vote count in favor of the pro-slavery ticket. These groups also rode about the countryside of eastern Kansas, impressing upon the population their intent to control the election. This low-level violence was nothing near what would occur on the border in the years of the Civil War, but it laid the foundation of hatred that would later result in the "Jayhawking" that sparked the all-out guerrilla war of 1861-1865.

In May of 1856, Rueben Randlett was sent by leaders of the Free State Movement to Leavenworth in an attempt to determine the intentions of a group of Border Ruffians gathering there. Randlett infiltrated the group and verified that they were bound for Lawrence, with the mission of punishing the occupants of the town for being at the center of the Territory's anti-slavery movement. Randlett was able to escape from the group of ruffians as they began their circuitous march towards Lawrence. He warned the occupants of the targeted town, allowing them the opportunity to prepare for the attack. Another man had been detailed to accompany Randlett, John E. Cook, but he fell ill during the journey and returned to Leavenworth. Cook would later be hanged with John Brown for his actions at Harper's Ferry.

Days before the attack on Lawrence, Randlett was sent with Cook and Charles Stewart to check into a reported murder by the Border Ruffians. While enroute to the reported site of the murder, Blanton's Bridge, they encountered two mounted men who they stopped to question. The incident ended in gunfire between the two groups and the death of Stewart. The mounted men escaped, though without their horses or firearms. While this incident is a far cry from the death and mutilation that would have occurred eight or nine years later out of a similar encounter, it was violent for a part of the country that was not at war. The violence learned here would breed far more brutal acts in the years to come.[2]

On May 21, 1856, the group Randlett infiltrated, numbering 600-800 ruffians, entered Lawrence with a red banner inscribed with the words "South Carolina" on one side and "Southern Rights" on the other, bent on destroying the Free State Hotel and two local newspapers that sided with the Free Staters. The assembled manpower of the Free Staters was around 150, a difference that resulted in the defenders opting not to put up a defense and they withdrew out of town. The Missourians came to the center of town, destroying the newspaper offices of the *Herald of Freedom* and the *Free State*. The newspaper offices out of the way, they tried to knock down the hotel with their three-pound brass cannons, but found them not up to the task. Finally, after placing their flag on the roof of the hotel for a time, a barrel of pitch was rolled into the hotel and with the aid of the furnishings was set on fire, gutting the structure. At least two witnesses indicated that the only casualty that the Missourians suffered was a man killed by a brick falling from the chimney to which the flag was attached.[3]

While the average soul in Kansas during the latter part of the 1850s was just trying to eke out a living, a number of individuals who would have great parts to play in history were living here on the edge of civilization. John Brown, soon to provide a deadly spark to the sectional controversy, operated with the Free State forces in many small skirmishes throughout Kansas, before embarking on at least one massacre of slave owners prior to the attack on Harper's Ferry. One of his companions in Kansas, Jim Lane, would become a dominant figure in Kansas for the next 10 years and be involved in much of the Jayhawk violence that set off the guerrilla campaign. Another Kansan, James Montgomery, led raids into southwestern Missouri to free slaves there and bring them to freedom in Kansas.

Many of these staunch Unionists lived for a time in the same town as one young man whose name would soon become a household name in America. He was William Clarke Quantrill and had come to Kansas from Canal Dover, Ohio. He made his living for some time as a schoolteacher, but eventually fell in with some bad company. He made a slight reputation with the anti-slavery community in Kansas, operating with them to liberate slaves from Missouri. This thin young man soon found his loyalties on the other side of the border and began a career that made him one of the most reviled men in Civil War history. While still living in Kansas, he wrote a letter to his mother that clearly identified which side of the coming conflict he would support. Quantrill alluded to the fact that pro-slavery forces were condemned for their violence, "but when one once knows the facts they can easily see that it has been the opposite party that have been the main movers in the troubles & by far the most lawless set of people in the country. They all sympathize for old J. Brown, who should have been hung years ago, indeed hanging was too good for him."[4]

As noted earlier, Lawrence had been attacked in May 1856 and some offending establishments destroyed by the Missourians. Little could anyone know the future place that Lawrence would have in the history of Kansas and the Civil War. Skirmishing between the Free Staters and Border Ruffians would continue through the latter years of the 1850s. John Brown, mentioned in the Quantrill letter above, would contribute to this bloodletting with his butchery of five proslavery men along the banks of Pottowatomie Creek on May 24, 1856. His violent attack was a harbinger to his raid on Harper's Ferry and an excellent example of the volatile nature of the border in the pre-Civil War period. It was in this environment that bitter hatreds and personal feuds were begun. Men who would soon be on opposite sides in a true war were pitted against each other in what would prove to be merely a precursor to the most violent episode in American History.

Civil War

With the coming of secession and the bombardment of Fort Sumter, the inhabitants of the Kansas Territory looked with apprehension to the east. Their relationship with their Missouri neighbors was barely a speaking arrangement and many feared that the new state could be totally cut off from the Union if Missouri went "out with the South." Many men remembered the violence and outrages of "Bleeding Kansas," and while most of the population consisted of reasonable, law-abiding citizens, there was an element in Kansas that sought revenge on the Missourians. A number of these men were hard-core abolitionists, with a burning desire to free Missouri slaves and rid the world of this "peculiar institution." Just as many were bandits, lawless men who saw the outbreak of war as an opportunity to plunder and rob at their leisure, possibly with the sanction of the State or Federal Governments. Concern about military affairs in Missouri, as Sterling Price began operations, led to a clamor for militia units in Kansas.

Jim Lane, an opportunistic politician, sought permission to raise a brigade to protect Kansas, though the real reason appears to be the strengthening of his power base in Kansas politics. Through skillful maneuvering, he received permission to muster in this organization and assumed command of it at Fort Scott in August 1861.[5] The unit, known as the "Kansas Brigade" or more accurately "Lane's Brigade," gathered at Fort Scott and anticipated action after the defeat of General Nathaniel Lyons at Wilson's Creek. The leadership of Lane's Brigade was a mixed lot, who would receive much press coverage in the ensuing years.

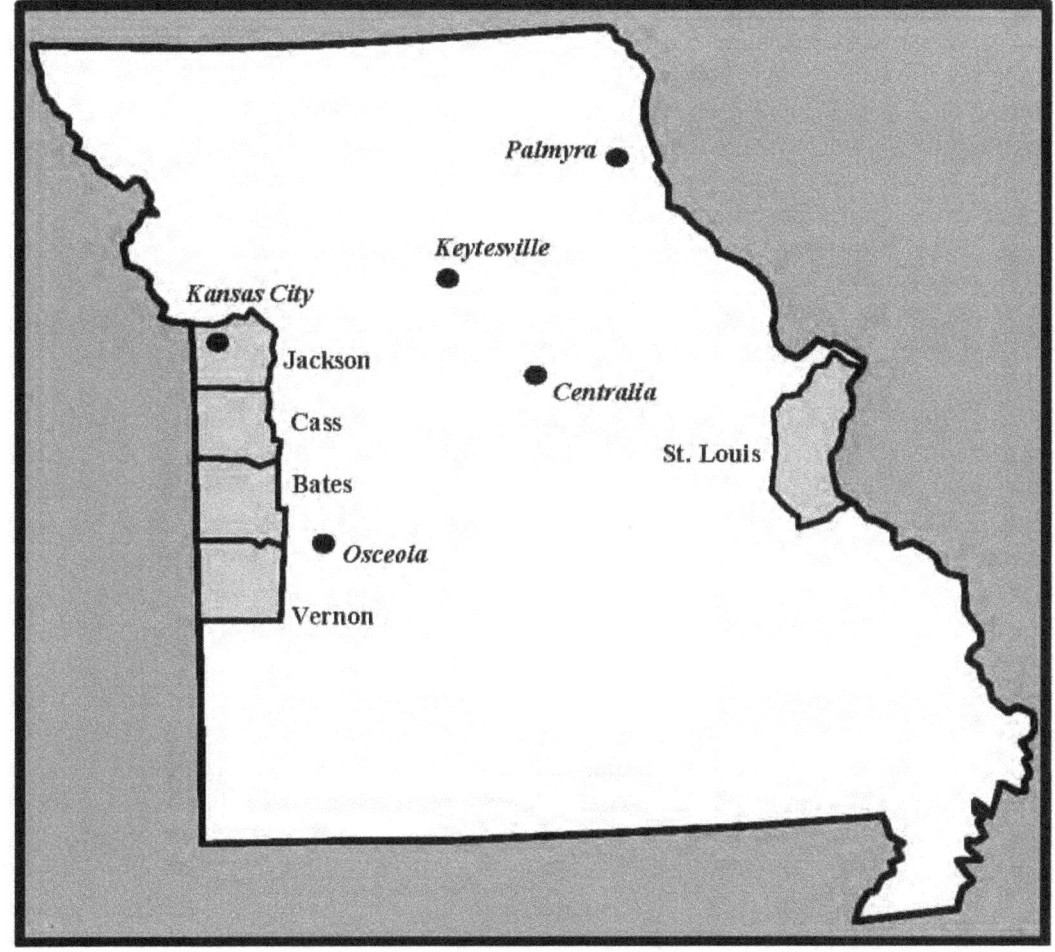

Map 4. Missouri Area of Operations.

James Montgomery had been commissioned a Colonel by the Governor of Kansas and was appointed second-in-command. Other members of his raiding parties from before the war, like Charles Jennison, were also appointed as officers over organizations that more closely resembled bandit hordes than military units. These men were as much interested in personal gain as they were in the protection of the law-abiding citizens of Kansas.

A scouting expedition from Sterling Price's army made contact with the Brigade and called for assistance from the main body. With the approach of Price's superior force, Lane fell back and Price turned his attention to more important quarry. Lane had no desire to attempt open combat with a regular force and thus left the field while he could. In a portent of what was to come, the detachment of Jennison's command, which had been left to guard Ft. Scott, looted the town after it had been evacuated by its occupants. Lane's Brigade never missed the opportunity to turn a profit on any military mission.

On September 10, 1861, Lane opted to start north along the Missouri border to clear out the secessionist element that inhabited the western counties that adjoined Kansas. His force of about 1,500 men set out to burn and plunder everything in their way, destroying anything of value to Price's army and to the secessionists who lived in that part of Missouri. How exactly they decided who was a secessionist and who was a unionist is still a mystery and one that plagued warriors on the border for the next four years. Lane's raid was the beginning of a policy of slash and burn that ran rampant between the western counties of Missouri and the eastern counties of Kansas for the remainder of the war. Ostensibly, the raid was to protect Kansas, but revenge for the actions of Border Ruffians in previous years was a much more prevalent motive. The Kansans now had the Federal Government behind them and they intended to give Missourians a taste of their own medicine.

Lane's Brigade continued their march through the Osage Valley and finally, on September 23d, reached the city of Osceola. Finding supplies for Price's army there, Lane allowed his men to loot the town and then burn it almost completely. The quantity of liquor consumed by the Brigade appears to have been excessive and the lack of control by their officers led to the destruction of an innocent town. The valuables from Osceola were piled in wagons before the destruction and most of the goods from this Missouri city were to end up in the homes of Kansans in the days that followed. This destruction of a barely defended city would fan the flames on the border and though Lane would try to defend his actions as being militarily justified, it served only to increase the level of violence on the border. Albert Castel, an active historian during this Kansas period, maintained that "Lane's Brigade was an irresponsible mob which looted and burned Osceola out of a wanton lust for plunder and a self-righteous desire to injure the Missourians." This was not a military expedition in the vein of Lyon and Price's meeting at Wilson's Creek, but a raid intended to punish and rob the Missouri populace for perceived wrongs of the territorial period. Lane wanted to strike not at Price, but at the people of Missouri and their society, to include their slaves. Its effect was to drive a greater wedge between these two types of people and stir the hatred of Kansas in the hearts of Missouri youth.[6]

The raid on Osceola was Lane's final act of consequence in command of his Brigade. While Lane no longer played an active role in field operations, other units of the Brigade continued this form of warfare against the people of the Missouri border counties. The most infamous of them was undoubtedly Charles Jennison and his Seventh Kansas Regiment, known more popularly as Jennison's Jayhawkers. The term "jayhawker" became the most commonly used and popular term for Unionist raiders coming out of Kansas. While it originated with Jennison and Montgomery some years earlier, it came into common use to mean any band of Kansan raiders who happened to ride into a Missouri or Indian Territory city bent on its destruction and plunder. While plunder and arson were the mode of operation for Lane's Brigade, Jennison would take the theme to much higher levels, adding murder to the list of approved activities whenever his Jayhawkers were dealing with any people he deemed to be disloyal. Jennison had been liberating slaves for many years on the Kansas-Missouri border and the conditions on the border now allowed him to perform his violence with an air of legitimacy. His raiders descended upon Jackson County, Missouri, and proceeded to burn and steal their way from one end to the other. Individual farms and small towns alike found Jayhawkers in their midst, taking what they wished and punishing anyone who tried to stand in their way.

Jennison had been commissioned by Governor Robinson in an attempt to control his outrages, but it became obvious in a very short period of time that nothing would ever control his lust for plunder. The Seventh Kansas included a unit commanded by the son of John Brown, a unit that was every bit as driven as the elder Brown, and they set out to punish slaveholders wherever they found them. Other officers in Jennison's regiment were equal to the commander himself in their zeal to punish and steal. Marshall Cleveland and D.R. Anthony (brother of Susan B. Anthony) commanded portions of the undisciplined organization in the field, and whether because of a total lack of moral fiber or a zealous commitment to abolitionism, these men were equally as quick with the torch on the possessions of Missourians. Some of the most zealous arsonists in these bands were actually unionist Missourians themselves.

As the war broke out, unionists and secessionists lived side-by-side in Missouri, held together by the bond of statehood and common social backgrounds. It was only when the firing on Fort Sumter forced individuals to take sides that problems became evident in Missouri society. Many unionist residents of the western counties were forced to move to Kansas by the actions of their secessionist neighbors, particularly after the success of Sterling Price at Wilson's Creek. These people had very personal scores to settle and many of them flocked to the Kansas regiments as an opportunity to even some of these scores and serve the Union they supported. In an interview with a victim of Jennison's violence, William E. Connelly commented that while Kansans had for years been abused by Missouri border ruffians, with the change in national administration the Jayhawkers had seized their opportunity to even the ledger and had taken the violence to a new level. While sounding almost proud of the violent accomplishments of the Jayhawkers, Connelly did admit that "the most deplorable result of both the border ruffian and the Jayhawker was the suffering entailed upon the innocent and those who had no desire to engage in lawlessness in either Kansas or Missouri..."[7]

While Connelly is an apologist for the actions of the Jayhawkers in his history of the border wars and the guerrilla violence during the Civil War, he adequately captured the essence of the irregular violence of the border. Missourians had preyed upon Kansans in the 1850s and now Kansans were preying on Missourians in the opening months of the Civil War. Action had brought reaction and the border would not be the same for many years to come. Perceived and actual wrongs were avenged and in a society filled with this type of personal violence, a vicious breed of man rose to the top. On the Union side, the type is best evidenced by Charles Jennison, but on the Confederate side it would soon be epitomized by the man most associated with the guerrilla violence in the Trans-Mississippi West, William Clarke Quantrill.

Jennison and the other members of Lane's Brigade fall under the category of Partisan Rangers, as their actions were officially sanctioned by the Federal Government and they were a duly constituted unit. On the other side, Quantrill and most of the Confederate guerrillas must be classified as war-rebels at best. While he claimed a commission from the Confederate Government and often acted in concert with the Confederate army, the Richmond Government did not claim his actions as their own at anytime. That he, and other guerrillas in Missouri, fought on behalf of the Confederacy is difficult to dispute, but they had no official claim to legitimacy in their actions.

Biographies on Quantrill have been the standard guerrilla fare for Civil War readers for over 100 years. His legend is one of the best known, and yet least understood, in the annals of this purely American war. A variety of authors each gave him their own slant, and while the work of Albert Castel has given us a more balanced view of his life, he is still a central figure in any discussion of guerrilla warfare in America. The truth is that while Quantrill is the best known and most storied practitioner of this violent military art form, he was one of many in Kansas-Missouri and the other states on the border. His story does lead the reader through the violence in this region better than any other and for that reason he will be at the center of this study on the Confederate efforts at irregular warfare.

Quantrill burst onto the scene as an active player in the deadly warfare on the border in March 1862. He and his band of bushwhackers burst into the Johnson County, Kansas, town of Aubrey at about dawn. They were looking for Jayhawkers and apparently left three dead in their wake. The story lives on largely for two reasons: Quantrill himself saw someone looking out the frost-covered upper window of the town's hotel and fired a round at the face. It struck the onlooker, but the glancing blow only stunned him for a short time. Upon the man's recovery, he was brought before Quantrill and turned out to be Abraham Ellis, the superintendent of schools in Miami County, Kansas, where Quantrill had once taught. Quantrill liked Ellis and after insuring that he was all right, allowed him to retain his possessions with the exception of some money that had already been taken from him by the bushwhackers.

The other interesting issue deals with Lieutenant Reuben Randlett, who was mentioned earlier as a scout for the Free Staters in the territorial period. Randlett was enroute back to his regiment from a leave of absence and was staying in the same room as Abraham Ellis when the raid began. He surrendered to Quantrill's men and after being threatened with a gun in his mouth and one to his ear, was taken to see Quantrill himself. The guerrilla chieftain had plans for Randlett and spared his life and that of the other regular Union soldiers who were present in Aubrey.[8]

Randlett would remain Quantrill's prisoner for eleven days, as the guerrilla leader attempted to exchange him for a bushwhacker who had been captured and was sentenced to be executed at Leavenworth. Quantrill was attempting to act as a regular soldier in this instance; at least to the extent that he had paroled the Union soldiers captured at Aubrey and was attempting to exchange Randlett. The Union authorities would have nothing to do with the attempted exchange and, even though Randlett was released to try and reason with the Union leaders, Quantrill's man was executed at Leavenworth. Randlett never returned to Quantrill's control after his attempt to be exchanged, but also never returned to Union service. His interview with William E. Connelley revealed a dissatisfaction that the Union authorities, apparently General Sturgis, refused to do what Randlett believed to be the honorable thing. Randlett could not understand why Sturgis would not exchange the soldiers. It was a common practice in the Civil War at this point and he would have received the life of an officer for that of a bushwhacker; by Randlett's estimation it was more than a fair trade. However, Sturgis would not exchange the guerrilla because he could not deal with Quantrill as though he were a regular officer. To have done so would have afforded Quantrill recognition as a combatant, rather than the outlaw that the Federal Government believed him to be. Sturgis' actions were in keeping with the legal opinions mentioned earlier from Halleck and Lieber and certainly met the letter of the law under General Orders No. 100, though that order was yet to be published.

With the appointment of Major General Halleck to command of the Department of the Mississippi on March 13, 1862, the unofficial rules of warfare on the border dramatically changed. The second act that Halleck took, after publishing his assumption of command order, was to issue General Order 2 of the Department of the Mississippi, which officially placed irregulars outside of the law and required them to be treated as outlaws. This meant that if captured, they would not be accorded protection as Confederate soldiers, but executed as common criminals.[9] Quantrill and his men had regularly paroled Union prisoners and it had not been unusual for Union officers to parole or exchange bushwhackers, though the informal rules of warfare forbade it. But with the official no-quarter order issued and abided by in the Kansas-Missouri area, the scene was set for violence of such proportions that many modern scholars find it suspect. There would be no more prisoners on either side, just a body count to see how many could be killed or executed. The raid on Aubrey had once again caused the tide of violence to ebb across the Kansas border, a trend that would occur more often in the months to follow. After the Aubrey raid, Quantrill and his men went "to ground" back in their haunts in Jackson County, Missouri, and the Sni-a-Bar Hills. The geography of this part of Missouri made it perfect to hide small bodies of men for extended periods of time, and as many of the men that rode with Quantrill had grown up here, it was nearly impossible to capture them. Many of the families of the guerrillas lived on this land and provided food and intelligence to the band as they avoided the Federal patrols. This was a key element in guerrilla warfare along the border, with the help of the population being an important ingredient in the recipe for guerrilla success in Missouri and other states.

A key element, if not the key element, in any guerrilla conflict is the population that is caught between the regular and irregular forces. On the Kansas-Missouri border, this included a mixed population of unionists and secessionists, living together in far less than harmony. With the advent of an unrestricted, no-quarter policy on both sides, violence accelerated against the entire population. Where plunder and murder had existed to this point, there was no longer any compelling reason, beyond whatever personal morals the participants exhibited, to deal anything but death to the enemy. Regular army units and Jayhawkers alike were permitted, in fact expected, to execute irregulars when captured.

Faced with this prospect, Confederate irregulars and bandits had no reason to confine their warfare to any limits of decency. General Halleck's decision, while being within the laws of war as he saw them, had the impact of exponentially increasing the pain and suffering felt by the civilian population along the border. From this point on, the violence would continue to increase in frequency and barbarity, running the gamut from murder of innocent civilians, on both sides, to the forced depopulation and wholesale pillaging of entire counties, to the final barbarous acts of Bill Anderson around Centralia, Missouri, in 1864. The restraints that generally confined traditional nineteenth century soldiers had been loosened, as they had been in Napoleon's Spanish Campaign, and normally moral men from both sides acted in a manner unheard of in American History since the French and Indian Wars.

One of the central questions surrounding this violence was how to identify people as unionist or secessionist. What part of the population would be held responsible for the acts of Confederate guerrillas? Who would the guerrillas hold responsible for the atrocities committed by those claiming the protection of the Federal Government? These questions held true in Kentucky, Arkansas, and the Indian Territory. The population of the entire border was caught between two armed forces, and faced danger from both sides. If you failed to assist the military you were of questionable loyalties and if you wouldn't assist the guerrillas that roamed the woods, you were a dreaded unionist and might well forfeit your life. The people of the border were trapped between two warring parties and there was very little that they could do to solve their problem. Inevitably, people were held accountable not for their actions, but also for their politics, and merely being perceived as a secessionist or a unionist could be reason enough to win a bullet or noose if you were at the wrong place at the wrong time.

Death was not the only problem for secessionists along the border. Union commanders, like General John M. Schofield, took whatever steps they believed necessary to combat the irregular violence they found in Kansas and Missouri. In the summer and fall of 1862, Schofield lacked the troops he needed to deal with the widespread guerrilla raids and had no chance of obtaining them from the Federal Government. His solution was to ask the Governor of Missouri to enroll the militia of the state to fight these shadowy enemies. What might seem to have been a simple and effective solution to this problem, turned out to cause Schofield even more problems. The population of Missouri was a diverse mix of southern and northern men who, left alone on their farms, could live in relative harmony. But with the general calling for the state militia, secessionist sympathizers of military age were asked to take sides against a cause in which they believed. While their personal beliefs allowed them to stay home and not help the Union, they could not bring themselves to openly fight against the Confederacy. The result was that they had only two viable choices: they could go south into Arkansas or Texas and join the regular Confederate armies operating there or take to the bush and join the irregular warriors that carried on the battle against the Union in Missouri. As a result, the Union commanders now faced an increased number of guerrilla bands throughout the state and a greater pool of local citizens willing to assist these guerrillas with food, shelter, and intelligence.[10]

In a report to higher headquarters, Schofield also discussed the growing involvement of the militia. His ability to equip and arm these units was severely limited and his search for a way to accomplish this finally came to rest with the idea of making the disloyal members of the state pay the cost. He imposed the cost of policing the guerrilla bands on the secessionists of the state. He specifically started in Saint Louis County and proceeded to raise $500,000 to support the active militia. Unfortunately, the determination of one's political sympathies was very subjective and rarely accurate. Determining who must pay the assessment was an inaccurate science and in Saint Louis County the method used was the appointment of a five-man committee to determine who was disloyal and would be assessed. This economic retaliation, while possibly necessary in Schofield's mind, served to drive a wedge into the population.[11] Committees such as this throughout the border area could be counted upon to settle old grudges and be utilized to legitimize the harassment and ruin of personal and political opponents. While assessments may have been effective in raising necessary monies, they simply served as another reason for families to turn against the Union.[12]

In the wake of mobilization of the militia and assessment of "disloyal" members of society, questionable deaths occurred with consistency across the border, sanctioned by Union authorities with little regard for anything resembling a burden of proof. One such incident occurred in Missouri in the fall of 1862 and serves to illustrate the violence of the region and clumsy way it was often utilized by Union officials. It is particularly interesting in light of the issue of how to classify units, in this case a Confederate army organization specifically assigned to perform activities consistent with the actions of Partisan Rangers but treated by the Union authorities with the same disdain normally reserved for Quantrill's unit.

Following a raid on the town of Palmyra, Missouri, by Confederates under the command Colonel Joseph C. Porter, an elderly unionist named Andrew Allsman was reported missing and presumed kidnapped by Porter's command. Evidently, this was correct and Allsman had been taken unknown to Porter and murdered by members of his command. Palmyra is in northeast Missouri, distant from the Kansas border and the haunts of Quantrill and the more well-known guerrillas of the border. Porter was a commissioned Confederate officer operating under the command of General Hindman, who had sent forces behind Union lines specifically to disrupt communications and command. In this way, Porter's mission was very similar to that of Colonel Benjamin Grierson during his famous raid into the Confederacy. Regardless of how Porter was perceived by General Hindman and the Confederate Government, he was merely a guerrilla in the eyes of the Union Army with no more official protection than the groups operating with Quantrill.[13]

In retaliation for the kidnapping and presumed death of Allsman, the provost marshal of the district that included Palmyra, W. R. Strachan, informed Colonel Porter that he would execute 10 men who were supposedly members of the offending command. Whether or not these men were actually members of Porter's unit is in dispute. Obviously, the Union correspondence maintains that they were, but no attempt was made to insure that they were anything but secessionists living in the wrong location.[14] Regardless of their true affiliation, Strachan marched them to a predetermined location and forced the 10 men to sit on their own caskets and had them shot. The deaths were neither clean nor quick and this poor performance of an already questionable action caused the killings to be viewed as murder by secessionists and the Confederate Government alike. President Jefferson Davis demanded the delivery of General McNeil, Strachan's superior, to the Confederacy to answer for what his government considered an atrocity. Failing this, he ordered Confederate commanders to execute the next 10 Union officers captured in the Trans-Mississippi.[15] Dedicated Unionists within Missouri believed that the men had gotten what they deserved and wrote to President Lincoln, maintaining that not only was the action legal, but necessary. Referring to Allsman's death and the execution of the 10 Confederates, they indicated that it was not just about justice, but "was, additionally, to vindicate the power and authority of law and the Government; to strike terror into the hearts of those whom no sentiments of right, honor, or justice could reach. It was to give safety and peace to this distracted country, and to assure the now almost incredulous people that the Government was not utterly powerless for their protection." They further expressed their satisfaction with the actions of Mr. Strachan, claiming that "the act has achieved its desired purpose. The law and the supremacy of our Government are vindicated."[16]

Writing this letter in January 1863, little could these men know that the action of General McNeil and Strachan had not put an end to the violence on the border, but was merely one of many actions which would cause it to accelerate. Confederate violence may have temporarily subsided in the northeastern counties of Missouri, but the spring and summer of 1863 would see an increase in the frequency and brutality of the irregular war.

The late winter and spring of 1863 saw a steady stream of reports of guerrilla activity along the border. Brigadier General Ben Loan, Missouri State Militia, communicated regularly with the commander of the Department of the Missouri, Major General Samuel Curtis, concerning problems with bands of irregular warriors. On January 19, he conveyed that intelligence reports had identified a guerrilla band of between 200 and 500 operating near Warrensburg, Missouri. The information indicated that the organization was under the command of Quantrill, but most likely it was simply well populated with former members of Quantrill's organization, many of whom had come home from serving with Jo Shelby in Arkansas.[17] At this point, almost any guerrilla band was believed to be headed by Quantrill. A February 26th letter from Loan to Curtis would outline the continuing problems Loan was encountering in trying to calm down the border area. In a discussion of his decisions to reorganize his troops for defense of his area of responsibility he reiterated the ever present problem that occurs when differing groups live in close proximity. Admitting that the Union population was torn, he wrote Curtis that they were often targets of guerrilla depredations from the Missouri side of the border, but also that "the citizens here require as much protection from the *Red Legs* of Kansas as they do from the bushwhackers of Missouri."[18]

Loan's comments reflect clearly the sentiment amongst Missourians of the border at this time, that they had as much or more to fear from uncontrolled Kansans as from Missouri guerrillas. These were the people that were caught in the middle and the true victims of irregular warfare.

Irregular violence would continue throughout the spring, with a growing belief on the Union side that they must somehow curtail the support given to the guerrillas by the local populace. In a clear expression of his guidance on the problem, Halleck wrote Major General E. V. Sumner at St. Louis, indicating that as the entire state of Missouri was under martial law, anyone who was in the state or came into it and either took up arms against the Union or provided support to those in rebellion were "military insurgents or military traitors." He directed that people falling into this category forfeited their property and possibly their lives.[19] This guidance gave the commanders in Missouri considerable latitude in arresting persons they believed to be aiding southern guerrillas, a common practice among secessionists in many of the counties along the border. Utilizing this guidance, family members of known guerrillas were arrested and confined, or banished from the area.

Union commanders in Missouri began to take an even harder line with the activities of guerrillas, as indicated in the following telegraph from General Loan to Curtis:

> I write this now to say that there can no longer be any question but that the contest for the supremacy in this State must be made a war of extermination; that is, one party, either the loyal or the disloyal, must be permitted to hold exclusive possession of the country. It is utterly impossible for both parties longer to dwell together. The guerrillas and the rebel sympathizers are waging a relentless, cruel, and bloody war upon our unarmed and defenseless citizens, and are determined to continue it until the last loyal citizen is murdered or is driven from his home to escape being murdered.[20]

Loan goes on to say that Washington believed his actions to have been too extreme and seeks guidance from Curtis on what would be the proper response. He outlines his preference by allowing that if ordered he could do enough damage to guerrillas in his district that "in forty days an honest man can ride from one end of it to the other without question or being harmed..."[21] Loan and other commanders along the border had begun to seek a more permanent solution to the guerrilla problem. The no-quarter edict issued earlier by Halleck did not go far enough for them, and they desired to divest western Missouri of all secessionists, leaving the countryside safe for loyal Union citizens. Curtis had also become more intent on upholding the no-quarter edict and reiterated the Union policy in a telegram to General Bartholow, pointing out that "Death to bushwhackers is the order. Have a commission always ready to try, determine, and execute immediately, if they are unfortunately taken alive."[22] Similar orders from General James Blunt, the commander of the District of Kansas, instructed the commander of the Ninth Regiment Kansas Volunteers that "when such persons are taken prisoners, which should as much as possible be avoided, they will be summarily tried by a military commission...and, if found guilty, must be executed by hanging or shooting, without delay".[23]

Commanders on both sides of the Kansas-Missouri border had obviously gotten the message and were intent on diligently imposing the no-quarter rule on suspected guerrillas. The most colorful statement of this intent was written by General Curtis, who advised General Loan that "We must not allow the vipers to make their nests, or, if they do, we must crush the eggs before they hatch."[24] This was the mood of the border as the summer of 1863 came to a close, in an August that would never be forgotten.

Against this specter of officially sanctioned extermination, William Clarke Quantrill planned his most notorious operation. Having returned from a trip to Richmond, supposedly in search of a commission as a colonel of partisan rangers, Quantrill decided the time was right to seek revenge on Kansans for all the evils of the territorial period and the early years of the war. The prospect of revenge, combined with a hearty desire to increase the weight of his men's pocketbooks, focused him on the obvious target of Lawrence. While well inside the bounds of Kansas, Lawrence had been the center of radical abolitionist sentiment since the early days of the territorial conflict and was very familiar to Quantrill. That James Lane lived in Lawrence made it all the more appealing as a target. Quantrill began planning the raid in the summer and held a final council of war with his lieutenants on 10 August, where he laid out his plans for the daring raid.[25]

Three days later, a building being used in Kansas City to house female sympathizers of the guerrillas, arrested under the guidance from Halleck, collapsed. A number of the women were killed and many others injured severely. Prominent in the list of dead and injured were the sisters of Bill Anderson, one of Quantrill's lieutenants, and a young lady who was related to both John McCorkle and Cole Younger. The news of this accident caused extreme anger in the guerrilla camp. Rumors spread that the building was deliberately sabotaged, but no evidence exists of such a plot. The collapse apparently was an accident, but one that would have effects well outside of Kansas City. The citizens of Lawrence, Kansas, would feel the anger of the members of Quantrill's band in less than two weeks. While some documents have indicated that the Lawrence raid was in revenge for these deaths, Quantrill's council of war held days earlier indicates that it was not. What it would do, however, is impact the mood of the guerrillas when they rode into Lawrence, insuring that they would do far more than just sack the town and loot it. Instead of simply destroying the town and pillaging it, these irregular warriors would visit death on the male members of this Kansas town, leaving only a few alive when they were finished.[26]

The level of violence displayed on August 21, 1863, during the second Lawrence made the first look like a skirmish by comparison and changed the dynamics of the war on the Kansas-Missouri border with a single stroke.

The reaction to this Lawrence raid by the citizens of Kansas and the Union authorities in the border area was predictable. Outrage at this violence caused a cry against all Missourians, with even the Governor of Kansas placing the blame squarely on their shoulders in a letter to Major General Schofield. Governor Carney informed Schofield that "I must hold Missouri responsible for this fearful, fiendish raid....such people cannot be considered loyal, and should not be treated as loyal citizens..."[27] Carney called on Schofield to take drastic actions against the border counties of Missouri, surmising that Quantrill could not have effectively staged the raid without more than just a few Missourians knowing of the force's plans. Carney's rage was augmented by the embarrassment of the commander of the District of the Border, Brigadier General Thomas Ewing. Having command over the area around Lawrence and the border counties from which the raid was staged, Ewing came under significant political and public pressure because of this event. An inquiry into his actions was demanded by the civilian leaders in Kansas and Ewing personally requested a board of inquiry be appointed to deal with the blight on his reputation. Union soldiers had two missions in the weeks following the raid; first to hunt down the guerrillas responsible for the atrocity, and second, to prevent armed Kansans from overwhelming the border counties of Missouri in personal revenge.

Knowing that he had to act to appease the people of Kansas and to settle the guerrilla issue on the border, General Ewing issued General Orders No. 11 on August 25, 1863. For some time Unionists along the border had maintained that the guerrilla force could not be dealt with as long as it was allowed the sanctuary of secessionist support. As with any guerrilla movement, support of the local populace was a key ingredient and the border of Missouri was no exception. General Orders No. 11 required everyone living in Jackson, Cass, and Bates Counties and a portion of those living in Vernon County to leave their homes within fifteen days. If they were able to prove their loyalty to the closest Union commanding officer they could move to a military installation anywhere in the state, with the exception of the St. Louis area. Those that could not be certified as loyal would have to move out of the district with the presumption that they were disloyal.[28] The intent of the order was clearly the depopulation of the power base of Quantrill's band and the resulting loss of effectiveness for the guerrillas, opening the door for the war of extermination that General Loan had called for, months before.

General Orders No. 11 has been the subject of considerable controversy and was the inspiration for George Caleb Bingham's celebrated painting of the same name. Albert Castel compared it to the confinement of Japanese-Americans during World War II and called the execution of Order No. 11, "the harshest treatment ever imposed on United States citizens under the plea of military necessity in our nation's history."[29] These counties would come to be known as the "Burnt District" because of the violent execution of this plan. While General Schofield attempted to soften the call for the destruction of these counties, with the movement of supposedly disloyal families, their homes and barns were burned, crops either stolen or destroyed, and families financially destroyed because of the location of their homes or slightest possibility that they were in support of Quantrill's guerrilla forces. This act of reprisal exemplifies the true victim in the guerrilla warfare of the American Civil War — the populace of the affected area. General Ewing maintained in a letter to General Schofield that virtually all the families remaining in these counties were disloyal and that the loyal families affected would be fewer than twenty.[30] While many of the citizens displaced were clearly loyal to the Confederacy and undoubtedly helped the guerrillas, there was no way of measuring it. Even the determination of loyalty was no clear assumption, as it was done by men advised by locals who had personal issues and fights to resolve.

While Ewing was confident of the nature of the people he displaced, General Schofield was not quite as definite in his report to Washington. Noting that the idea had come up between he and Ewing previously and was not just a reaction to Lawrence, he went on to lament the "utter impossibility of deciding who were guilty and who were innocent" and the fear of reprisal by the guerrillas on any who were left in the counties. Schofield also recognized the role that the historical hatred between Kansas and Missouri, dating from the territorial period, had in the violence here. He blamed the "old border hatred intensified by the rebellion" for the problems in these counties and those surrounding them.[31] There was no telltale sign to identify the disloyal people in this instance, no racial, ethnic, or religious delineation that could be used. Hundreds of families were sent into exile, with the resulting effect that many young men would have to once again decide whether to go south to the regular Confederate forces or cast their lot with the guerrillas in the bush. This order created a further division between the Union and the occupants of the border and left a legacy of hatred and mistrust.

The early fall passed in Missouri with less irregular activity, largely because of the continuing efforts to ferret out those responsible for the Lawrence raid. With the effects of Order No. 11 beginning to show in the loss of support structure and the falling of the leaves so valuable for concealment, many of the guerrilla warriors gathered under Quantrill and began the trek south to winter in northern Texas. The trip would take them through parts of Kansas, Arkansas, and the Indian Territory. Those events, which occurred south of Kansas will be covered in later chapters, but Quantrill would make one more mark on the Kansas-Missouri border region before entering winter quarters in Texas.

On October 6, 1863, Quantrill's advance party reported finding a Union camp, busily engaged in building a fort near Baxter Springs, Kansas. The guerrillas had not known of its existence, which was not surprising as the instructions to construct the fort as a way station for an express route between Fort Scott, Kansas, and Fort Gibson, Indian Territory, had only been given on August 26, 1863.[32] Quantrill laid out a plan to attack the fort utilizing an enveloping force of cavalry. The initial attack on the fort met with resistance from Captain James Pond and the few troops assigned on work detail. The force at the site was small as they had just recently sent out most of the men on a foraging expedition. Having some cover in the partially completed fort and a single artillery piece, these soldiers defended themselves credibly. Quantrill's enveloping force had gone a bit too wide and came out beyond the clearing where the fort sat, only to find a larger column of wagons and cavalry. This column turned out to be the personal escort of Brigadier General James Blunt, enroute to Fort Smith. His escort consisted of companies of the Third Wisconsin and Fourteenth Kansas Cavalry, numbering approximately 100 men. As the guerrillas emerged from the wood line and organized into battle lines, Blunt thought them to be an honor guard from the fort that had come to escort him. Dismounting the carriage in which he was riding and mounting his horse, he realized that these were not Union soldiers and called his escort forward. His Adjutant, Major H.Z. Curtis, formed the units in battle lines and had them prepared when the guerrillas charged. The Union cavalry wavered and, when the first volley of fire erupted from the guerrilla ranks, the cavalry line broke and ran for cover. The guerrillas pressed on, chasing individual soldiers down and killing them, including Major Curtis. The General's personal band was in their band wagon, horns out to play for Blunt's arrival, and sought to escape the attack. Their attempt failed and as a guerrilla rode up alongside the wagon, one of the bandsmen shot the Confederate. This was an unfortunate decision for the band members, as the guerrilla's friends observed the event and killed everyone in the wagon, setting fire to it and bodies in retaliation for the perceived brutality. General Blunt escaped death, as did a few members of his escort, and an officer's wife who was traveling with him to Fort Smith.[33]

In all, General Blunt was only able to rally 15 soldiers after the melee, indicating that approximately 85 were killed during the conflict. Much has been made of the conflict at Baxter Springs, often referring to it as a massacre with the same kind of anger that is reserved for events like the Lawrence raid or the Alamo. The basis for these accusations is the fact that almost all of the Union soldiers found dead had received a bullet to the head, as if they had been executed. With the burning of the bandwagon as additional grist, the irregular force was painted with the same brush as the one that sacked Lawrence. This was not an accurate assessment of the event, however. Blunt and his men were part of a force that had sworn a no-quarter oath against the men who rode with William Clarke Quantrill, and based on the guidance from Blunt himself and other leadership, they would have been required to execute any of the guerrillas they took prisoner. Therefore, the irregular warriors were also engaged in a similar campaign of extermination, just as was called for by General Ben Loan. Article 62 of General Order No. 100

indicates that "all troops of the enemy known or discovered to give no quarter in general, or to any portion of the Army, receive none."[34] Based on their own general order, the Union soldiers or high command should not have expected anything but a no-quarter action from the irregular warriors at Baxter Springs. General Blunt was merely the victim of the orders of Henry Halleck and every other Union general officer on the border. The picture that Blunt would paint in his reports after the conflict was colored by his own embarrassment at losing his escort, his flags, and his general officer's commission. Quantrill would indicate in a rare communication with Major General Sterling Price that he had taken some prisoners at Baxter Springs and on the trip through the Indian Territory, but had "brought none of them through."[35] This should have been considered acceptable to a Union army that was given guidance by the father of Major Curtis (Major General Samuel Curtis) that "death to bushwhackers is the order."[36]

Quantrill and his men would spend the winter of 1863-1864 in Texas, causing problems for the Confederate authorities there. While in Texas the group began to splinter and Quantrill lost control of large portions of the irregulars. Upon their return to Missouri in the spring and summer of 1864, the principal groups were led by George Todd and Bill Anderson, with Quantrill out of the limelight. Todd and Anderson's actions became gradually more violent and less controlled, and though they were ostensibly operating in conjunction with the regular Confederate force under Sterling Price in an effort to cause confusion behind Union lines, their excesses would go beyond even the violence of Lawrence.

Union communications concerning the efforts of these guerrilla bands certainly indicate that they had the attention of the militia and regular forces in central and north central Missouri. Included with the bands of Todd and Anderson was one led by Major John Thrailkill, whose group rode under a Confederate flag and conducted themselves quite differently from the former Quantrill men. Numerous entries relating to Thrailkill can be found in the *Official Records*, but the most telling deals with his efforts in the town of Keytesville, Missouri. On September 20, 1864, Thrailkill rode into Keytesville under the Confederate battle flag and demanded the surrender of the garrison there, promising parole for the soldiers. In a very controversial decision, the commander of the garrison surrendered his blockhouse and 35 men to Thrailkill, apparently from pure fear and lack of military ardor. The Confederate response to this action was markedly different from that expected of Todd or Anderson. Thrailkill paroled the entire garrison, with some men joining his band, and burned the fortified courthouse. While two Union men were killed, they were not amongst the soldiers who surrendered and thus not protected by Thrailkill's guarantee to the commander. Again the difference between the Quantrill's guerrillas and other irregular Confederate forces was visible, but totally lost on Union authorities. Thrailkill's actions would indicate he was operating as a partisan ranger and within the laws of war as he knew them, but the Union reports clearly indicate he was considered the equivalent of Anderson.[37] Information on Thrailkill shows that he was guilty of what Michael Fellman termed "guerrilla double-mindedness," as he operated with the guerrillas, yet often acted as a regular Confederate officer. Thrailkill was captured in July 1863 and after a court-martial in St. Louis was determined to be a combatant rather than a guerrilla. Though Fellman's sources indicate Thrailkill was imprisoned for the remainder of the war, he was active once again in September 1864. The "double-mindedness" to which Fellman referred is obvious in Thrailkill's parole of soldiers at Keytesville and subsequent activities with Todd and Anderson.[38]

The culmination of this reign of terror came at Centralia, Missouri, in late September, 1864. Anderson's band, with their trademark of scalps affixed to their bridles, rode into Centralia for information about Sterling Price. Alcohol flowed steadily and they stopped the train coming through from St. Louis. Approximately 20 soldiers were on the train and forced to dismount. After looting the train, the soldiers were "paroled" with the help of the Navy Colts of Anderson's men. The Union reports vary from 20 to 30 soldiers killed, but the closest number appears to be 20. Anderson and his bushwhackers left town and returned to the nearby camp to join the groups of Todd and apparently Thrailkill. Close behind them were portions of two Union companies commanded by Major Johnson of the 39th Regiment, Missouri Volunteers. Johnson had his men form a line of battle and dismount in an attempt to make best use of the range of their muskets. While Todd and Thrailkill's forces circled to the left and right of the Union position, Anderson's men charged in a frontal assault. The volunteers were no match for the fast riding guerrillas, armed with multiple pistols and greater firepower. The Union command was decimated with the official reports stating approximately 130 killed. What followed was a battle cry for Union forces in Missouri, similar to Lawrence, Kansas. Anderson's men killed all prisoners and then proceeded to begin to mutilate the bodies. Heads were cut off and switched to other bodies, noses and ears cut off for souvenirs, and even genitals were torn off and stuffed in the mouths of the corpses. This disgusting conduct marked the low point of guerrilla actions in Missouri during the war, going far beyond the killing of the enemy in self-defense or even for revenge. For Anderson, the conflict had degenerated into barbarism and even if it was fueled by his anger over the death of a sister and crippling of another, he had crossed the line from hardened guerrilla fighter to psychopath.[39]

Todd and Anderson were dead within thirty days of the Centralia affair and Sterling Price's invasion failed to bring the state of Missouri under Confederate control. The worst season of guerrilla war in Missouri and Kansas was over and most of the big names in the guerrilla ranks were gone, either dead or moved out of the state. As mentioned earlier, Quantrill went east, eventually meeting his demise in Kentucky. The legacy that these violent men left behind, along with the legacy of the Union officers who so violently sought them, was that of death, misery, and hatred.

The grudges and hatred that had existed between Missouri and Kansas before the war were not gone with the end of guerrilla war. The violence between the two sides had been too deadly and progressed too far. Small bands would continue to be active along the border for some time to come, ending the violence only when most of the irregular warriors were allowed to come out of the bush to pardons after the war. Even with the pardons, violence would continue as men settled old scores from the war in the post-war period. Many of those who rode in irregular bands would move on, finding their lives destroyed in the border area and no safety in their homes. Many had come from the "Burnt District," which offered no hope at the end of the war, because all that was left standing were stone chimneys. The people of Kansas and Missouri would rebuild and continue on, however, no longer caught between two forces conducting absolute war.

Notes

1. *Official Records*, Series I, Volume 22, Part I, pp. 572-593; Leslie, pp. 245-255; Connelly, pp. 398-420.

2. Rueben Randlett interview, William E. Connelly Collection, Western Historical Collection, University of Oklahoma, Norman.

3. Randlett interview; William Crutchfield interview, William E. Connelly Collection, Western Historical Collection, University of Oklahoma, Norman.

4. William E. Connelly, *Quantrill and the Border Wars*, (Ottawa, KS: Kansas Heritage Press, 1992), p. 90.

5. Albert Castel, *A Frontier State at War: Kansas 1861-1865*, (Lawrence, KS: Kansas Heritage Press, 1992), pp. 49-50.

6. Castel, pp. 54-55.

7. John P. Duke interview, William E. Connelly Collection, Western Historical Collection, University of Oklahoma, Norman.

8. Thomas Goodrich, *Black Flag: Guerrilla Warfare on the Western Border, 1861-1865*, (Bloomington, IN: Indiana University Press, 1995), pp.29-30; Randlett interview, Connelly Collection, pp.14-17.

9. *Official Records*, Series I, Volume 8, pp. 611-612.

10. *Official Records*, Series I, Volume 13, pp. 10-11.

11. This type of division and the problems it can cause military forces when trying to deal with irregular warfare is evident in the recent war in Iraq. The Sunni, Shiite, and Kurdish populations of this country were already at odds with each other and opportunities for one group to gain at the expense of the other two were far too common. American Forces that must deal with a split in society like this must be careful to make deliberate decisions so as to avoid inflaming tensions in the area unnecessarily.

12. *Official Records*, Series I, Volume 8, p. 12; Series I, Volume 22, Part II, pp. 17-18.

13. *Official Records*, Series I, pp. 12,13, 33, and 45.

14. *Official Records*, Series I, p. 719; Edward E. Leslie, *The Devil Knows How to Ride: The True Story of William Clarke Quantrill and His Confederate Raiders*, (New York, Random House, 1996), pp. 150-151.

15. Jefferson Davis, *The Rise and Fall of the Confederate Government, Volume II*, (New York: De Capo Press, Inc., 1990), p. 600; *Official Records*, Series I, Volume 22, Part 1, pp. 816-819.

16. *Official Records*, Series I, Volume 13, p. 5.

17. *Official Records*, Series I, Volume 22, Part I, p. 63; Leslie, p. 160-163.

18. *Official Records*, Series I, Volume 22, Part II, p. 125.

19. *Official Records*, p. 159.

20. *Official Records*, p. 183.

21. *Official Records*, p. 183.

22. *Official Records*, p. 184.

23. *Official Records*, p. 222.

24. *Official Records*, p. 279.

25. Connelly, p. 311.

26. Connelly, pp. 301-304; Leslie, pp.196. Leslie's version of what happened appears to be the most sensible. The plans to raid Lawrence had been made well before the building's collapse and, while it may have caused the violence level to be increased during the Lawrence Raid, it was not the proximate cause of it.

27. Connelly, p. 576.

28. *Official Records*, Series I, Volume 22, Part II, p. 473.

29. Albert Castel, "Order No. 11 and the Civil War on the Border," *Missouri Historical Review*, vol. 57 (1963), p. 357.

30. *Official Records*, Series I, Volume 22, Part I, p. 584.

31. *Official Records*, p. 575.

32. *Official Records*, Series I, Volume 22, Part II, p. 478.
33. *Official Records*, Series I, Volume 22, Part I, pp. 688-700.

34. *Official Records*, Series III, Volume 3, p. 155.

35. *Official Records*, Series I, Volume 22, Part I, pp. 700-701.

36. *Official Records*, Series I, Volume 22, Part II, p. 125.

37. *Official Records*, Series I, Volume 41, Part I, pp. 424-426.

38. Michael Fellman, *Inside War: The Guerrilla Conflict in Missouri During the American Civil War*, (New York: Oxford University Press, 1989), pp. 107, 206n.

39. Leslie, pp. 319-329; *Official Records*, Series I, Volume 41, Part III, p. 488.

Chapter 3

Indian Territory-Arkansas

As the armies of the Confederacy and Union surged back and forth across Arkansas, depredations from irregular forces were common against sympathizers of both sides. It is difficult to draw definitive timelines on the violence in any specific area, as the amount of guerrilla activity was often linked to the number of troops assigned to an area and their allegiance. On March 27, 1863, Colonel William Phillips reported to General Curtis that the "guerrillas have been pretty well driven out of this section."[1] Four days later, Colonel William Weer reported to General Schofield that in the vicinity of Carrollton, Arkansas, the Union population was having significant trouble and, in some cases, individuals were forced to flee to avoid attack. Finally, he advised Schofield that "the guerrillas who traverse the country shoot every Union man they see mercilessly...The operations of the enemy's guerrillas in Arkansas are far more vindictive and remorseless than anywhere else under my observation."[2]

Colonel Weer's problems with guerrillas appear to have gotten worse as time passed. On April 2, 1863, he reported to General Schofield that he was "enveloped in a cloud of guerrillas." Weer lamented that he could not control the area around his encampment due to the boldness of the guerrillas and the secessionist leanings of the surrounding population.[3]

The irregular war in the Indian Territory and Arkansas has not had the well publicized history of the Kansas-Missouri area just to the north. These two entities, a territory and a state, had been reasonably quiet in the 1850s. While the political tension in the Indian Territory had been palpable, the civilization on this portion of the border had been able to avoid open violence to solve political issues.

Just as the adjoining states of Kansas and Missouri were dealt with together, so will the Indian Territory and Arkansas be joined. The violence that beset them was very similar and, because of their ill-defined border, it surged from one to the other without even the participants knowing for sure whether they were committing depredations in the Indian Territory or Arkansas. Indians and Whites alike populated these two areas and both were the victims of the sometimes random violence that permeated the border.

Indian Territory

Few American students have not at least heard the outlines of the story of the "Trail of Tears." It is part of an ugly episode in American History, where members of the Indian tribes that had occupied the southeastern portion of the United States for many years were forcibly evicted and consigned to a new home farther west. The reasons for their being compelled to move were simple, white men wanted the land on which they lived and were concerned with the social implications of having these Indians within their midst. That is the basic story taught to school children, but from the perspective of at least one of the tribes involved there is a deeper, more divisive tale. That tale is at the root of much of the violence that beset Oklahoma during the years of the Civil War.[4]

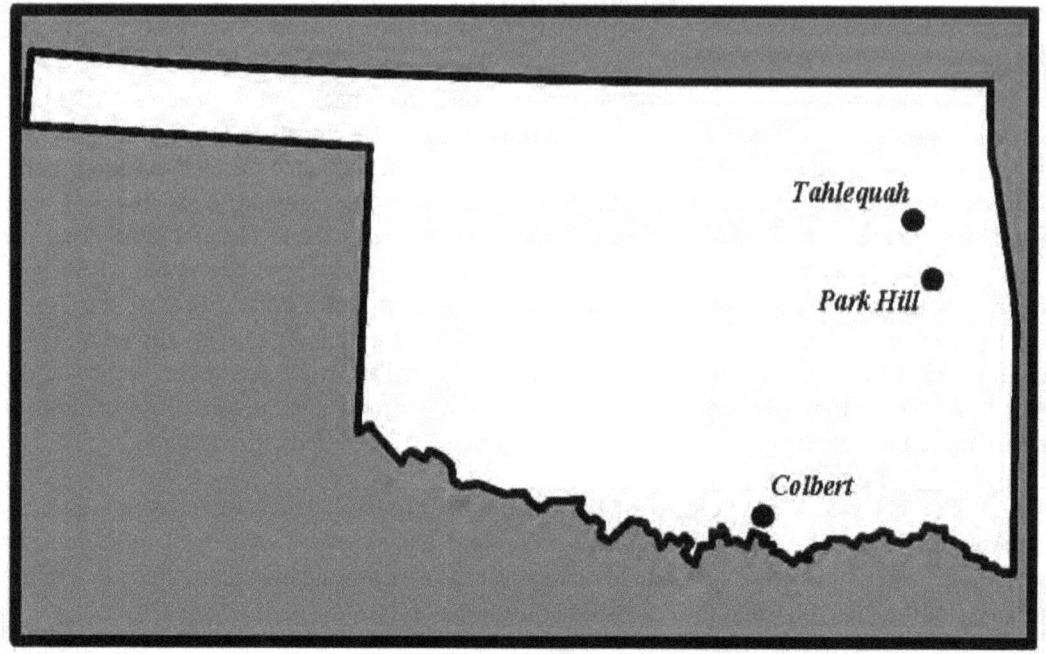

Map 5. Oklahoma Area of Operations.

As white settlers moved westward, they inevitably came into contact and conflict with Indian tribes that already occupied the land. One of these tribes, the Cherokee, was a resilient group who ceded lands to the encroaching settlers in an attempt to save at least part of what had been theirs. Early on, some members of the tribe opted to move to the west, occupying lands in Arkansas that provided better hunting and farming opportunities than their home lands in Georgia or Mississippi. Thus, the Cherokee Nation was divided into two geographical groups: the "Cherokee West," constituted by the early settlers in Arkansas, and the more populated "Cherokee East" that was made up of those who had opted to stay put in the southeast, on the lands they had historically occupied.

Problems were not far away though. Based on an agreement between the State of Georgia and the United States Government, known as the "Georgia Compact of 1802," the United States agreed to remove the Indians from the lands of the State of Georgia. By the middle part of the 1820s, Georgia wanted this agreement carried out and the leaders of the Cherokee Nation foresaw the coming storm. Though the Nation reorganized in an attempt to avoid displacement, setting up a government more like that used by the White governments around them, they found that by 1830 the chances of staying on their lands were slim.

It was in this timeframe that the seeds of violence in Oklahoma were planted. As with any group of people, different attitudes towards the displacement were evident within the Cherokee Nation. The Principal Chief, John Ross, was opposed to removal from the traditional tribal lands and was apparently supported in this position by the majority of the Cherokee people. A smaller group, led by a quartet of men; Major Ridge, his son John, Elias Boudinot, and Stand Watie believed that the removal was inevitable and the best way to avoid the problems attendant to living in an area while surrounded by a hostile populace was to cede their lands and move to those occupied by the Cherokee West. By now the West tribe had been coerced into leaving Arkansas and relocate to the Indian Territory. It was to this land that the Ridge-Watie-Boudinot group wished to move the Cherokee East Nation.

To affect this move, the supporters of removal signed the Treaty of New Echota with the US Government, and though they were not the elected representatives of the Cherokee Nation, the Congress of the United States quickly ratified the treaty, sentencing the Cherokee to a westward movement. From this signing in 1835, the Ridge-Watie-Boudinot group would be known as the "Treaty Party" and would be the opposition party in Cherokee politics. As should be expected, many of the Cherokee Nation believed these men to be traitors, who sold out the heritage of the tribe. They had allowed their people to be forcibly pushed to the Indian Territory on a march that cost the lives of many of the weaker Indians. This hatred would simmer for years to come, occasionally rising into a bubbling pot of violence and discord that would mar the peaceful existence in the Territory.

The first such episode occurred in 1839, when three of the quartet who orchestrated the Treaty of New Echota were murdered on the same day. Only Stand Watie avoided death and ascended to the leadership of the Treaty Party in a Cherokee Nation that was now permanently divided into hostile camps, which centered around the issue of removal. The majority faction was headed by Chief John Ross, still the elected Principal Chief of the Nation. While it may appear that this violence was nothing more than a local political squabble, its effects were felt in the upper echelons of national politics. Watie and members of his faction wrote to important Americans to enlist their assistance, including Andrew Jackson.

Jackson informed Watie on October 9, 1839, that he had written—

> a letter to the president of the United States in as strong language in your behalf & that of your friends as the facts and the outrageous & tyrannical conduct of John Ross & his self created council would authorize, & I trust the president will not hesitate to employ all his rightfull power to protect you and your party from the tyranny & murderous schemes of John Ross.[5]

He continued to give his counsel to Watie, enjoining him to "appeal & resort to all peacefull means to obtain justice..." before allowing violence to rule the day. In the final lines of his correspondence, Jackson advised the Treaty Party leaders that if they found peaceful means within the bounds of the legal establishment insufficient to bring the murderers of their leaders to justice "then and not until then will the great and good Spirit smile upon your exertions by force to obtain justice by freeing yourselves & people from oppression."[6] Jackson had counseled patience and the use of peaceful means to solve the dispute between the Watie and Ross Factions, but left the door open to the use of force if peaceful means were inadequate.

The period that followed the murders of the Ridges and Boudinot indicates that Watie was apparently unable to deal with the issues that confronted him through peaceful means. Violence followed this incident and blood flowed on both sides of the argument. Murder was the reply to murder and the hatreds that were the result of personal vendettas created a worsening situation in the Cherokee Nation. This violence merely set the stage for what was to come in later years. When the "white men" to the east could not control their political processes and solve their problems without violence, they engaged in civil war. The smoldering conflict that plagued the Indian Territory was fertile for such violence, even 21 years later. The Cherokee Nation, and those of the Creeks and Seminoles, split along historical and political lines when the war came, plunging the Indian Territory into an irregular battle involving Indian and "white" guerrillas that rivaled the violence in Kansas to the north.

As the United States became a divided nation, beset by a civil conflict between the Union and Confederate forces, decisions had to be made within the Indian Nations. They were located between Union Kansas and Confederate Texas, a geographical location that would obviously put them in contact with forces of both sides. The Five Civilized Tribes had come to the Indian Territory from the Deep South and had brought many of its institutions along on the trip. Most of the Nations kept black slaves and, though slavery was not totally accepted in the Territory, it was just another part of the southern culture that tied the Indian Nations to the South. Chief John Ross, seeing the dangers of alienating either of the governments (Union and Confederate), counseled neutrality for the people of the Cherokee Nation in an effort to spare them from the violence and possible future retaliation that could come with taking sides.

John Ross' efforts to keep his people out of the American Civil War were relatively short-lived. He would, by August of 1861, lead his people into an alliance with the Confederate States that would further tear apart the Cherokee Nation. It is not hard to understand John Ross and his desire for neutrality. All of the border states, which were part southern and part northern, had similar problems maintaining peaceful coexistence between the politically disparate portions of their populations. The Indian nations had the additional problem of not being "white," a fact that would undoubtedly slow the reaction of the Union Government to any calls for assistance. Washington was unable to protect the Unionist people of Missouri from the Confederate army or guerrillas who soon possessed the southwestern portion of the state. Surely John Ross had to see the difficulty of maintaining a position of neutrality when only one side in the conflict was truly interested in possession of the Indian Territory. The Confederate Government appointed a commissioner for the Indian Territory, Albert Pike, who oversaw the creation and administration of treaties with the Indian nations on behalf of the Richmond government.[7]

Ross was undoubtedly sympathetic to the Union cause, as his actions in the years that followed confirmed, but the situation in the Indian Territory left him little choice but to lead his people into the Confederate fold. The earlier mentioned interest on the part of the Confederacy meant that the military forces in Texas, Arkansas, and Missouri were a true threat to Ross if he chose to side with Washington or even maintain neutrality. These forces nearly surrounded his tribal lands and the possibility of reinforcement from Kansas was slim, as the Union forces there were occupied with Missouri raiders and the Army led by Sterling Price. Throughout the spring of 1861, Confederate emissaries met with John Ross in attempts to convince him to align his nation with that of the Confederacy.

Significantly, in July, the Union forces were defeated at the Battle of Bull Run and just over a month later Sterling Price claimed victory at Wilson's Creek, a battle virtually "just up the road" from the home of the Cherokee people. The Choctaw and Chickasaw Nations had severed their relations with the United States Government and tossed their lot in with the Confederacy earlier.[8] John Ross was faced with the option of opposing the Confederacy, either openly or through continued neutrality, or joining with the government that appeared to be on the verge of winning its independence from the Union. His position as Principal Chief was firm, but the members of the Treaty Party were already committed to the Confederacy and failing to go with the South would have led to armed conflict between the rival factions and, possibly, with the Confederate forces poised in and around the Indian Territory. On August 21, 1861, John Ross succumbed to the mounting pressures and withdrew his objections to joining the Confederacy. The Cherokee Nation had joined the Choctaws and Chickasaws in looking to the South for their future.[9]

While Chief John Ross and the Cherokee had chosen to ally themselves with the Confederacy rather than risk intratribal warfare, the leader of the Creek Nation, Opoth-le-yo-hola, chose to continue his loyalty to the Union. He sent a messenger to the US Commissioner for the Creeks and Seminoles, requesting assistance from the Union Government. The Commissioner, E. H. Carruth, was able to send only his assurances of Union support and a future movement of Union forces south from Kansas to support the Creek leader.[10] The Creeks, like the Cherokee, were divided in their loyalties and a faction of the tribe was determined to sever their treaty ties to the Union and join the Confederacy.

Throughout the fall of 1861, Confederate leaders in the Indian Territory attempted to bring Opoth-le-yo-hola to an agreement that would align the entire Creek Nation with Richmond, but to no avail. In November, Confederate forces consisting of Indian troops from the Creek, Chickasaw, Choctaw, and Cherokee Nations, along with Confederate-aligned troops from Texas, set out to force the Creek leader to surrender his resistance or bring him to battle. The Unionist Creek forces fought a running battle with the Confederates in late November and into December, finally losing so many supplies and warriors that they were forced to retire into the safety of southern Kansas. This defeat cleared the Indian Territory of Union forces and left the Confederacy in tentative control.

The spring of 1862 would demonstrate, however, that no one was in control of the Cherokee Nation or, for that matter, most of the Indian Territory. As has been written about extensively in Kansas and Missouri, areas on the border in which believers from both sides of the question resided, were seldom controlled. The feud between the conservative elements of Cherokee society and the Treaty Party had been only thinly veiled since the Ridge-Boudinot murders, and the coming of the "white man's war" to the Nation merely provided the excuse to engage in more open warfare. The Union-leaning conservatives, who were largely full-blooded Cherokee, had formed an organization known as the "Pins" in the pre-war years, an organization that espoused the importance of the tribe's old customs and was substantially anti-slavery. While the southern portion of the Cherokee Nation organized home guard companies and, eventually, the regiment of mounted riflemen commanded by Colonel John Drew, the conservative elements either moved north to join the Unionist Indians in southern Kansas or formed irregular companies to beset the southern sympathizers in the Nation.[11]

While Stand Watie and Drew were supporting the Confederate army in the Arkansas-Missouri-Indian Territory vicinity, the residents of the major towns of the Cherokee Nation, Tahlequah and Park Hill, were experiencing the kind of violence and terror that would beset innocents everywhere along the border. Reverend Stephen Foreman, a self-proclaimed half-breed minister in Park Hill and a strong supporter of secession and Stand Watie, wrote extensively of the problems that plagued he and his family during the spring and summer of 1862. He was distraught over the unsettled state of the Cherokee Nation, fearing at anytime that either Pin Indians or Jayhawkers from Kansas would visit Park Hill and exact a heavy price on the residents for their support of the Confederacy.

In April 1862, he wrote Reverend L. S. Wilson in Columbia, South Carolina, complaining that "on account of the unsettled state of affairs in the Nation...I have not been able to preach...I have made two appointments...which I failed to fill on account of the jay-hawkers who were expected among us, to rob and to commit other depridations."[12] Rev. Foreman continued his lament, revealing to Rev. Wilson the concern that he harbored for the future of the Cherokee Nation. Now that the Cherokees had cast their lot with the Confederacy, the issue was settled for him and his only worry was whether or not the South could successfully prosecute the war. He showed some concern over the Union victory at the Battle of Elk Horn and what it meant for southern sympathizers in the Indian Territory. If this was the beginning of a negative trend for the Confederacy, he worried that "the Cherokee Nation shall be in constant dread, not knowing what moment the Jay-hawkers may be among us, robbing and killing." His concern was evidently not just Jayhawkers from Kansas, but the previously mentioned Creek Indians who had followed their leader into southern Kansas and the service of the Union Army. In his closing line, Rev. Foreman summarized the fears of many in the Territory, correctly identifying that "if the Northern army comes into the Nation, those of us who stand up for the South expect but little mercy shown to them."[13]

Foreman is an articulate spokesman for the supporters of the Confederacy in Park Hill and the overall Cherokee Nation. The proximity of Kansas and the existence of the Indians who openly sided with the Union created an atmosphere that violence was always just a hoof beat away, only awaiting the arrival of an irregular Union warrior, Indian, or "white man," who would bring death, destruction, or robbery to the Southern sympathizers. Foreman's concern in April was well-founded, as his later letters and those of others clearly indicate. In July, Foreman received news of the murder of his brother, Alex, and another Park Hill resident, Abijah Hicks. They were murdered in separate incidents and Foreman indicates that initial reports showed that Hicks was killed by men associated with Stand Watie. The motive for Hicks murder was murky, as Foreman indicates that he was an "inoffensive man" and must have been killed for his property or his "abolitionist sentiments." Either motive is credible, as Foreman lamented that "no one who has a good horse or any good property is safe, though I have heard of no one being killed yet for his sentiments, still I should not be surprised if it came to that."[14]

Rumors that Chief John Ross and other members of the Cherokee leadership were attempting to contact the Union, supposedly to renew the recently severed treaties, were evident in the Nation. Southerners among those at Park Hill and Tahlequah were concerned that a plot was underway to turn the towns and the Cherokee Nation over to the Federals. Stephen Foreman was concerned about these rumors and sought an audience with John Ross to inquire about his intentions. He went to Ross' home on July 7th and spoke with the Chief about his apprehensions. He pointed out to Chief Ross that he had heard reports that portions of Drew's regiment would soon be defecting to the Union Army and that the leadership must take steps to insure that the Nation was united. Foreman was unconvinced by the answers he received from John Ross and indicated so in his diary. He perceived the Ross Party and Pins as one and believed the evidence strongly indicated that "a plan was on foot for the whole Pin Regiment and all others of the same stripe to join the Northern Army and that the time was now at hand..." Foreman was convinced that Ross was no longer loyal to the Southern cause and would soon openly be reunited with the Federal Government.[15]

From mid-July on, Foreman's diary is filled with tales of the Pin Indians and the fear and depredations that they brought to "Watie men" like Rev. Foreman. Foreman's frustration at being singled out amongst other leaders who were also supposedly of southern sympathies is evident in his words. He admits to being a Southern man, but maintains that Chief Ross and other Baptist preachers professed to be Southern men. Finally, he reaches the conclusion that the issue is more than just being a Southern man. As mentioned earlier, the Pins grew from their support of the old customs of the Cherokee Nation and they stood with the pure blood Indians of the Nation. His concern was obviously about his blood line, stating that "they themselves had drawn a line of distinction between themselves and the half-breeds, and being a half-breed, I naturally fell on the Watie side."[16]

The importance of the old feuds, stretching back to New Echota, is evident once more. Much of the division within the Cherokee Nation continued to be based on long-smoldering problems, which the Civil War had rekindled, causing additional suffering and destruction amongst the Indians. Foreman was not just a southern sympathizer, but a Treaty Party man. While the Jayhawkers from Kansas would rob him and conceivably kill him for that allegiance, the Pins would make another distinction and abuse him for his ties to that portion of the Cherokee Nation that had brought about removal.[17]

Reverend Foreman had early on been a vocal opponent of the Pin organization and by mid-July 1862 was beginning to fear for his life because of this opposition. He mentioned the organization regularly in his diary and equated it and its ideals to the party of Chief John Ross and the National Council.[18] The diary is filled with references to the violence committed by Pin raiding parties, who "pass about in the neighborhood hunting Negroes, horses and Watie men." He detailed the creation of a Pin headquarters, at the Ross home, and assumed that the raiding parties were extremely effective as "they have quite a lot of Negroes and horses at Chief Ross's." Rev. Foreman summed up his opinion of the situation on July 1862, when he wrote that "all who do not belong to their party, and who have not fled to them for protection are robbed of everything and shot down whenever met with. So to be a Watie man or an anti-pin is to be under sentence of death."[19]

Foreman's fear and bitterness is obvious in the pages of his diary, along with a frustration at the state of affairs in the Park Hill area. He related a concern for the people of the area and what appears to be a sincere desire for peace, regardless of the cost. Though a devout Southerner, he continued to seek intervention to bring peace to the Nation. He wrote that "It does seem to me that either the North or the South ought immediately to take possession of the country and control affairs, so as to stop this killing and robbing which is carried on so boldly in different parts of the Nation." He carefully notes for posterity that this comment does not indicate that he is uncaring about the Southern cause and that he has for some time been an ardent foe of Northern principles and the attitudes of abolitionists. He reiterates his support for the Confederacy and his desire to see them victorious. His fear and concern seem to compel him to believe that "It is from considerations of humanity alone that I wish for some authority to interfere and control affairs here."[20]

Foreman was a man, like many others along the border, who was tired of the random violence that beset areas that were alternately occupied by the North and South. These areas saw the ebb and flow of the war and were exposed to violence from every quarter. No one was safe from this violence, depending on which force was in control of their town on that particular day. Also in Park Hill were many Northern sympathizers, as Foreman clearly portrayed Chief John Ross. One such individual was Hannah Hicks, the widow of Abijah Hicks, of whom Foreman wrote earlier. She was a woman of Northern sympathies, as it appears was her husband, and though acquainted with Foreman, had many differences of opinion with him on loyalty issues. Hannah was not as vocal as Rev. Foreman, probably because a widow along the border without the protection of a husband had little choice but to quietly try and make it through each day. Even though she was not a Southern woman, her fear of the Pins was also evident. Often it mattered not whether someone was Northern or Southern, as it was not until after the violence was over that their true sympathies were revealed. Information came to Mrs. Hicks that "my poor husband was killed by the 'Pins,' but through mistake intending to kill another man. If it was a mistake 'twas a terrible one for me. It is strange, very strange anyway."[21] Later that month, Hannah Hicks would lose her home to a fire, apparently set by Pins who believed it to be the home of a Watie man and wished to punish him.[22] The lines of allegiance all along the border blurred as they obviously did in Park Hill, with the innocent suffering right along with the guilty.

The proximity of Northerner and Southerner in the Cherokee Nation is clearly shown in the relationship between Rev. Foreman and Hannah Hicks. Foreman indicated in his diary on July 19, 1862, that rumors were around Park Hill that he had something to do with the death of Abijah Hicks, but was content that Mrs. Hicks knew the rumors to be false. His relationship with Hannah Hicks appeared to be friendly and on July 20th he wrote of hiding in her garret to escape capture and murder by the Pins. His relationship with Mrs. Hicks is illuminated later in that entry when he referred to Hannah's father as a dear old friend, submitting that his relationship with her father was the reason that she hid him from his own people, who were now out to kill him.[23] A check of Mrs. Hicks' diary indicates circumstances that are perceived much differently. Her entry of September 19, 1862, indicates that Rev. Foreman and his family had left Park Hill for the Creek Nation and allowed that she hoped he found better friends there. Her notes went on to reveal some strong feelings towards Foreman that weren't obvious to the

Reverend. She indicates how happy everyone was to see Foreman depart and how bitterly he treated those who disagreed with him. She laments having provided him shelter and food in her garret for a number of days, but at the end of that time found him to be just as bitter to those who protected him as he was before. Evidently those who sought him believed that he had a hand in the murder of her husband, Abijah Hicks, and intended to make him pay a price for that involvement. Her feelings towards Rev. Foreman are solidified when she shares that "I do believe that his influence helped to cause the murder of my husband, and the arrest of brother D.D. You will think this dreadful, Ann Eliza, but, believe me, we have sufficient cause. Oh the fearful things that were spoken by him and his."[24]

Both Rev. Foreman and Hannah Hicks lived in Park Hill during the summer and early fall of 1862, but their perceptions of what happened and who was to blame are markedly different. Their opinions were obviously determined by what side of the conflict they supported, which should not be surprising. The amazing thing is that while they supported different sides in the violence around them, they were so closely connected and had such intimate contact. While enemies deep inside, they had to live side-by-side and did what was necessary to keep life going until relief came in one form or another. This relationship is at the heart of the uniqueness of the irregular warfare that permeated the border region in the West. The lines of battle weren't clearly drawn and easily definable, as they were on the fields of Gettysburg or Antietam, but blurred into a violent haze that put enemies into daily contact. The question each day was which side would apply the violence that all had to look forward to and fear. Many would die because they met the wrong side on a particular day and were unable to convince them of their true loyalties. It is hard to imagine that kind of fear and how it had to affect adults and children. The animosity that Hannah Hicks felt for Stephen Foreman is obvious in her diary, but she dared not express it openly as tomorrow could be the day that his side held temporary sway and she could not afford to alienate a man who could bring her such violent problems.

The violence in the Indian Territory was not confined to the Park Hill and Tahlequah area. Interviews with survivors of the war and their descendants are filled with tales of wanton killing and robbery at the hands of bushwhackers from both sides of the conflict. One interviewee admitted that his father was a bushwhacker and that "in other words he was one of the men that played both sides in the War."[25] This belief among descendants of the victims of the war in Arkansas and the Indian Territory, that the bushwhackers were not representatives of any particular side, is evident in the interview with William L. Cowart. He indicated that his father was a Confederate soldier and that his family suffered at the hands of bushwhackers, but that they were not members of the Union forces. He described the bushwhackers as men who "took out their spite on the helpless non-combatants and robbed and burned and committed crimes, as there were no civil officers and no law in the Cherokee Nation at that time, and the Bushwhackers operated unmolested, where and when they pleased."[26] These men often had no political side in the conflict or just changed sides as the situation suited them. One such combatant, named Jesse Russel, was originally with the Pin Indians, but chose to leave them and join with the Southern forces. The Pins waited what they believed to be an acceptable period of time for him to return to them and when he didn't they hunted him down and killed him.[27] Apparently, changing sides was not uncommon, but could be deadly if those that you left were still in the immediate area.

Much of the violence that has been portrayed thus far was committed by the Pin Indians, ostensibly in support of the Union forces in the War. Violence of this type was not restricted to the Northern side or to Indians. Stand Watie's men also conducted raids of this sort and, while they could be considered regular soldiers in some instances, their warfare in general lends them to the classification of irregulars. Watie's adjutant described the force that Colonel Watie commanded in October 1863 as "a crowd of Cherokee, Creeks, Chickasaws, and white vagabonds and Border Ruffians." This is apparently the force that Watie had with him when he was at Park Hill in November 1863. He wrote his wife, Sarah, about his scout there explaining that they "killed a few Pins in Tahlequah. They had been holding council. I had the old council house set on fire and burnt down, also John Ross' house. Poor Andy Nave was killed. He refused to surrender and was shot by Dick Fields. I felt sorry as he used to be quite friendly towards me before the war but it could not be helped."[28]

While the preceding pages have painted the picture of the violence that went on between Union and Confederate Indians, these were not the only irregular warriors active in the Indian Territory during the war. Jayhawkers from Union Kansas rode into the Cherokee Nation and exacted a price from those they perceived to be Confederate sympathizers. Rev. Foreman's diary indicated his fear of these raiders and placed them in bands with the Pin Indians that raided their fellows in the towns of Park Hill and Tahlequah. These men were constant threats to the population of the Cherokee Nation, creating a pall of unrest that hung over the country like a dangerous cloud.

An even more violent threat entered the Indian Territory on the evening of October 6, 1863, in the form of William Clarke Quantrill. After the infamous raid on Lawrence in August 1863, Quantrill's men had gone to ground for a period of time. Reorganizing and setting out on a renewed campaign, Quantrill came upon Brigadier General Blunt's command near Baxter Springs, Kansas, on the 6th and decimated the Union force. From Baxter Springs, Quantrill set off south down the Texas Road into the Indian Territory, apparently in the belief that Union reinforcements would soon follow after the fight at Baxter Springs. As usual, his entry into any area was bloody and savage, with his official report citing the capture of about 150 Indians and Negroes, none of which apparently lived to relate their experience with the king of civil-war-era guerrillas.[29] One of Quantrill's guerrillas accounts for some of these 150 when he details an attack on Indians in the early days of that movement through the Indian Territory. Quantrill's band came upon a wagon train of Pin Indians on the second evening of the trip and charged the column, apparently killing them all, as the author points out that "in a short time, they were all good Indians."[30] Quantrill and his band would continue to raid into the Indian Territory for the next six months, operating either on their own or loosely in concert with larger Confederate raids organized by Stand Watie or other southern forces. While his forces provided a hard-fighting company of men to the Confederacy, they were uncontrollable and left destruction and bloodshed wherever they went. Obviously, those individuals in the Indian Territory aligned with the Federal Government were given no-quarter when they fell into the hands of this guerrilla leader, but the pain that he inflicted was never limited to the enemy.

In February 1864, Quantrill and his band stopped in the town of Colbert, situated in the Chickasaw Nation, close to the border with Texas. Here he forced the occupants of the Isaac Albertson farm to serve dinner to him and his soldiers. The women of the house, apparently Confederate sympathizers, prepared the guerrillas food and drink and gave them the hospitality of their home. Quantrill returned the favor from these southern women by taking all the livestock on the farm with him when he left. Shortly after this episode, Quantrill's men killed a Confederate officer, Major Butts, in the Chickasaw Nation.[31] While it was to be expected that the enemy would have much to fear from the guerrilla violence of William Clarke Quantrill, it is obvious that no one was safe in his presence. Things grew so bad between Quantrill and the Confederate leadership, in the late winter and early spring of 1864, that Quantrill was forced to flee back to Missouri, where he ultimately lost control of his guerrilla band.

Obviously, classification of these irregular warriors is complex, with units like Stand Watie's operating as regularly enrolled soldiers while using guerrilla tactics. Others can be defined, by their actions, as falling into the category of war-rebels, while some certainly merited the term of outlaw that was applied to all guerrillas by the Union authorities. While some areas of the border held more of one category or another, they all generally possessed many of the same characteristics.

Arkansas

As was the case all along the border area, the day-to-day war in northern Arkansas was a scene of terror and depredation. While the battles of Pea Ridge and Prairie Grove are the part of the Civil War that appears in most histories of Arkansas, the people of the state had to deal with the petty war continually. The war was not restricted to the battlefields, but was evident in the streets of most towns and in the barnyard of most farms. War on a mass scale tends to be impersonal, but the irregular war, on the other hand, is one of personal violence and terror. The story of one woman in Arkansas is illustrative of this point; while Confederate soldiers had to worry about minnie balls and cannon shot, Mrs. Sallie Jordan's mother had her right foot placed into a bed of hot coals by Federal soldiers, bent on forcing her to reveal the hiding place of the family's money.[32] This is not the type of violence that was found on the battlefields of Pea Ridge or Shiloh or even Franklin, but it had a tremendous effect on the people that it touched.

The war ebbed and flowed across northwestern Arkansas, however, and at any given time the area could be controlled by either the North or the South. Within such a turbulent environment, and with the total lack of uniformity in military dress, citizens often were unable to determine the politics and military allegiance of a visitor until they questioned him. It was by no means unusual for Confederate soldiers to wear Union blue that they had captured, as their own government was unable to provide them with adequate protection against the elements. The noncombatants, caught in the middle between two rival armies, wondered constantly whether they would live to see another day or whether they would lose everything they owned to the next group of riders to come galloping up the lane.

One writer, a retired schoolteacher named Robert Mecklin, remained at home in northwestern Arkansas throughout the war and his letters revealed how families survived in this violent atmosphere. In a letter, dated August 30, 1863, Mecklin explained the exploits of a Confederate officer named Captain Buck Brown, who, with about 120 men, operated in the vicinity of Fayetteville, Arkansas, hitting exposed Union patrols and supply trains. With the fall of Little Rock only ten days away, Captain Brown was operating many miles in the rear of the main Union force, utilizing the classic tactics of the guerrilla to cause as much consternation as possible among the Federals.[33] Mecklin goes on to talk of the quality of Brown's organization and that of another Confederate officer, noting that "better officers and braver soldiers could not be left us."[34] Obviously, Mecklin believed these irregulars to be Confederate soldiers, involved in a fight to protect the southern sympathizers of the area from Federal troops.

Map 6. Arkansas Area of Operations.

These men, which southern sympathizers regarded as soldiers of the southern cause, were perceived as renegades by the Union authorities and failed to recognize the legitimacy of irregular warfare anywhere along the border. Based on General Order No. 100, they were defined as outlaws, bushwhackers, and brigands, and stood to forfeit their lives if they were captured under arms against the Federal authorities. To be recognized by the Federals as partisans, a term which provided for treatment as prisoners of war, the soldier had to be part of a force detached from a main body and wearing the uniform of his army. In the fall of 1863, it was difficult to determine if there was a main Confederate army in Arkansas and the armed men of southern sympathies were treated under Article 82 of the General Order, which deemed them to be pirates and highway robbers, and were liable to summary execution.[35] A resident of the ravaged area showed how tense the situation was in a letter in which he detailed meeting Federal soldiers while he was out chopping wood. He did not at first recognize them as Federals, but knew as soon as he heard them speak. They passed him by, but he confided to his correspondent that "had [I] been found with a gun instead of an axe, trying to shoot a hawk for carrying off our chickens...or a turkey to get a little meat for my family, I would have perhaps been shot down as a bushwhacker."[36] In this environment of fear and violence, families could not even perform the tasks that were natural to their everyday existence, the hunting of food, or the protection of their belongings. Weapons were hidden, for discovery with arms was an admission of guilt and a ticket to prison or death.

While the most active area of guerrilla activity was northern Arkansas near the Missouri border, other areas of the state were affected also. General Blunt, in command of the District of the Frontier in July 1863, informed Schofield that guerrilla bands were extremely numerous in southwestern Arkansas hunting down Union men who had fled there for the protection of the mountains.[37] The problem in Arkansas was that the Union forces were never able to fill the state with adequate troops to truly control the countryside. Major General Frederick Steele, commander of the Arkansas Expedition, indicated this when he wrote to the Sixteenth Army Corps Commander, Major General Stephen Hurlbut, informing him that as soon as his troops departed an area the guerrillas would flow back in and control the terrain and his lines of communication.[38] More open proof of this conscious decision on the part of Washington is found in correspondence from General Halleck to Schofield. Halleck expressed his displeasure that Steele continued to retain forces in Arkansas, directing that since "only guerrilla bands will be left in Arkansas" Steele's forces are not to "be parceled out to merely to protect the country." Halleck wanted these troops for operations with General Nathaniel Banks along the Red River and apparently saw no pressing need to protect the Union citizens of Arkansas.[39]

The communications between headquarters involved in operations in Arkansas paint a picture of a sea of guerrilla manpower that parted as the Union forces moved through an area, then surged back as the end of the Union columns disappeared over the last hill. General McNeil, who enamored himself to the Confederacy by his actions at Palmyra, Missouri, attempted to use the Union First Arkansas Cavalry to police their home state, imploring them to get off of the main roads and seek out the guerrillas along the mountain paths that were known only to local men.[40] Other Union commanders sought and received permission to raise local Federal militias to fight the specter of irregular violence, believing that the locals would be much more motivated and adept at combating the guerrillas.[41]

The Union commanders weren't the only ones concerned with irregular warfare in Arkansas. Confederate leaders indicated similar problems from irregular Union forces operating in their midst. Brigadier General William Steele, a division commander in the Trans-Mississippi Army, complained of a guerrilla force that was cutting off his line of communications following the retreat of General Hindman's forces south. He blamed rogue Texans and local Unionists for the problems, citing the common problems of trying to bring to battle irregular forces when they are well mounted and working in rugged terrain. Just as the Union forces gave irregulars no military standing, Steele referred to these forces as "lawless bands of robbers and murderers," further indicating that they were committing countless depredations on the local Confederate population.[42] Indications from Confederate correspondence show that the sea analogy is consistent for them also, with Steele's adjutant informing his higher headquarters that "it has been impossible to leave this portion of the country up to the present time without abandoning all this country to our enemies, or rather that which would prove more destructive than an organized enemy – bands of traitors who are about in this vicinity."[43]

Even Confederate Secretary of War James Seddon expressed concern over the impact of this guerrilla violence in Arkansas in a letter to Lieutenant General E. Kirby Smith. The letter asked Smith to take a personal role in the state of affairs in Arkansas, lamenting that the people are represented to him by good sources as being without basic subsistence and nearing starvation, with what little they have being plundered by "gangs of lawless marauders and deserters."[44]

While guerrilla activity in Arkansas never reached the levels of intensity and violence that was found in Kansas and Missouri, the violence of the border spilled south. As Confederate and Union forces roamed the countryside, they preyed on citizens they considered disloyal to their cause. Quite often the Confederate guerrillas would take the opportunity to serve with Jo Shelby or John Marmaduke conducting raids into Missouri.[45] These irregular soldiers moved in and out of the Confederate service as suited their needs, rarely under control of their commanding officers. In addition to these forces nominally working under command of Union or Confederate officers, the problem of desertion, raised earlier by General Steele and Secretary Seddon, contributed significantly to the unrest in the countryside. As soldiers, tired of war or simply seeking plunder, left the control of regular forces they tended, all along the border, to turn to murder as their mode of operation. Though hard to pin down, complaints of these "lawless bandits" were commonly heard.

Both while the Confederate army was in the state and after they had departed, the people of northern Arkansas were besieged by violence from both sides and victimized by lawless individuals who fought for no cause except their personal aggrandizement. The fear and tension are evident in the words of Robert Mecklin, who indicated that if he was caught away from home he would likely be killed and if he was to avoid such an end, his lot would be time in the guard house. He shared that he was convinced that he would stay in the guard house, unable to help his family, until such time as he bowed to the lewd comments of his captors and took "the oath of loyalty to Mr. Lincoln's government."[46] As a man of Southern sympathies, he feared Union supporters around every corner.

This violence in Arkansas continued throughout the course of the war and contributed not only to the death toll, but to the unrest amongst the civilian populace of the state. Guerrillas attacked a Union officer in February 1865 on the road from Fort Smith to Van Buren. He was lucky and all they did was threaten him and take everything he had, to include his pride. Not as fortunate was a Union Private named Williams, who was killed by partisans within half a mile of his unit's camp.[47] These soldiers were victims of painful encounters with irregular warriors late in the war in Arkansas, but as seen earlier it was more often the civilian population that suffered the most. The population around Fort Smith was unable to effectively grow the crops necessary to feed themselves because of the presence of guerrillas in the area. They petitioned the Federal Government for protection and arms with which to defend themselves. While no established Confederate army threatening Arkansas, the specter of violence from sympathizers and partisans continued to create fear and tension in the populace.[48]

The Indian Territory and Arkansas were not critical battlefields in the grand scheme of Civil War history. What happened there did little to affect the final outcome of the war and the collapse of the Confederacy. The events in these areas were, however, critical to the Americans who populated the towns and farms there. They lived in fear of violence for years and many encountered that deadly violence first-hand. Even the families of the guerrillas faced these dangers, because while Quantrill on the Confederate side or many of the Union soldiers were not from Arkansas or the Territory, most of the irregulars that fought here were members of the communities in the local border area. Some of their families were left at home to take their chances, while others were displaced to Texas to live a camp life that was itself a great psychological burden. With the end of the war, all these families were losers in one way or another and the small war in the Territory and Arkansas solved little, but caused immense pain.

Notes

1. *Official Records*, Series I, Volume 22, Part II, p. 181.

2. *Official Records*, p. 186.

3. *Official Records*, pp. 189-190.

4. Much of the information for this introduction concerning the historical background of the Cherokee Nation was drawn from Edward E. Dale and Gaston Litton, *Cherokee Cavaliers: Forty Years of Cherokee History as Told in Correspondence of the Ridge-Watie-Boudinot Family,* (Norman, OK: University of Oklahoma Press, 1996).

5. *Cherokee Cavaliers*, p. 17.

6. *Cherokee Cavaliers*, p. 17.

7. Wiley Britton, *The Union Indian Brigade in the Civil War,* (Ottawa, KS: Kansas Heritage Press, 1922), p. 25.

8. Britton, pp. 25-26.

9. Britton, pp. 28-29.

10. Britton, p. 34.

11. Britton, p. 33.

12. Stephen Foreman to L.S. Wilson, April 2, 1862. Stephen Foreman Collection, Western Historical Collection, University of Oklahoma, Norman, OK.

13. Stephen Foreman to L.S. Wilson, April 2, 1862.

14. Foreman Diary, July 6, 1862.

15. Foreman Diary, July 7, 1862.

16. Foreman Diary, July 16, 1862.

17. This dual threat to Foreman as both a Southern sympathizer and a Treaty Party man points out the importance of understanding the culture of a populace in the midst of irregular violence. Union soldiers from the north would not have understood this dynamic, but it was apparent to members of his cultural community. US Army forces have just recently begun to take an interest in the culture of the populace in which they operate, after seeing its importance displayed so prominently in Iraq and Afghanistan. Professional military education institutions in the Army are focusing much more clearly on the importance of culture and language so as to better understand the civilians and irregular warriors with whom they have to deal.

18. Foreman Diary, July 16, 1862.

19. Foreman Diary, July 17, 1862.

20. Foreman Diary, July 18, 1862.

21. The Diary of Hannah Hicks, (Tulsa, OK: The Thomas Gilcrease Institute of American History and Art, 1972), p. 8.

22. Hicks Diary, p 8.

23. Foreman Diary, July 20, 1862.

24. Hicks Diary, p. 9 and note #5.

25. John Silk interview #6005, Oklahoma Indian Project, Oklahoma Historical Society, p. 492.

26. William L. Cowart interview #7901, Oklahoma Indian Project, Oklahoma Historical Society, p. 69.

27. Hicks Diary, p. 4.

28. *Cherokee Cavaliers*, pp. 142-145.

29. *Official Records*, Series. I, Volume 22, Part 1, 700-1.

30. John McCorkle, *Three Years with Quantrill: A True Story Told by his Scout John McCorkle,* Norman, OK: University of Oklahoma Press, 1992), p. 142.

31. LeRoy Fischer and Lary C. Rampp, "Quantrill's Civil War Operations in Indian Territory;" found in the John W. Morris Collection, Western History Collection, University of Oklahoma.

32. Belser, "Military Operations," p. 643.

33. W.J. Lemke, ed., *The Robert Mecklin Letters*, (Fayetteville, AR.: Washington County Historical Society, 1955), p. 11.
34. Lemke, p. 13.

35. Hartigan, pp. 60-61.

36. Lemke, p. 25.

37. Lemke, p. 411.

38. Lemke, p. 444.

39. Lemke, pp. 709-710.

40. Lemke, p. 518.

41. Lemke, p. 533.

42. Lemke, pp. 774-775.

43. Lemke, p. 778.

44. Lemke, pp. 802-803.

45. Lemke, p. 219.

46. Lemke, p. 13.

47. Fort Smith *New Era*, Feb. 11, 1865.

48. "General Bussey Takes Over at Ft. Smith;" found in the A. M. Gibson Collection, Western Historical Collection, University of Oklahoma.

Chapter 4

Texas

In his work on the Great Hanging at Gainesville, Texas, Richard McCaslin observed that few of the approximately 42 prisoners who were executed at Gainesville in 1862 were guilty of the treason or insurrection with which they were charged. Southern leaders in this north Texas city and county were striving for a level of security for their citizens and did not hesitate to use the rope and the hanging tree to try and cut out what they viewed as a potentially dangerous part of society. Their actions were bred of fear; fear of what could happen if Union sympathizers were able to operate in the county and create unrest among the population and slaves. In the end, their actions were accepted by the people of the county, though they were, in most cases, not within the bounds of existing law.[1]

The state of affairs in Texas during the war was at once similar and different from the other border states in this study. Violence on a low, personal level was common throughout the state, driven by political perspectives and a simple desire for personal enrichment. Conversely, the violence in Texas was not exactly that found in Kansas or in Kentucky. Organized or semi-organized guerrilla bands opposing the government in power were not a common problem anywhere in Texas. Most of the violence driven by political perspectives was based on the perception of disloyalty and the fear of actions, rather than on concrete actions by Union guerrillas. This subtle distinction, while important, does not make the violence in Texas any less bloody or dangerous. A continuing focus on the border population and the impact of this violence on that society is just as important in a society filled with violence based on perceptions or misperceptions, as one filled with guerrillas. The Texans who were hanged at Gainesville died as surely as if they carried a Union battle flag, the distinction as to whether they were trying to engage in the Union fight mattered not to them.

Civil wars are by their very nature bloody and personal. Baron de Jomini characterized this type of war as a "war of opinion." In discussing the violent nature of such wars, Jomini wrote that these type of wars "…result either from doctrines which one party desires to propagate among its neighbors, or from dogmas which it desires to crush, in both cases leading to intervention. Although originating in religious or political dogmas, these wars are most deplorable; for, like national wars, they enlist the worst passions, and become vindictive, cruel, and terrible."[2]

It was the propagation of doctrines and dogmas amongst the population of Texas, perceived or real, that brought on the violence examined in this chapter. Jomini's contention that these wars are particularly cruel and vindictive was born out in the Civil War experience in Texas. It was very hard for citizens to remain quiet and at ease when they perceived a threat in close proximity to them. This type of fear was rampant whenever the group in power, be they Union or Confederate, believed that the population, or a portion of it, was disloyal to their cause. Disloyalty covers a broad scope of offenses and feelings. A German citizen of Fredericksburg or Comfort had only to be "soft" on slavery or secession to be considered disloyal, and therefore dangerous to the public good. Non-Germans around Gainesville found the same to be true in another section of the state. Overt acts were not necessary to bring the weight of "justice" down upon the heads of the offenders. Any accusation or suspicion was enough to warrant arrest, incarceration, or hanging from the nearest tree. Some of those considered disloyal to the Confederate cause were afforded the luxury of due process, but they were the lucky ones. Others were left hanging over the road, swinging from a tree limb, or were shot and thrown into the nearest stream.

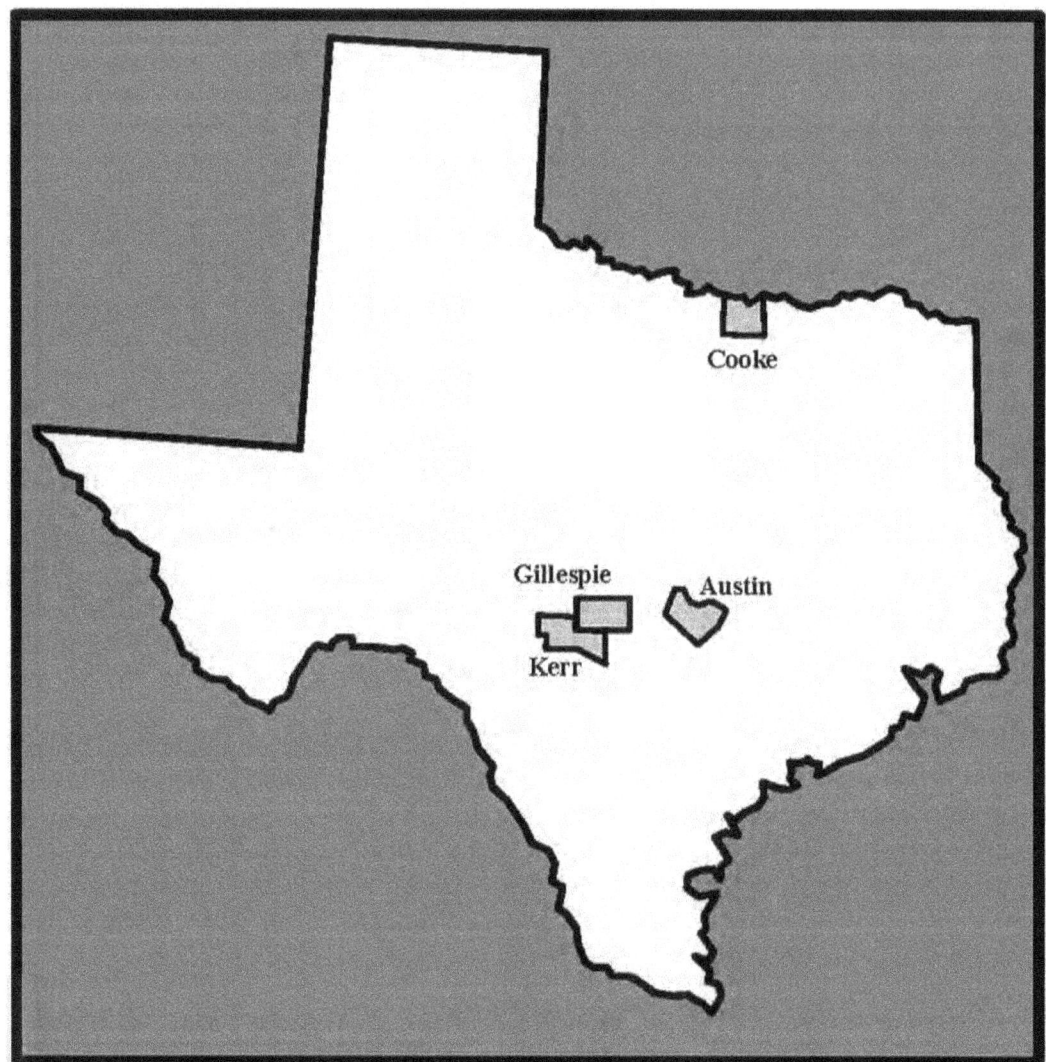

Map 7. Texas Area of Operations.

This type of violence and the fear that it breeds does not die out quickly. Men who died on the field of battle did so in a rather impersonal way. They seldom knew the individual soldier in the other uniform — he was just another Yankee or Reb — so their scars healed a little quicker when the war was behind them. Unfortunately, the type of personal violence, which is detailed here, creates scars that take generations to go away. The scars are healed now, but the wounds are not covered as deeply as 147 years of history would suggest. The violence that occurred in these counties had a lasting effect upon the history of Texas and many of those who lived through it went on to serve in positions of importance in Texas government. How could perceived unionists such as Jacob Kuechler and Edward Degener, who suffered physical attack, incarceration, and the loss of loved ones, easily forget the men whom they knew were responsible for these acts? Radical reconstruction in post-war Texas eventually offered these men the power that they needed to even the score with their antagonists.

The counties in the area between Austin and San Antonio were not inhabited by strong secessionists. In fact, 10 counties voted against secession and five more proved to have nearly 50 percent of their voters in opposition to the ordinance.[3] The agriculture of much of this area did not readily support slave labor and the Germans who inhabited a great deal of the land opposed the institution. Many had fled Europe for political reasons and felt a continuing allegiance to the Union that had accepted them when they were homeless. They were not a firm part of the southern mentality that was so prevalent in the states of South Carolina, Alabama, or Georgia. They were a predominantly well-educated group that had no desire to leave the Union, but if that was the route Texas chose, they wanted to be left alone, hoping to avoid an active role in the war that was inevitable. In June of 1861, a group of men from the counties of Gillespie, Kimble, Kendall, and Kerr felt the need to band together, for the defense of their homes on the frontier. They formed an organization called the Union Loyal League whose—

> "…objects and purposes were, not to create or encourage strife between Unionist and Confederate sympathizers, but to take such action as might peaceably secure its members and their families from being disturbed and compelled to bear arms against the Union, and to protect their families against hostile Indians."[4]

As 1861 progressed, the group continued its campaign to avoid bearing arms against the Union, increasing its numbers to nearly 500 Unionists by the summer of 1862.[5] Though this group was, ostensibly, not intended as a threat to the Confederate authorities, they came to view it as such and took action against it.

Apparently, the group came to the attention of the authorities in San Antonio because of recruiting irregularities in the frontier company that was being organized by Captain Jacob Kuechler. In a petition to the Governor, members of the Fredericksburg community, who held secessionist views, bitterly complained that Kuechler was only recruiting men he knew to be unionists and that the organization would not be willing to fight for the Confederate cause.[6] Similar meetings occurred in other parts of central and southern Texas, some for the purpose of joint protection and others merely to discuss opposition to the conscription laws, or petition the governor for relief. While not all of the participants were German, they were generally identified as such.[7]

So much were those in opposition to the conscription laws identified with the German community that General J. B. Magruder issued instructions to the Superintendent of Conscripts in Austin County, Texas, to "cause all persons of foreign birth who exhibit opposition to the enforcement of the conscript law to be sent from this state..." The superintendent was cautioned to do it quietly, however, to avoid creating a group mentality towards the Germans. The commanding general was concerned that "difficulties from this cause also may arise between our native-born citizens and those of foreign birth." Magruder's concerns were valid; a line between the German residents and the rabid Confederates had already been drawn and was regularly being crossed with violent results.[8] One report indicates the crossing of the line, with references to a petition to General Magruder from the women of Austin County. The report indicated that the officer responsible for enrolling conscripts went to the households of German citizens for the apparent purpose of enrolling the men. Led by some disreputable members of the community, who were obviously anti-German, the squads reportedly struck women and children at will during their attempts to locate and take into custody the German men. The Confederate government did not condone these excesses, at least not the commanders at Magruder's level and up, but that does not reduce the violence suffered by the German community of central Texas.[9]

During the loyalty trial of Philip Braubach, a potential Lieutenant in Kuechler's company, Charles Nimitz was sworn in to testify. Nimitz was the individual in charge of conscription and enrollment in Gillespie County, and one of the originators of the petition, which was forwarded to the Governor. During Nimitz's testimony, he stated that Braubach had raised men in secret, though customarily such companies were raised by public notice. He further indicated that the company took actions that he believed were intended to hide their meetings from public scrutiny. Finally, as the individual in charge of enrollment, he indicated that "I never had a list of men in my hands showing the progress made by the accused in raising the Company. I call myself loyal...I call all those loyal who worked to break up that Co. by petition to the Governor."[10]

It was this type of suspicion that prompted the disbanding of the Frontier company that Kuechler had been authorized to enroll. No tangible evidence was presented before the Military Commission beyond the testimony of Nimitz and other secessionist members of the Fredericksburg community. Heresay and supposition were the standard fare for the Military Commission during its period of justice. Another witness, Frederic Fresenius, added to the comments of Nimitz by restating the accusations that the members of this company were raised in secret and worked diligently to disguise their meeting times and places. He further provided his opinion that "He is now considered as disloyal by the loyal people of the town, the others may consider themselves as loyal to Lincoln. One of the young men who joined the Co, said that their object was to join and when the Yankees come they would lay down their arms. I take it that those men were disloyal from the fact that as soon as Martial law was declared, they all put out, and have not shown themselves since. Those men have shown their disloyalty ever since Secession, but after that Co.was broken up, they have shown their disloyalty and insulted us."[11]

Obviously, the loyal secessionist men of Gillespie County and Fredericksburg perceived these Texans with unionist sentiments as a distinct threat. Confederate military authorities, such as Colonel H. E. McCulloch, voiced the opinion that this sentiment would have "to be crushed out, even if it has to be done without due course of law..."[12] As with the rest of the country during this trying time, there was no middle ground allowable on the question of slavery or secession. The mere inference that a man was soft on the secession question, or unwilling to fight actively for the Confederacy, was enough to brand him as a Black Abolitionist and open him to attack from all quarters. The environment became one in which a man had to take a stand, neutrality was not an option. Most of the members of the Union Loyal League were unwilling to bear arms against the Federal Government, but they had no firm intentions of bearing arms against the Confederacy. A prominent story of this period concerns a group of men who started for Mexico and were caught by Partisan Rangers on the banks of the Nueces River. The exact sequence that led to the death of many of these men is a subject of debate. Some maintain they were simply running from conscription, while others are convinced that they were enroute to join the Union forces in New Orleans. While it is true that some of the survivors did join the Union army, others did not.[13] Men like Jacob Kuechler stayed in Mexico, and though they disagreed with the Confederacy and its ambitions, they did not put on a uniform and take the field of battle against the South.

This discussion of the Nueces group will continue later, but more important is the fact that of the nearly 500 members of the Union Loyal League, only 61 attempted to flee to Mexico in this group.[14] The remaining Unionists either slipped into Mexico unnoticed, in smaller groups, or took to the hills as was alluded to in the testimony of Fresenius. The actions of these men who took to the bush tended to be more in line with the ideas of the League as stated by John Sansom. They appear to have been much more interested in avoiding conscription into the Confederate service than in carrying on a war against the secessionist element. Almost without exception, the reports of violence that can be found concern attacks upon Unionists or suspected Unionists by Confederate soldiers and their sympathizers. In the rest of the Trans-Mississippi the violence was two-sided as both the Unionists and Secessionists carried on campaigns of violence against the other. Violence by one side was sure to bring on a reprisal by the other. In Gillespie and surrounding counties, there was considerable fear and violence, but it was remarkably one-sided. While researching the irregular violence in central Texas, no record of an unprovoked attack by Unionists was ever found. These German and American Unionists didn't attack railroad lines or Confederate garrisons; they appear to have been too busy trying to stay out of the path of Partisan Rangers like Captain James Duff.

In response to the Union Loyal League, and the complaints of loyal secessionists such as Nimitz, the Commander of the Sub-Military District of the Rio Grande, Brigadier General Hamilton P. Bee, declared martial law to be in effect in the area under his jurisdiction. The order, dated April 28, 1862, included the counties mentioned earlier.[15] Just over a month later, on May 30, 1862, Brigadier General P. O. Hèbert, the Commander of the Department of Texas, extended the martial law order over the whole of the State of Texas.[16]

This martial law edict took the law in Gillespie County, and others, out of the hands of the civil officials and turned loose a rule of military violence that had lasting effects on the German community. The same day the proclamation took effect, Captain James Duff rode into Fredericksburg to begin his duties as the Provost-Marshal for the area.[17] Duff had been born in Scotland in 1828 and later emigrated to the United States. The best information regards him as a soldier of fortune and maintains that upon his arrival he enlisted in the Federal Army. He was apparently charged with a rather serious offense and dishonorably discharged. He came to San Antonio in 1860, making his living as a merchant. Whether or not his previous military record was concealed is still in question, but he was able to secure a commission as a Captain in command of a partisan ranger unit known as Duff's Partisan Rangers.[18]

Ordinarily, the imposition of martial law upon a community which, in name, was loyal to the Confederate cause was onerous enough, but by placing James Duff in charge of military justice, General Bee sentenced a large number of citizens to incarceration or death. Historians have not treated Captain Duff well, often referring to him as a mercenary or murderer. One young historian wrote that, "According to various descriptions of his character and conduct, Duff must have been a military 'hero' beside whom Santa Ana would look pale by comparison."[19] Others, many of whom were contemporaries of Duff, have been no less critical in their description of the man who held absolute sway over Gillespie County. R. H. Williams, a member of Duff's partisan ranger unit remembered him as a man "who on foot resembled a bullfrog, and on horseback Sancho Panza." As to Duff's performance in policing Gillespie County, Williams wrote that "he exercised [his martial law powers] to their fullest extent, committing atrocities that even his superiors in San Antonio would not have sanctioned."[20] The diary of another Confederate soldier, assigned to Fort Martin Scott (Camp Davis), just outside of Fredericksburg, has numerous entries that betray his feelings toward James Duff. On August 5, 1862, Desmond Hopkins wrote "As our regular scout came in today they found a man hanging right over the trail, with his throat cut from ear to ear, later learned his name was Sewell — hung over our trail by some of Duffs men, for the purpose, first to leave the impression, that our boys done it — and second we would have to bury him, d--d scoundrels — and sure enough the order came from old Duff..."[21]

Five days later Hopkins again commented on Duff, this time lamenting the fact that his unit had been placed under his control. "No inspection today, in fact we have had no inspection since we were placed under command of old Jim Duff, he keeps our men on the jump, while he and his men lay in camp and drink good whiskey, and smoke the best cigars."[22]

It is evident that this Scotsman, Captain James Duff, was a hard man with whom to deal. He sent the summons to all men over 16 years of age to come to Fredericksburg to take the loyalty oath and register, but few of these men appeared. To counter this problem, Duff sent out two parties of rangers to scour the hills and bring in those who had refused to answer the summons. These groups reportedly ransacked homes of suspected Unionists to the point that they were no longer habitable. They brought in a few men and eight women and children who were placed under guard in the camp and Fredericksburg.[23]

About a month before Desmond Hopkins was writing in his diary about Duff, a group of men who were members of the Union Loyal League met on July 4th to expand the organization. They organized three companies, for the purpose of self-defense, with Major Fritz Tegener being elected to command the battalion. This meeting brought the relations between the German Unionists and the military government to a critical point. On July 20, 1862, Major Tegener learned that his county and the others that composed the Union Loyal League were considered to be in open rebellion, and that Captain Duff had been given orders to do whatever was necessary to deal with the situation.[24] Knowing full well what measures Duff would take, Tegener and others determined the best course of action to be a departure from the area. Sixty-one members of the League started from Kerr County, enroute to Mexico, on August 1, 1862.[25] Though they have been portrayed as dangerous and violent by the men who pursued them, a close reading of the literature indicates that most of them desired only to cross the border into Mexico and stay there until it was safer for them to return home. They were armed with rifles and some handguns, but this was not unusual for men living on the frontier of Texas. If these men were expecting trouble, they did a very poor job of preparing for it. Their camp ground was in an area lending itself to an easy ambush; they failed to post an adequate guard force, and had done nothing to ascertain whether they were being followed. Their actions resemble those of men on a hunting trip more than those of a military unit.[26]

The story of what happened on the tenth of August in 1862 has been written many times in Texas history. The Confederates, under command of Lieutenant C. D. McRae, attacked the Unionist position, routing the Germans from their encampment. The best information indicates that 33 of the Germans escaped, 19 were killed, and nine were wounded so badly that they could not flee.[27] This action in itself was not a violation of the rules of war, or decency, though a more compassionate commander might have given the party the opportunity to surrender. The term "massacre" can only be applied to what was to follow during the day of the tenth. Numerous sources indicate that the Confederates, with the express knowledge of Lieutenant McRae, executed the wounded prisoners they held.[28] Though McRae's official report indicates only that there were no prisoners, even the Confederate authorities and soldiers knew something was not exactly right.[29] Desmond Hopkins' diary again provides a different perspective on the actions of the rangers. "Today our big scout got in from the bushwhacker fight, on the Newases river the men in the fight on our side were made up from different companies of our regiment... there were two men killed and eighteen wounded on our side, and thirty on the other side, and a number of prisoners taken, but the prisoners all managed to make their escape, so the boys said, and I know they would not lie about a little thing like that."[30]

The incident at the Nueces River was a violent act, set in a very violent time. There is no excuse for the murder of wounded men, but it would be hard to fault the Confederates for their pursuit of the armed group. Most of the literature has treated the incident in isolation from the violence that preceded it, and would follow it. In reality, the massacre was simply one link in a chain of violent, terrible events that occurred during the war. Just 12 days after the massacre occurred, and prior to the return of McRae's unit, more violence was felt in the hill country around Fredericksburg. Hopkins, while noting that the scout had just returned, wrote that "we are having a tough time in this neck of the woods just now, I counted seven dead men, all hung on one limb...cut down, and thrown over a bluff in to Spring Creek, one old gray headed man named Nelson, was over eighty years old. After he had rose to the top of the water some woman came up, and lifted him out in a sheet, and buried him."[31]

Hopkins' mention of an elderly man named Nelson is particularly interesting in light of the report which Captain Duff filed with his headquarters in San Antonio on June 23, 1862. In this report he noted that he found the people of the area to be "shy and timid" and reported that "In Kerr County there are a few men who are bitterly opposed to our Government. These men are headed by an old man by the name of Nelson. I took care that he and his party should be notified in good time to report to the provost-marshal. This they failed to do and Nelson sent me a defiant message. I then sent a detachment of State troops kindly placed at my disposal to arrest him, but he had taken to the cedar brakes and escaped."[32]

It appears that although Captain Duff's troops missed Nelson in their June attempt, they were finally able to lay their hands upon him in late August. If this case can be used as an example of Duff's prevailing brand of justice, it is understandable why suspected Unionists chose to stay in the cedar brakes.

The problems of Gillespie and other counties did not culminate in the Nueces River Massacre, but continued through the war's end. One outstanding example, to support the conclusion that the Massacre did not happen in a vacuum, can be found in the "Records of the Confederate Military Commission in San Antonio, July 2-October 10, 1862," which were edited by Alwyn Barr in the late 1960s. Taken by themselves, the transcripts of these loyalty trials are interesting examples of martial law justice, but taken in conjunction with the Massacre and the hangings about which Hopkins wrote, they are further evidence of the physical and mental terror that the people of these counties must have felt. The commission was convened by Brigadier General Paul O. Hèbert, and was in session from July 2d until martial law was ordered rescinded by President Jefferson Davis on October 10, 1862.[33] The commission sat in judgment on at least 15 cases, mainly involving German and American citizens from Gillespie and surrounding counties.[34] The record of the trial, as edited by Professor Barr, reveals a community in Fredericksburg where everyone was constantly looking over their shoulder or worrying about who might overhear what they said. The owner of a bookstore, William Gamble, was charged with the crime of "Keeping and circulating Abolition books." His crime stemmed from a single book in his store, a British book entitled Hochelaga, or England in the New World, which contained about six passages that could be construed to be in opposition to the institution of slavery. For this crime Gamble was sentenced to three months confinement and banishment from the Confederacy.[35] No other books were found in his store of an Abolitionist nature, though according to the defense counsel the "vigilant acting Provost Marshal...whose duty it has been to examine and report any Abolition Books found in the collection and yet zealous and prompt in his detective duties as he is known to be he has been able to produce no other book, pamphlet or paper ...of an objectionable nature."[36]

Other defendants, such as William McLane, were placed on trial for disobeying the martial law stipulation against not accepting Confederate currency.[37] One of the truly outstanding cases was that of Julius Schlickum, who had been arrested by Captain Duff in June, 1862, reportedly because he had been in touch with the Hill Country Unionists and the North. He was accused of disloyalty and singing Yankee songs while drunk. No testimony actually linked him with any dangerous persons, but his overall conduct was discussed through heresay and implication. For this dastardly crime, Schlickum was sentenced to imprisonment for the duration of the war because "in his general deportment he is calculated to create discontent and dissatisfaction with this Government and its currency."[38] Others were tried for similar crimes, but this type of justice is not unusual during martial law and military rule. It is not the inequity of the justice in this case, but the effect that justice of this sort had upon the community.

Knowing that they were being watched and that, possibly, their actions and language were subject to the close scrutiny of a man of Duff's caliber, was enough to create fear and mental duress in anyone. If a man had a few too many beers in the local drinking establishment and said things that could be construed as Unionist, or at the very least not totally in support of the Confederate cause, he had to fear trial before such a court in San Antonio or the fate of the venerable Nelson. Living on the frontier of Texas was not an easy life in peacetime, but how could a man of conscience risk being taken off to jail in San Antonio and leaving his family to fend for themselves?

Thus far, this study has examined the physical violence, fear, and mental anguish with which the inhabitants of the Hill Country had to contend with from the Confederate authorities. With the abolishment of martial law on October 10, 1862, Captain Duff's brand of violence and terror no longer reached into these settlements.[39] This might have been the end of problem, but for a group of lawless men who continued to prowl the area until after the war. This group, led by J. P. Waldrip, was commonly known as the Haengerbande, and consisted of extremely violent men who, though not officially affiliated with the Confederate Government, were rabidly anti-Unionist in their thinking.[40] At another time and place, these men would have been considered common criminals; many had been just that before the war, but they now formed a vigilante organization to terrorize the German community for many years.

It is ironic that one of the dominant members of the Haengerbande, a former Lieutenant with Duff's Rangers, William Banta, chose to dedicate his life story to "The women of the Frontier of Texas, exposed to every danger from ruthless savage and wild beast, suffering untold hardships in an uninhabited wilderness, brave as lions when in danger, yet tender, loving and true..."[41] The irony lies in the fact that, although Banta is referring to Indian depredations when he speaks of savages and wild beasts, there were many of these frontier women who would quickly classify him and his cohorts in the same way. The Haengerbande, whose given name actually means band of hang men, took what they wished and hung whom they wished for the next few years.[42] They developed a sophisticated spy network, enabling them to determine, at least in their own minds, who was a Unionist or who had uttered treasonous statements.[43] Upon arriving at a suspect's name they would then ride out and mete out the justice they saw fit — usually with a rope or gun.[44] They were actively pursuing these "bushwhackers," as the Unionists who had fled to the bush were called, and when they found men that they suspected to be bushwhackers, they gave no-quarter. Banta describes such a raid in which his German friend, Joe Freece, was killed: "The scout came up where they were camped as day was breaking, and the bushwhackers made their way into a thicket and the scout surrounded them, and at daylight the bushwhackers fired from the brush, killing two men and wounding two others. Poor Joe Freece was one of the killed. But the bushwhackers paid dearly for it, as there was not one of them left to tell the tale."[45]

The reference to no one living to tell the tale appears to have been the rule with this vigilante organization, not the exception. In his narrative, Banta provides a chilling description of the state of affairs in Gillespie County during this time. He describes the terror and violence, but maintains that it was the work of the Union bushwhackers. Of these groups he wrote: "The object of these outlaw gangs was not to assist the North; their object was to murder and rob the almost unprotected citizens of that vicinity; and many a poor woman had to stand out in the chilly night and watch the little house, a few moments before they had called home, burn to the ground, while her husband was in the army or ranger camp, or lay stiff and fast growing cold at the feet of his murders. Reader, this is no idle dream, but a terrible reality. Such was the work of the German and American bushwhackers."[46]

Banta's narrative gives further shape to the picture of violence and terror, but it does not agree with other available sources as to the perpetrators. All the other accounts of the happenings in Gillespie County show these same events to be occurring, but they uniformly portray the violence to be against the Unionist element. Even R. H. Williams, a member of Duff's Rangers, and Desmond Hopkins, the Confederate soldier who kept such a valuable diary, indicate that the men who were hanged and shot were Unionist. There is not a single incident recorded in Hopkins' diary of an attack by bushwhackers against Confederate troops or sympathizers. A careful reading of the *Official Records* supports this judgment. In Kansas, the Union correspondence was filled with tales of the death meted out by the guerrillas, but the references by the Confederate officials in central Texas are focused on opposition to conscription or Unionist sympathies, not violence directed against southerners. Based on the historical record, Banta is correct in his account of what happened, but somewhat misguided as to who was responsible.

In 1865, the Civil War came to an end, but a final chapter in the violence of the Hill Country was still being written. In the fall of 1865, 25 men were indicted for outrages committed during the war. Included in these were Waldrip, Banta, and Cadwell.[47] Only seven of the fugitives were taken into custody, including Banta and Cadwell. While these seven were in jail awaiting trial, the violence they had left so free flowing in Fredericksburg came back to haunt them. A group of citizens, estimated by Banta to be about 200, stormed the jail where they were being held and began to fire into their cells. Before the mob could murder all of the men, the Sheriff arrived with another group of men and dispersed the crowd. In the mob scene, three of the prisoners were killed, along with one member of the attacking mob. Two of the other prisoners were seriously wounded and the two that escaped unhurt "owe[d] their escape to Providence, the darkness and the powder smoke."[48] Banta and his fellows were released for their own safety and never brought to trial.

It has been written that violence tends to breed violence. Though this was true in the fall of 1865 in Gillespie County, the amazing story is that it had not been true earlier. The record depicts a community that was terrorized for many years because of their Unionist tendencies. While it was true that the county had voted overwhelmingly against secession (398-16),[49] it does not constitute Unionism. There were other places in the South where a large portion of the population did not favor secession, but once the vote was counted they supported the Confederacy. The vote in Gillespie County, used as a barometer of loyalty, could well have been misleading. A number of historians, including Egon Richard Tausch and Hubert Heinen, have made strong cases showing that the labeling of all Germans as Unionists was a misconception.[50] Many Germans served in the Confederate armies, and those that didn't were not necessarily Unionists. Many simply chose to stay at home to protect their families from the Indians and vigilante violence raging across the frontier. This vigilante violence, whether done outside the law or cloaked in the veil of authority, was present farther north in Texas along the border with the Indian Territory. Here the victims were not of any particular national group, but identified only by their perceived views on secession.

The land in north Texas would see as much or more violence than the hill country of central Texas. The victims here were members of the Peace Party, an organization originally planned to provide for the families of men sent off to war and insure their safety. The fear and uneasiness of Confederate sympathizers and particularly rabid secessionists led to killings with both the gun and the rope more widespread than anywhere outside of the Kansas-Missouri border. Fueled largely by one man, James G. Bourland, these border counties would be home to violence on a scale far beyond that inflicted on the Germans around Fredericksburg.

The violence in this part of Texas began as vigilantism in the early months of the war. As in most other border states, this part of Texas was populated with citizens from the north and south, and with these differing roots normally came differences of opinion on issues such as slavery and secession. The conservative element of this population was the slave-owning southern man. These men were the more stable, long-time residents of the counties and many of those they feared were relative newcomers. The conservatives saw a border society that was filled with violence to the point of anarchy and sought to impose order upon it. Unfortunately for those whose politics differed from these conservatives, the methods of imposing order were extralegal and deadly.

As in the hill country of central Texas, the issue that most divided the society was conscription. While the newcomers who did not support the Confederacy could stand to remain on their farms if left alone, they were unable to bring themselves to fight against the Union. Some of the reluctance was based on the uncertainty for their families' welfare while they were gone, after all this was basically the frontier and life was more dangerous than in the east. The same conscription notices that were in effect in the German hill country were enforced in north Texas. Officials attempted to lighten some of the problems by getting reassurances that soldiers raised in this area would not be sent east of the Mississippi, but the assurances were not binding. Many soldiers chose desertion rather than resign themselves to stranding their families in the midst of chaos.

By the winter of 1861-62, these northern counties were filled with deserters, draft dodgers, and other individuals who were perceived as dangerous by the conservative element. Contributing to the unrest in the area was its proximity to the Indian Territory, which caused intense fear of raids by Union Indians or Jayhawkers. This unrest provoked increased violence as the spring approached in 1862, varying in severity from the knife slaying of a saloon owner in Cooke County and the subsequent lynching of the killers in retaliation, to a rash of fires that occurred in north Texas during the spring. Responding to the unrest and to enforce conscription, General Hebert imposed martial law on May 30, 1862.[51] This imposition of martial law and its requisite appointment of a provost marshal provided the catalyst necessary to ignite the growing sparks in the border counties. Just as Captain James Duff had policed central Texas with an iron and bloody hand, so too did James Bourland. Though the martial law edict made it clear that provost marshals were not to interfere with the normal pursuit of civil justice or inflict their violence upon loyal citizens, the areas outside of the cities of Texas were controlled almost totally by their provost marshals. Under Bourland's tutelage, Cooke County and those around it would be filled with violence and murder through the end of the war.

By the end of summer 1862, this area had become a maelstrom of turmoil over the issues of secession and conscription. Those favoring the Union saw Bourland and his supporters as a threat to their well-being, which was patently true, and formed the Peace Party. The more conservative element saw the threat very differently and classified all who were even perceived as soft on secession as traitors, deserving only of punishment. In September 1862, information came to Bourland and the conservative element that a secret organization existed and included in its designs were plans for violent actions against the Confederates. This threat provoked the violence that would come to be called The Great Hanging and put Gainesville, Texas, on the Civil War map for good.

The story of The Great Hanging is masterfully told by McCaslin and needn't be repeated here in detail. The importance for this study is that just as in central Texas and the other border states of the Trans-Mississippi, citizens were killed in an effort to preserve order through fear and violence. Many of those convicted by the Citizen's Court were guilty of conspiring to commit violent acts, but they were punished by a court that had no legal right to pass judgment. Beyond the nine men sentenced by the Citizen's Court were at least 33 others who were hanged by mob decree, without even the semblance of due process. Remembering Henry McCulloch's missive to crush out this dissent, even if it had to be done without due process, this should not be a surprise.[52]

Men who are fearful will resort to any means for their self-preservation and the conservatives of north Texas believed that these means were justified. The vigilante methods of disposing of dangers to their society were outside the law and often punished men who were no danger to them, but they were condoned by the Confederate leaders in Texas and ignored by President Davis.[53] The same fear that allowed Union commanders in Missouri to enforce a no-quarter policy towards secessionist threats, allowed James Bourland and his followers to hang men in Gainesville for not believing in the Confederacy.

The violence in north Texas did not begin or end with the Great Hanging. Bourland's rule would become even more tyrannical, culminating in accusations that he had many prisoners murdered while in custody, rather than allow them to go to trial in a civil court.[54] His violent actions did not bring order to north Texas, anymore than the violent retaliations by Union generals in Missouri did. Violence normally leads to more violence and this was the case in Texas. While the Germans of central Texas rarely fought back, the men who escaped the noose at Gainesville and the many deserters in the area remained a threat to secessionists through the end of the war. While the violence here was nothing like that farther north, the population that remained in these counties had to spend their nights wondering when a knock would come at the door and which side would be coming to visit. Chaos and near anarchy reigned as a succession of Confederate commanders tried to use Bourland as their bludgeon to beat north Texas into line.

Adding to the chaos and violence in this part of Texas in the years after the Great Hanging was the arrival of William Clarke Quantrill and many of his followers. Following the Lawrence Raid and the destruction of Blunt's forces at Baxter Springs, Quantrill and his men continued into Texas to spend the winter. They bivouacked in these same north Texas counties and, though ostensibly amongst friends, caused considerable problems. McCulloch attempted to use them to capture deserters, but found that their prey rarely came in alive. This was merely an example of the inability of the regular Confederate army to control Quantrill and his men. Finally, following the murder of a Confederate officer by a member of Quantrill's band, the guerrillas would head back to Missouri to escape the wrath of McCulloch and Bourland.

The participants in the irregular violence in Texas were mainly a mixture of Confederate Partisan Rangers and vicious outlaws, as evidenced by Duff's unit and the members of the Haengerbande. While Quantrill's war-rebels spent time in north Texas, their part of the story is a brief one. Texas was the only state along this border region that would remain in the Confederacy throughout the war. The irregular violence that was perpetrated in the Lone Star State was not the work of Union armies that chased down secessionists protecting their farms and families. This violence was perpetrated by secessionists and the Confederate government upon Texans who were perceived as not totally supporting the Confederate cause. Once again a population along the border was forced to endure four years of violence, misery, and death, though the war between the main regular armies was far away. In Texas the post-war period would be different, as the winners would get their opportunity for retribution in the days of reconstruction. After all, in this case, the portion of the population that felt the biggest sting during the war turned out to be the winners in the end.

Notes

1. Richard B. McCaslin, *Tainted Breeze: The Great Hanging at Gainesville, Texas 1862*, (Baton Rouge, Louisiana State University Press, 1994), pp. 1-8.

2. Baron de Jomini, *The Art of War*, quoted in Robert B. Asprey, *War in the Shadows: The Guerrilla in History*, vol. 1, (New York: Doubleday & Company, 1975), p. 149.

3. Alwyn Barr, "Records of the Confederate Military Commission in San Antonio, July 2-October 10, 1862," *Southwestern Historical Quarterly* 71 (October 1967), p. 93.

4. R.H. Williams and John W. Sansom, *The Massacre on the Nueces River: The Story of a Civil War Tragedy*, (Grand Prairie, TX: Frontier Times Publishing House, ca. 1911), p. 25.

5. Williams and Sansom, p.25.

6. Barr, p. 263.

7. *Official Records*, Series 1, Volume 15, pp. 887, 925-929, 945-946.

8. *Official Records*, p. 890.

9. *Official Records*, pp. 981-982, 989-990.

10. Barr, p. 263.

11. Barr, p. 264.

12. *Official Records,* Series 1, Volume 9, pp. 704-705.

13. Williams and Sansom, p. 36.

14. Williams and Sansom, p. 25.

15. Barr, p. 94.

16. *Official Records*, Series 2, Volume 4, p. 785.

17. *Official Records*, Series 2, Volume 4, p. 785.

18. Don H. Bigger, *German Pioneers in Texas*, (Fredericksburg, TX.: Fredericksburg Publishing, 1925; reprinted., Austin, TX: Eakin Publications, 1983), p. 59; Eldon Stephen Branda, ed., *The Handbook of Texas: A Supplement*, Volume III, (Austin, TX: The Texas State Historical Association, 1976), p. 255.

19. Gerald Gold, "Gillespie County in the Civil War," Junior Historian 25 (January 1965): 30.

20. Williams and Sansom, pp. 6-7.

21. Hopkins Diary 1862-1865, Desmond Pulaski Hopkins Papers, p. 74, Barker Texas History Center, Austin, TX.

22. Hopkins Diary 1862-1865.

23. Williams and Sansom, p. 8.

24. Williams and Sansom, p. 25.

25. Egon Richard Tausch, "Southern Sentiment Among the Texas Germans During the Civil War and Reconstruction," M.A. Thesis, The University of Texas at Austin, 1965, p. 13.

26. *Official Records*, Series 1, Volume 9, pp. 614-616; Williams and Sansom, p. 14.

27. Williams and Sansom, p.14.

28. Williams and Sansom, pp. 18-19, 34.

29. *Official Records*, Series 1, Volume 9, pp. 614-616.

30. Hopkins Diary, p. 81.

31. Hopkins Diary, pp. 81-82.

32. *Official Records*, Series 2, Volume 4, pp. 785-787.

33. *Official Records*, Series 1, Volume 9, p. 735.

34. Barr, p. 95.

35. Barr, p. 301.

36. Barr, p. 297.

37. Barr, pp. 247-250.

38. Barr, pp. 253-258.

39. Barr, p. 95.

40. Corinne Cameron, "Haenger Bande," Paper found in the Gillespie County Collection, Pioneer Memorial Library, Fredericksburg, TX: undated, p. 2; Meyer, Verdie, "Buergerkrieg Terror in Gillespie County," *Junior Historian* 22 (November 1961): 23.

41. Banta and Cadwell narrative, dedication page, Barker Texas History Center, Austin, TX.

42. Cameron, p. 1.

43. Meyer, p. 23.

44. *Pioneers in God's Hills: A History of Fredericksburg and Gillespie County People and Events*, Vol. II, (Fredericksburg, TX: Gillespie County Historical Society, 1974), p. 39.

45. Banta and Cadwell narrative, p. 181.

46. Banta and Cadwell narrative, pp. 223-224.

47. The name, Cadwell, is derived from the primary source. Most of the secondary sources identify this individual as J. W. Caldwell, Jr.

48. Banta and Cadwell narrative, pp. 227-230.

49. Frank H. Smyrl, "Unionism, Abolitionism, and Vigilantism in Texas, 1856-1865," (M.A. Thesis, The University of Texas, 1961), p. 85.

50. Tausch, "Southern Sentiment Among the Texas Germans During the Civil War and Reconstruction."

51. McCaslin, *Tainted Breeze*, p. 55; *Official Records,* Part 1, Volume 9, pp. 715-716.

52. *Official Records*, Part 1, Volume 9, pp. 704-705.

53. McCaslin, p. 113.

54. McCaslin, pp. 143-146.

Chapter 5

The Impact of Irregular Warfare

The recurring theme throughout this study has been the effects of the irregular violence, the Third War, which daily occurred along the border against the population that inhabited these states. All of the Border States were beset with similar problems, though the two with the most in common were Missouri and Kentucky. Both nominally Union states, they had Confederate governments in exile and were represented by stars in the Confederate flag. Of the states in this study, Kentucky received the least attention by scholars of irregular warfare. The effects upon the local society that appeared in the Trans-Mississippi were invariably repeated in the Bluegrass State. In examining the fear and violence that afflicted all of the Border States, this chapter focuses on Kentucky, using it as a thread of continuity to accent the problems along the western border.

It is within a framework of national violence that the guerrilla war must be examined. Violence tends to breed violence, and it is unimaginable that the death and destruction of a conflict such as the American Civil War could have been confined to the fields of battle on which massive conventional armies faced each other. Violence was the norm along the border, a state-of-being expected by the residents.

Kentucky was by no means unique in the homespun violence with which she was beset. Conventional battles filled Virginia, Missouri, and Tennessee with the same struggles and outrages that characterized the war years in the Bluegrass State. These states were the battlefields of the war, as they lay in the precarious position of border areas. As the buffers between the North and the Deep South, they bore the brunt of the combat in the early stages of the war. The most heralded of these must, of course, be Virginia. Here was where the headliners, Generals Grant and Lee, faced each other and the conclusion of the war was finally determined. The other border areas, which have taken a back-seat to Virginia for many years, were each touched in their own way by the war.

Bruce Catton captured the essence of the border conflicts the best when he wrote "Here it was a battle in which ill-equipped armies learned their trade in blundering action; there it was a matter of shadows in the dusk, neighbor ambushing neighbor, hayrick and barn blazing up at midnight with a drum of hoofbeats on a lonely lane to tell the story, or a firing squad killing a bridge-burner for a warning to the lawless."[1]

The war along the border, just as Catton maintains, took its own peculiar twist in the different states and areas. The thread of continuity that exists among all of these areas is the awful violence that pervaded society at every level. In Texas it was marked by disloyalty trials in both Gainesville and San Antonio, run by the Confederate authorities, and lynchings in both the hill country northwest of San Antonio and north Texas.[2] The Texans, like the other inhabitants of the border, were simply unable to deal with the mix of Unionist and Secessionist in a non-violent fashion. In Missouri and Kansas, the actions of Jennison's Jayhawkers and

Quantrill's sacking of Lawrence is representative of the violent nature of the war away from the formal battlefield.[3] The much heralded rules of war gave way to hatreds and personal vendettas that proved too powerful to control.

During the war, newspapermen from both the North and South chastised Kentuckians for not flocking to their flags in large enough numbers. To these contemporaries the lack of Kentuckians in northern or southern armies was a mark of cowardice or lack of spirit for the cause. Some modern day historians have perpetuated many of these same feelings, making much of the spirit of compromise that has long embodied the Kentucky heritage. They point out the failure of Bragg's army in 1862 and the lack of the support, which John Hunt Morgan had assured him the Confederates would find. While researching this volume, another reason for Kentuckians who decided not to join one of the main armies became apparent.

Shortly after the initial invasion of Kentucky soil by the Confederate army in 1861, the Bluegrass State found itself inundated with fighting men of both sides. For a time the state was divided geographically, with the Union holding much of the northeast and the Confederacy the southwest. Federal and Confederate units alike were formed and sent off to join the main armies. The state supplied many troops in these earlier days, some choosing to go with the blue and some with the grey. After these initial enlistments, when it became obvious that the war would not bring quick success for either side, recruiting slowed. Men began to take stock of the situation and ask questions as to what would be the fate of their families if they chose to go off to war. With the imposition of martial law upon the Bluegrass State, the decision became even tougher. The people of New York or Alabama would find it hard to comprehend, for when their men went off to war; they could feel certain that the families they left behind would be safe. It is true that the rigors of war caused economic hardship in states north and south, but it was in the Border States that men had to fear for the very lives of their loved ones at home. A Union man in Kentucky in 1861-1865 could look around his beloved state and see it filled with Confederate guerrillas, striking out at Unionists and the Federal authorities with impunity. To leave for the front meant exposing his family to these dangers without the benefit of protection. This could not have been an easy decision for a man to make. On the other side of the coin, the secessionists in Kentucky — and there were many — faced a state under the martial law powers of the dreaded Yankees. Civil rights had been suspended and meetings of the Democratic Party were broken up by military units.[4] Even worse, in the latter stages of the war, the troops used to police the state were predominately black. Though it is often hard for modern students to comprehend, for a man who still believed in the image of the southern cavalier there could be nothing as awful visited upon a people. The number of men who failed to enlist for these reasons cannot be accurately numbered, but it was undoubtedly substantial.

This problem is mirrored in the State of Missouri. Sterling Price repeatedly attempted invasions of his home state, convinced that he had only to show the Confederate banner to raise a strong Missouri force. While Bragg was trying to recruit in Kentucky, Price was doing the same in Missouri. For most of the reasons stated in regards to Braxton Bragg, Price too was unsuccessful.

For these same reasons, and others associated with the war itself, many men from both sides deserted and returned to the Bluegrass State. These men, who had faced each other in mortal combat on other fields, could hardly be expected to forget all the passions that led them to enlist in the first place. The close proximity of people whom they considered the enemy presented another means of carrying forth the war. This question of proximity was a common problem throughout the border areas, for just as they were the meeting place of the two foes geographically, they were also the location of a mixing of the societies and politics of the two areas. Men of the northern persuasion and others of the southern lived side-by-side, often times a part of the same family. Geography and fate had placed these states in the middle of the largest conflict in America's history, and they paid dearly for this distinction.

Likewise, deserters filled the border areas of the Trans-Mississippi, most notably in Texas. Their presence in these states fueled the irregular war by placing armed veterans in the midst of already flaring violence. The effect was similar to pouring gasoline on a small fire.

The imposition of martial law is onerous in any democratic society, but few other actions carry as dark a name in the American psyche. Our nation was founded upon certain principles, which have been considered virtually sacred down through the years. In the nineteenth century these principles were not mere rhetoric, but carried close to the heart of most Americans. One of these basic ideals was the subordination of the military to the civil authority. The standing army had been a dreaded fear for many years in this country and when it was finally organized in the first decade of the nineteenth century its position as the servant of the people was loudly stressed.

It is of little surprise that the people of Kentucky reacted as they did to the imposition of martial law and the suspension of the writ of habeas corpus. On June 25, 1864, General Henry Halleck informed the Union commander in Kentucky, Brigadier General Stephen Burbridge, that "It has been represented that disloyal persons in Kentucky...are giving aid and assistance to armed rebels...The Secretary of War directs that...you arrest and send to Washington, under proper guards, all persons so inciting insurrection or aiding and abetting the enemy...You are expected in this matter to act with discretion, but at the same time promptly and energetically."[5]

Shortly after this sweeping instruction, on July 19, 1864, President Lincoln suspended the writ and proclaimed martial law to be in effect in the Bluegrass State. The reasons given for this action were similar to those found in Halleck's instruction to Burbridge. The proclamation maintained that the guerrillas had been assisted by "disaffected and disloyal citizens of the United States residing therein" and that the insurgent forces had "overborne the civil authorities and made flagrant civil war, destroying property and life in various parts of that State."[6]

Lincoln and his advisers recognized that the petty war in Kentucky was getting out of hand and the imposition of martial law was intended to stem this tide. In this way martial law appears to be a direct result of the guerrilla war, not a cause, but it only contributed to a further worsening of the war in Kentucky. Men who would have remained at home prior to this suspension of their rights and held even the mildest of southern views turned away from the

Union. As if General Burbridge did not have enough problems in the state, he soon faced even greater troubles.

As stated above, the imposition of martial law upon the people of Kentucky was not well received. If its imposition had been effective in the suppression of the guerrillas, the people of Kentucky might have been able to overlook the suspension of their rights. After all, warfare brings with it certain unpleasant aspects even to those not directly involved in combat. Unfortunately, martial law and the men who carried it out were ineffective in dealing with the problems that had worried the President. George Prentice, the outspoken editor of the *Louisville Daily Journal*, complained of this ineffectual performance in an October 1864 editorial, "What is martial law good for in Kentucky when it offers not a shadow of security against all-sweeping depredations and other outrages constantly going on throughout our State? We are to a great extent deprived of our civil rights, and what do we get to compensate us for the deprivation?"[7]

Martial law had been declared much earlier in the Trans-Mississippi and by both Union and Confederate officials. The people of Missouri or Texas could certainly empathize with the Kentucky newspaper's lament about its lack of effect. Martial law did little to stop irregular warfare and, in fact, normally had the opposite effect. When the men given the power to supervise martial law were of the caliber of James Blunt, W. A. Strachan, or James Bourland, little good could come of it. Their actions penalized the population far more than the actual irregular warriors. Acting with inadequate information, normally based on accounts of men who stood to profit, these men used and abused their martial law powers to settle scores and stifle dissent, while providing precious little protection.[8]

The inability of the martial law government to deal with the guerrilla problem in Kentucky and elsewhere accomplished the opposite of what the edict was intended to do. With enlistments down, the Union resorted to the draft in order to fill the quotas that had been imposed upon Kentucky. The draft in Kentucky, just as martial law, was a failure. Very few of the men drafted ever made it into the Union armies, some providing substitutes, but an even greater number choosing to go with the South if they had to fight. The ranks of the guerrilla bands swelled greatly as a result of the Union draft. After all, service with the partisan rangers or the likes of Sue Mundy allowed men with Southern proclivities to remain in the area of their homes and still take the war to the Federal Government. In Owen County, 1,360 men were drafted in October of 1864, but according to the Deputy Provost Marshal, only 200 reported for service. Newspaper accounts of this county's condition maintained that "unquestionably the guerillas will get three times as many of the drafted men as the Federal Government will."[9] The lack of success from martial law and the manner in which Union authorities carried it out caused the ranks of guerrilla units to grow and simply reinforced the infrastructure of support for these warriors, which already existed in the Bluegrass State.[10]

This problem of getting adequate troops from Border States through conscription was particularly keen in Texas. The most common complaint from Confederate commanders in Texas was their inability to get the residents to register as required by the conscription laws. The Great Hanging at Gainesville began with an instance of this resistance to conscription, as did the violence in the Texas hill country. As in Kentucky and Missouri, where men became guerrillas rather than join Union forces, many Texans who were not in agreement with secession, or refused to leave the family alone on the border, sought ways to escape the draft.

From the time of the Emancipation Proclamation, the Unionists of Kentucky had begun to wane in their devotion to the Union at all costs. Kentucky was a slave state, and although the Proclamation had no legal effect in states not in rebellion, many intelligent men saw the writing on the wall as to the future of their slaves. Though the institution of slavery had lost importance in Kentucky during the 1850s, it was still a part of the economic landscape. As freed slaves from the Deep South fled through Kentucky they found themselves returned to bondage in the Bluegrass State. These actions were as much based on the fears of racial problems as on the need for slave labor. Large numbers of blacks living free in Kentucky was considered to be an untenable situation, just as it was in Indiana or Illinois. This influx of blacks into the border areas caused much disgust and consternation among the citizens of the states that experienced it.[11]

Though the Civil War would end slavery in the United States forever, it was unable to stem the racial prejudice that accompanied the institution. This change in the structure of the southern fabric added to the unrest already felt in Kentucky, and provided a fertile recruiting ground for guerrilla soldiers.

In 1897, one of the great Kentucky historians, Nathaniel Shaler, wrote that "Although there was a certain amount of disgust when the Emancipation Proclamation came out, it did not make an enduring impression on the minds of the Union men; but when, in 1864, the government began to enlist negro troops in Kentucky, the people became greatly excited over the matter."[12]

Shaler wrote of the Union people of Kentucky, those who had supported Lincoln and the Union against the Richmond Government. Even these men and women, loyal to the northern position and desiring to maintain the Union, found it difficult to contend with the order to enlist black troops. That order was conveyed to Brigadier General Burbridge in a July 5, 1864, communication from Secretary of War Stanton, which directed the Kentucky commander to "protect loyal citizens, and carry into effect the enlistment of troops, white or black, and suppress treasonable and disloyal practices..."[13] This decision, to utilize black troops in the Union army and in Kentucky, had lasting effects upon the state and its people. As with other decisions made by the Union command in the state, it served to swell the ranks of the Confederate units operating in or around Kentucky. Many men, who might have remained at home peacefully or supported the Union cause, could not live with blacks being placed in positions of power and authority. The thought of slaveholders or other white Kentuckians being arrested by black troops or guarded by them in the Lexington prison, was unconscionable to many citizens. Two young men from Henry County, William Martims and William Pollard, displayed the mood of many of their contemporaries. They joined Colonel Jessee's band of guerrillas in September 1864, citing as the reason "that they could not remain quietly at home and be forced to submit to the insults frequently offered by negro soldiers."[14]

The violence of the war, the social and political turmoil which Kentucky's geographical position demanded, and the volatile questions of martial law and race created in Kentucky, as in the other Border States, an atmosphere that fed guerrilla warfare. The Union people of Kentucky grew concerned because the authorities could not protect them and those who supported the Confederacy often provided open support to the guerrillas who sought to do as much damage to Unionists as possible. John Jeffries, a Kentucky merchant, summed up the situation in his home state quite well when he wrote his friend Mick and confided that "the feeling in Kentucky is getting more and more bitter everyday; if pretty soon the men of the State do not take up the Confederate Cause, the women will shed their hoops and go at it themselves."[15]

In assessing the impact of the guerrilla war on the border, scholars of the Civil War have long dismissed the petty war as a sideshow, without military importance or legitimacy. These historians have dismissed the guerrilla activities entirely or at best given them scant mention, largely because this type of combat bears so little resemblance to the main body of the war. The relationship that guerrilla activities bore to the bloody battles of Franklin or Gettysburg had no bearing on the impact they visited upon the people of Kentucky or Missouri. Although the eventual insurgent violence in Iraq bore little or no resemblance to the conventional war that led to the fall of Baghdad, both conflicts inflicted pain and suffering upon the people who lived through them.[16] True, the Great War was gone from Kentucky soil by the spring of 1864, and that is the war of which these scholars wrote, but another war — more personal and perhaps more deadly — lived on in the Bluegrass State until well after the surrender of the main armies of the Confederacy. Shaler placed a bit more emphasis on the guerrilla violence, if not more space. He wrote that "The desperation to which the people were brought by the system of guerrilla raids can hardly be described. In the year 1864, there was not a county in the State that was exempt from their ravages. The condition of the Commonwealth reminds the historical student of that which came with the Thirty Year's War in Germany and with the latter stages of the war between the King and Parliament in England."[17]

The majority of historians of the American Civil War in Kentucky have not recognized the impact that these bands of irregular warriors had upon the state. It would be hard to dismiss the voluminous evidence that shows what the guerrillas accomplished, so this lack of recognition can only be attributed to what a noted historian perceives as their "lack of relationship to military operations."[18] The questions that spring to mind are, why must they resemble the grand armies of the war in order to have an impact on the border? Is it not possible that the operations of Adam Johnson, conducted in the heart of Kentucky, had more far-reaching effects upon the people of Kentucky than did the march of Sherman's army to the sea? And weren't the operations of Johnson, and even some of those guerrillas categorized here as war-rebels, conducted along the lines of military operations? The fact that Quantrill or Anderson were not treated as regular soldiers did not keep them from having a more vivid effect on Kansas and Missouri than any regular Confederate forces.

For many years the history of military activities was written in a vacuum. It was a dry recitation of flanking movements and thrusts. It dealt only with soldiers and armies, not with the effects that these individuals had upon the societies around them. Similarly, historians have shied away from looking at the society's impacts on the military. Since the mid-1950s, some historians have approached military history in a different way, attempting to place the experiences and actions of military men in the context of their effect on society. In dealing with the Border States in this vein, the historian can look into the impact of regular battles such as Wilson's Creek and Perryville, or delve into the smaller war of guerrilla warfare.

Guerrilla warfare is by its nature very personal. It is a one-on-one exchange, devoid of cannon fire and mass assaults, primarily characterized by personal violence. It has tremendous effects on the people it touches in both a psychological and social sense. While it is true that a Union soldier, standing behind the battlements at Franklin, Tennessee, may have been psychologically affected by the murderous fire that he and his fellow soldiers poured into the attacking Confederates, this is part and parcel of being a soldier. More striking and devastating to society in general are the psychological implications of war and death being brought into the streets of one's hometown, or into a man's home itself. When a family cannot feel safe in their own home and citizens do not believe that they can safely travel in an area that is supposedly under the control of the government, and insulated from the battlefields, this places a psychological burden on the populace.

In a letter from a friend, identified only as C.Q.L., Richard Herndon of Meade County, Kentucky, was informed that his friend could not bring himself to visit due to the guerrilla problem. "While my heart yearns for the quiet home and pleasant companionship of your family circle, my excitable temperament shrank from daily shocks, occasioned by depredating bands." The letter goes on to lament the writer's inability to travel the approximately 100 miles from Fayette County to Meade County, because the worries of the guerrilla menace simply weigh too heavily upon his mind.[19] Countless other letters testify to the same predicament, Union citizens unsafe in their own homes and threatened by these guerrillas. Thomas Truitt, of Crittenden County, wrote to the Governor confiding that "guerrillas...are robbing stores taking arms and ammunition, taking horses and money from Loyal and peaceable citizens and have hung some worthy citizens till they were almost dead..they [the guerrillas] have threatened that Loyal citizens will have to cross the Ohio or be killed..."[20]

In yet another part of the state, similar threats were directed at specific individuals, not just to the loyal Unionist citizens in general. Dr. Glasscocke, a well-known Unionist in the small town of Bloomfield, was made to fear for his life by members of Sue Mundy's band. His wife wrote to Governor Thomas Bramlette in January of 1865, appealing for troops to protect her husband and citing the background for her request. She relayed an incident in which Dr. Glasscocke answered the door of his home and was confronted by what he thought were Union soldiers. Upon warning them of guerrillas in the area, he discovered them to be Confederate guerrillas and had to make a hasty escape to save his life. With him gone, Mrs. Glasscocke now feared for her life and their property as "they have threatened me also, that I cannot remain here, and they will 'wipe his habitation from the face of the earth,' if I do not insist on my husband's return."[21]

The Civil War that raged through this country threatened the lives of many men, but the type of threatened violence represented by Mrs. Glasscocke's letter strikes much closer to home. Not only was her husband forced to abandon his home, in the heart of Union-held territory, but his wife's life was threatened in his absence. This scene is reminiscent of the problems encountered by Reverend Foreman in the Indian Territory. Though his portion of the Cherokee Nation was supposedly controlled by Stand Watie's troops, the Reverend had to spend his nights hiding in the fields to avoid a probable death. It is part of a soldier's responsibility to deal with the threat of death, but the effect upon a society from threats to civilians is far greater.

This psychological impact was not restricted by the artificial limits of the Civil War. As Professor Harrison notes, the war "left some permanent cracks in the community solidarity that remained a bitter legacy of the Civil War." Many historians have noted the inability of Kentuckians, who had been on different sides during the war, to deal with each other when it was over, but seldom mention the role of the small war on this phenomenon.[22] If the fact that a man had fought for the Confederacy on the battlefields of Virginia made it difficult for Unionists to live and work with him, how hard must it have been for the Unionist people of Kentucky to live with Jacob Bennett after the war. After all, the first had been in the war — but in a faraway place and against unnamed faces — while Bennett had worked at his trade in the heartland of the state and could be personally identified with the death of many a person's father or brother. Taking this thread even farther, what of the families who had openly aided these guerrillas? Widespread guerrilla warfare cannot continue over an extended period of time, as it did in Kentucky and Missouri, without a support infrastructure among the populace. Families of secessionist beliefs provided aid and comfort to many of these irregular soldiers and were made to pay a heavy price for their support after the imposition of martial law. Could they and their Unionist neighbors simply forget the bloody violence of the war when their very presence served as a reminder of the bloodshed?

Obviously, the State of Missouri, which had endured irregular warfare for a longer period than Kentucky, had to experience similar or worse post-war problems than the Bluegrass State. The rebuilding of Bates, Cass, and Jackson counties alone was a momentous undertaking, both physically and psychologically. Families had been destroyed financially, with many sustaining multiple deaths. The scars from the Unionist-Secessionist split would take years to heal, if ever. In Texas it would be more pronounced, as those who had been the subjects of government-sponsored violence had come out on the winning side. More than one score would be evened by Unionists during Reconstruction.[23]

As with any event that affects the life of people in a nation, the Civil War had effects upon the economy of Kentucky. Economies are not artificial entities that carry on unrelated to events occurring around them. They are a part of the national fabric and as such respond to pressures from the forces within and outside the country. The big war had tremendous economic effects upon Kentucky and many historians have argued that one of the prime reasons for Kentucky staying in the Union was the possibility of economic enrichment.[24] There appears to be a great amount of truth in this conclusion. Situated in the middle of the two foes, with the Louisville and Nashville Railroad running north and south, and the Ohio River bordering the state to the north, Kentucky was in a perfect position to carry on a lucrative trade with both belligerents. But how did the guerrilla bands with which this volume deals figure into this economic question? They carried on no trade and were unable to establish anything permanent enough to contribute. While the guerrillas of Kentucky contributed nothing to the economy of the state, they did a great deal to restrict its effectiveness on a local scale. Figures are unavailable for the econometrician to accurately chart their impact, but the primary sources reveal the force they exerted on the agricultural industry in the state and the routes of commerce that led in and out of Kentucky.

In January 1865, Governor Bramlette admitted the economic problems that beset the Commonwealth in an address to the State Legislature. He lamented that "Our fields had been devastated by the sweep of armies, and homes desolated by rebel raids and guerilla depredations, to such an extent that a large portion of our productive labor had been driven from the State, and the arm of industry was greatly paralyzed by the destruction which menaced its labors..."[25]

Certainly, the whole of Kentucky's problems were not caused by the bands of irregulars that roamed her hills, the armies had long been gone by 1864, and no large scale rebel raids were carried out that could have had an economic effect. Another observer, the ever-watchful George Prentice, commented that "the outlaws are preying upon her [Kentucky's] vitals, and if a remedy is not soon applied, the disease will become hopeless. Lands are fast depreciating, property is going to destruction, and everywhere stacks the form of ruin..."[26] So how were these relatively small bodies of men creating such a negative impact on the economy of such a powerful state as Kentucky and what methods were being used to cause so many problems?

One answer had to be the psychological terror the guerrillas spread throughout the state. Men did not feel safe at home or on the road, and the normal pursuits of industry and agriculture became secondary to the protection of life and property. Farmers in the fields had more to worry about than just getting the ground broken or the planting finished. In June 1864, another letter to the State Adjutant General lamented the plight of farmers who were distracted from their work by the presence of guerrilla bands. Otho Miller wrote that "Robt. Cochran and his friends carry their pistols hanging to the harness of their plough horses" in order to protect themselves and their families.[27] In July 1864, the *New Albany Ledger* wrote that "it is useless to attempt to farm, as the scoundrels will be sure to destroy the crop."[28] Six months later things had not improved as guerrillas still terrified the farmers who attempted to raise crops in support of the commissary of the Union armies. A December newspaper article reported that "the guerillas along the Ohio River in the vicinity of Cloverport have threatened to burn all the hay that farmers may deliver upon the banks of the river for Government use. A great many farmers are afraid to move their hay from the barns, and those who were baling large quantities have ceased operations on that account."[29]

The states of Indiana, Illinois, and Kentucky were the breadbasket of the Union army. These states contributed agricultural goods in large quantities for the armies that were pushing south into the Confederacy. These Confederate bands sought to disrupt the supply of goods to those armies by cutting them off at the grower. Whether or not this tactic had much impact on the armies of the Union is hard to determine, but its effect in Kentucky is easy to see. Every farm in a county could not be guarded, and in large parts of Kentucky the guerrillas were more in control than the Federal Government.[30] Crops in the field were not the only target of these roving bands of Confederates. Kentucky has long been noted as center of the horse industry and this period of time was no exception. Guerrilla bands took horses for their own use and even more to send south to the Confederate Army. Forced to live in this environment, many Unionists chose to leave the state temporarily or shut down their businesses until after the depredations ceased. Entire towns began to feel the pressure of the guerrilla forces, such as the tiny town of Boston in central Kentucky. The *Louisville Daily Journal* commented in August 1864 that "the merchants of Boston have determined to abandon their business, as for the present there is no safety in property of any kind. The stores are being closed, and the village begins to wear a sad desolate look."[31] This terror and the reaction that it brought was not limited to the central portion of the state. Earlier, a letter from Hopkins County indicated that "our citizens a number of them are leaving the state & the time is coming when all the Union men will leave this part of the State."[32] With large numbers of Unionists leaving the state or their homes, the economy was affected at least by the disorganization that was evident throughout the state.

In addition to the farms and businesses disrupted by the guerrilla menace, the commerce of the rivers and railroads were particular targets of these small bands. Morgan showed the effectiveness of tearing up track and burning railroad bridges in his many forays into the Bluegrass State. The guerrillas who carried on his form of warfare in his absence proved to be equally adept at these skills. Sue Mundy, Jacob Bennett, and Henry Magruder were regular visitors to the tracks of the Louisville & Nashville — burning bridges, tearing up track, and firing into trains as they passed. All of these actions were intended to incite terror, disorganize the government support systems, and discourage commerce on the fragile situation of the rail lines.[33] Though unable to stop the flow of supplies south to Sherman's army, they were able to shut down the railroads for short periods of time and cause much uncertainty among the officers responsible for feeding and supplying the troops of the Union armies.[34] James Guthrie, the President of the Louisville & Nashville was concerned enough by the daily raids on his rail lines to communicate with Federal authorities demanding arms and ammunition to arm his trains. As it was put in a letter to the Secretary of War, Edwin Stanton, "the increase of guerrilla bands has been such that unless those engaged in running the trains are armed it will not be possible much longer to retain them in service."[35] In addition to these raids on the rail lines leading to the Union armies, the guerrillas regularly preyed on the riverboats that steamed up and down the Ohio River and the smaller streams in the interior of Kentucky. Boats that had utilized these waterways to move commerce for many years, found the rivers to be unsafe in the heyday of the guerrilla war. In July 1864, newspapers carried a story that was repeated many times during the year — "The guerillas are again on Green River committing depredations… Some fears are entertained as to the safety of the Dunkerson and R.B. Speed, as the guerillas are said to have declared their purpose to wait for the latter."[36]

While the R.B. Speed appears to have survived the war, other steamers were not as lucky. The steamer, Levi, was burned at Winfield after a band of thirteen guerrillas captured her with 40 Union soldiers aboard.[37] The only protection that could be afforded the river people was the presence of small gunboats from the "mosquito fleet," which patrolled the Mississippi and Ohio Rivers. Unfortunately, these gunboats could not be everywhere at once, and when they were called away to support combat operations or attend to guerrillas in a particular area, the remainder of the river became fair game for the guerrillas. A Kentucky merchant, John Jeffries, wrote to his friend William and confessed his concern over the safety of stores he had recently dispatched to Vicksburg on the river: "I have felt a little uneasy on the subject, for the new advance by Sherman's Corps up Red River is accompanied by all the gunboats; the Mississippi is now left open for the guerrillas."[38] Others were even more vehement about the problems the river commerce was experiencing. The *Journal* editorialized that "...the entire river border of Kentucky swarms with outlaw bands, and the citizens, left without protection...the trade of the river is ruined. No business can be transacted under the existing state of affairs...It was thought that when martial law was proclaimed in Kentucky, guerilla bands would be expelled from the State, and the people would be allowed to repose in quiet. Time has furnished a result entirely different. The State was never so fearfully disorganized as now."[39]

It would be imprudent to place too great an importance on the impact these guerrillas had on the economic portion of the Union war effort. Their effect on the armies, which were taking the war to the heart of the Confederacy, was probably minimal, but their effect on the people of Kentucky was not. As with every other aspect of life on the border, the day-to-day uncertainty about life and property took a heavy toll on the economy of the rivers and the farmlands of the western border.

Any discussion of the impact of the irregular military forces that inhabited the border would be incomplete without an examination of their affects on the military effort in the west and the war in general. Despite the problems that some historians have with the differences between the operations of these irregular groups and those of the regular armies, the guerrillas dictated the military situation on the border and had an impact on the general war situation far out of proportion to their numbers. W.T. Sherman recognized the problem that was coming for the invading Union armies. He characterized the situation in the west as one in which "though our armies pass across and through the land, the war closes in behind and leaves the same enemy behind," he continued noting that the Union would have to begin in "Kentucky and reconquer the country from there as we did from the Indians."[40]

The armies in the west were dependent on very fragile lines of communication, lines that could be easily cut by rebel raiders or the ever-present threat of guerrilla bands. Though guerrilla warfare is inherently afflicted with a limitation — an inability to seize and use, rather than destroy[41] — this limitation had no ill effects on the guerrillas' mission to interdict communications and supplies. Along with the destruction of rail bridges and steamboats, the guerrillas of Kentucky specialized in tearing down telegraph lines and destroying the instruments that carried the messages for the Union armies. To counteract this unlimited threat presented by Morgan, Forrest, and their less famous cousins, the Union high command was required to station large numbers of troops along these vulnerable lines of communications.

Herman Hattaway and Archer Jones, in their book, *How the North Won,* appear to have grasped the importance of the petty war better than most historians of the Civil War. They additionally examined the effects of these additional garrison troops on the Union war effort. They observed that "the impact of rebel raids and guerrillas caused a tremendous dispersion of Federals. Although the Union moved on the offensive with its main armies, it stood on the defensive in protecting its communications and its conquered territory...fifty-six thousand men were guarding Kentucky, West Virginia, and the line of the Baltimore and Ohio..."[42]

These thousands of troops were busy defending territory nominally under the control of the Federal Government. They were not contending with a Confederate army for the areas, but trying to hold onto them against elusive groups of shadow "soldiers," who continually harassed their communications and logistics. During his service in the West, General Don Carlos Buell was so impressed with the dangers of these raids and guerrilla bands that he recommended Kentucky be garrisoned by a force of 30,000 Federal troops.[43] In a war that was marked by high casualty rates and immense attrition, this large number of garrison troops had a significant impact on the outcome of the war. This is not to say that the outcome would have been different if these guerrillas had not existed, but how much quicker could Grant have forced Lee out of Richmond, or Sherman dealt with Generals Joseph E. Johnston and John Bell Hood, if they had been able to draw 20,000 more troops into their commands? By creating such havoc in the rear of the main armies, irregular soldiers effectively tied down the equivalent of an entire field army, relegating them to missions as policemen and security guards. Going further, Hattaway and Jones have determined that the force left to guard these rear areas numbered as high as 30 percent of the entire Union armies east of the Mississippi. By subtracting this 30 percent from the Union strength, they conclude that the relative strength of the Confederate armies to those of the Union was 80 percent. Considering the overwhelming superiority in population that the North enjoyed, the authors cite two reasons for the disparity in efficient use of the available assets. First was the Confederacy's superior mobilization, and second was the "Union's need to guard its communications from the guerrillas and from the very effective Confederate policy of cavalry raids."[44] The problem was of such significance that it preyed on the mind of Union leaders all the way to Washington. In a discussion with General William S. Rosecrans, President Lincoln confided that "In no other way does the enemy give us so much trouble, at so little expense to himself, as by the raids of rapidly moving small bodies of troops (largely, if not wholly mounted) harassing, and discouraging loyal residents, supplying themselves with provisions, clothing, horses, and the like, surprising and capturing small detachments of our forces, and breaking our communications."[45]

A less quantifiable impact of this type of warfare on the larger war is pointed out by Gerald F. Linderman in his study of the combat experiences of soldiers during the war. He found that the "desire to inflict punishment on Southerners" by Union soldiers in the years following 1862 grew much faster than could be controlled by the authorities. He attributes this growth of violence directly to the appearance of irregulars, not just along the border, but in the rear of Union armies as they continued to advance. The occurrences of irregular violence in the rear of these armies increased as they moved south, an increase that had significant psychological impact on the Union soldiers. His discussion of the difference in perception of irregulars in Union and Confederate minds is illustrative of the thorny issue of how irregulars were treated when captured. While a farmer shooting at a passing Union column was a murderer and bushwhacker to the Union troops, to his neighbors he was simply a man protecting his home from invaders. This may seem a hazy distinction, unless you are the farmer whose smokehouse is being raided and whose chickens are tied to the saddle of a looter. This impact on the war is intangible, but guerrilla warfare obviously generated retaliation during the war on the border and that retaliation took more individual forms when the Union army entered the South.[46]

While it is readily apparent that the guerrilla activity along the border had a serious affect on the communications, supplies, and manpower requirements of the Union armies operating elsewhere in the war, what of the effect within the bounds of the individual states? Historians are split on the military significance of the guerrilla units operating in the Commonwealth of Kentucky. While most appear unimpressed with their activities from a military perspective, one historian, Nathaniel Shaler, concluded that "the hundreds of skirmishes with guerrillas and raiding parties within the State were even more fatal than the regular warfare."[47] In the spring and summer of 1864, the military commander of Kentucky was forced to implement martial law and utilize troops to police the countryside as there were no regular Confederate troops operating in the Commonwealth and there had not been for quite awhile. These actions were taken specifically to combat the military necessities caused by the guerrillas and their sympathizers. Regardless of the editorials of George Prentice and the proclamations of politicians, these guerrilla bands operated as military units to a large degree and caused the same problems that similar sized forces from Wheeler or Forrest's divisions would have caused. To maintain that they had no military significance because they were not part of a large body of troops is folly. Though some were engaged in plunder and robbery, they also took action, on a regular basis, against the troops that occupied Kentucky. It is not characteristic of outlaws and highwaymen to take prisoners and administer paroles, but the irregular forces in the Commonwealth did just that. One of the many guerrillas, who fall into the war-rebel category, a man named Hamilton, captured a force of 150 men of the 48th Kentucky in January 1864. Contrary to the rhetoric of the day, the soldiers were paroled as required by the laws of war and they and their commander, Captain Gillum, were allowed to proceed to Union lines.[48] When the steamer, Levi, was captured (and eventually burned beyond use), a Union general officer, named Scammon, and 40 other Union soldiers and officers were onboard. Instead of following the no-quarter tactics, the guerrillas paroled the bulk of the Union soldiers. The Union general and three of his officers were mounted and sent off towards Confederate lines.[49] These acts are in keeping with the mission of a military force, not the senseless plunder of outlaws. It would appear evident that outlaws and those guerrillas who cared nothing for the Confederate cause would have avoided confrontations with large bodies of Union soldiers. They had nothing to gain and their lives to lose from such exchanges, but repeatedly, reports are found of troop columns being attacked by guerrilla units, resulting in capture or being chased back to their lines with their tails between their legs.[50]

Not only did the guerrillas engage in these hit and run tactics so reminiscent of John Hunt Morgan, but they were also capable of brazen acts of military force. A history of the war in Owensboro, Kentucky, contains a story of how "with only a few months until the war would be over, guerrilla leader Captain William Davidson burned the courthouse in January 1865. Enraged that black troops had been quartered there, Davidson marched into town with 300 men, captured the building, allowed records to be removed, and then burned the six-year-old, $100,000 building."[51]

Though a relatively non-violent incident, this story has all the markings of a military operation and none of an outlaw raid. Few outlaw gangs rode in groups as large as 300 and moved with the evident discipline of Davidson's unit. The mere act of allowing the records to be removed from the courthouse indicates an element of respect for the law, which would not be an element of the outlaw psyche. The scenario lends itself to an irregular military unit, similar to those earlier operations under the control of Adam Johnson, conducting a reprisal raid for a perceived injury — the use of black soldiers. While it cannot be refuted that a lawless group existed on the border whose only goal was personal enrichment and vengeance, indisputable evidence exists that large numbers of Confederate soldiers, some authorized and others acting on their own, operated in Kentucky and Missouri for the specific purpose of conducting military operations against Union forces and their civilian supporters. Their legitimacy in regards to prisoner of war status can be vehemently argued, but their military importance cannot. Regardless of uniform or rank or legitimacy, they did significant injury to the Federal Government and occupied troops far out of proportion to their own numbers. For this reason, these irregular soldiers deserve a place in the military history of the war.

As evidenced by the American experience in Afghanistan, a principal mission of guerrilla warfare is the destabilization of civil authority.[52] Though it would be presumptuous to conclude that this mission was one which was thought through by the border irregulars, they nevertheless were extremely successful in accomplishing it. In Afghanistan, the Taliban consistently attempt to accentuate the government's inability to protect citizens and property, thus eroding support for the regime at the grassroots level. Adam Johnson, William Quantrill, Sue Mundy, and many others in the guerrilla ranks accomplished this same objective through their operations in 1861-1865. So successful were they that these Confederate irregulars controlled much of the countryside and traveled throughout the border with impunity. State officials were unable to contend with their activities, and as a result, significant question arose as to whom was truly in control in parts of the affected states. So bad was the environment, that it prompted President Lincoln and various military commanders to declare martial law, removing control of the state from the hands of its elected officials and placing it with the military commanders.

This single act, the imposition of martial law, is ultimately important in assessing the political importance of the petty war and its supporters on the border. Lincoln's proclamation had specifically cited the fact that insurgent forces had "overborne the civil authorities," a statement that could only be taken as an indication of impotence on the part of the State officers.[53] As in any society where the elected officials prove to be unable to handle the tasks at hand, border residents questioned their elected leaders and the military officers who followed them. In September 1864, two months after the declaration of martial law, the editor of the *Louisville Daily Journal*, a staunch supporter of the Union (though no friend of Abraham Lincoln) complained that "still we must say that the long series of guerilla successes in Kentucky are either very creditable to the management of the guerillas or not very creditable to the management of much better men."[54] Richard Collins, in his *Annals of Kentucky*, was more specific in his disgust for the inability of the civil officials to deal with the problem and their willingness to turn it over to the military. He complained that "The proclamation delegates an assumed absolute power over the personal liberty of citizens to irresponsible military officers, and leaves them to select their victims; it provides no form of trial, requires no proof of guilt, indicates no redress nor relief, establishes no safeguards against personal vindictiveness and petty tyranny."[55]

All the states of the border experienced martial law, whether controlled by the government in Washington or Richmond. Its relative ineffectiveness is demonstrated by the persistence of irregular violence throughout the war years. Border residents were willing to pay the price for security and peace, but never got the expected return for their sacrifices.

If the actions of these guerrillas did not bring down the civil government entirely, they showed its inadequacy every day. State and Federal officials were unable to perform their jobs without the protection of troops. Sheriffs were unable to arrest felons or hold those that they did arrest, post offices were ransacked and postmasters threatened if they continued to perform their duties; even military officers, such as the Provost Marshal of the 5th Congressional District, Captain Womack, were bullied and threatened by guerrillas in order to exact oaths not to serve the Federal Government further.[56] When it became evident that the Government was unable to provide protection for its own officials in the Border States, support was eroded. The imposition of Federal or Confederate martial law and the violent occupation that accompanied it also contributed to the alienation of many residents well after the war was over.

The Americans who inhabited the Border States during this most violent period in our history bore the brunt of this war. On many a farm in any number of states, men and women lived a fearful existence awaiting the arrival of violent men who would ruin their lives. No other period in American History has so taken war into the streets and barnyards of this country and been felt so closely by our citizens at home. That is the issue that differs this war from others in our history, as non-combatant Americans suffered violence at home that was specifically directed at them and not just an accidental spilling over from a nearby battlefield.

Notes

1. Bruce Catton, *Terrible Swift Sword*, (Garden City, NY: Doubleday & Company, Inc., 1963), pp. 9-10.

2. Alwyn Barr, "Records of the Confederate Military Commission in San Antonio, July 2-October 10, 1862," *Southwestern Historical Quarterly* 70(1966), 71 (1967), 73(1969); Hopkins Diary 1862-1865, Desmond Pulaski Hopkins Papers, p. 74, Barker Texas History Center, Austin, TX.

3. Richard S. Brownlee, *Gray Ghosts of the Confederacy: Guerrilla Warfare in the West, 1861-1865*. Baton Rouge, LA; Louisiana State University Press, 1958, Louisiana Paperback Edition, 1984, p. 110-127.

4. Merton E. Coulter, *The Civil War and Readjustment in Kentucky*, (Chapel Hill: The University of North Carolina Press, 1926; Reprinted, Gloucester, MA: Peter Smith, 1966), p. 171.

5. *Official Records*, Series 1, Volume 39, Part 2, pp. 144-145.

6. *Official Records*, pp. 180-181.

7. *Louisville Daily Journal*, October 21, 1864. The problems created by the authorities' inability to maintain security for the people of the border areas served to fuel the guerrilla organizations and continually increase the pressure on the populace, government, and economy. Unable to feel safe in their own streets and homes, citizens turned away from the occupying Union forces and government; questioning where their loyalties should lie in the conflict raging around them. Aggressive measures taken by Union commanders often reaped few benefits, but contributed to the alienation of the more moderate forces in Border State society. It was this moderate portion of society that was necessary to stabilize the Border States; and reprisal killings and draconian measures (such as the use of black soldiers to police Border States and unsuccessful martial law) served often to drive them, if not into the guerrilla camps, at least out of active support of the governing body. These same problems were evidenced in Iraq and point out the requirement in a counterinsurgency environment to provide for the security of the population as a method of slowing the insurgent movement. As the American Army was unable to provide for the security of the streets and homes of Iraqi citizens, the problems of the insurgency grew.

8. No other lesson can be so clearly drawn from the study of guerrilla warfare on the border, and particularly in Missouri, than the importance of quality intelligence in the struggle with guerrillas. These irregular organizations had a natural network in the towns and countryside and only solid, timely intelligence allowed opposing forces the ability to effectively engage them. When that intelligence was faulty, often information inspired by an attempt to settle old scores amongst the population, anti-guerrilla operations was universal failures. This same problem is common in the historical literature of counterinsurgency warfare and the importance of intelligence is stressed in much of the present day writings of military scholars and leaders.

9. *Louisville Daily Journal*, October 18, 1864.

10. This same problem is reflected in the American experience in Iraq. Countless sources lament the fact that without the ability to consistently secure villages and towns in Iraq, the insurgent power in an area waited until American forces no longer posed a threat and then flowed back into virtual control of a town or province. As martial law failed to provide security on the border, our efforts in Iraq often failed to provide adequate security to the Iraqi population.

11. George C. Wright, *Life Behind a Veil: Blacks in Louisville, Kentucky, 1865-1930,* (Baton Rouge, LA: Louisiana State University Press, 1985), pp. 16-20.

12. Nathaniel S. Shaler, *Kentucky: A Pioneer Commonwealth*, (Boston: Houghton, Mifflin and Company, 1897), p. 349.

13. *Official Records*, Series 1, Volume 39, Part 2, p. 163.

14. *Louisville Daily Journal*, September 5, 1864.

15. John Jeffries to his friend Mick, July 17, 1864, Jeffrey Family Papers, Special Collections and Archives, University of Kentucky Libraries, Lexington, KY.

16. It has been argued that civilian leadership during the planning of Operation Iraqi Freedom did not fully comprehend the problems inherent in a potential insurgency after conventional combat ended. If this is the case, their thoughts were merely reflective of the historians mentioned whose tendency is to slight or ignore irregular warfare because it is not neat and easily understandable.

17. Shaler, p. 345.

18. Lowell H. Harrison, *The Civil War in Kentucky*, (Lexington, KY: The University Press of Kentucky, 1975), p. 75.

19. C.Q.L. to Richard Herndon, August 18, 1864, Herndon Family Papers, Special Collections and Archives, University of Kentucky Libraries, Lexington, KY.

20. Thomas Truitt to Governor Thomas Bramlette, June 13, 1864, The Quartermaster and Adjutant General's Papers, Kentucky Military History Museum, Frankfort, KY.

21. Thomas Truitt to Governor Thomas Bramlette, June 13, 1864; Mrs. Glasscocke to Governor Bramlette, January 2, 1865.

22. Harrison, p. 102.

23. An issue that became clear in this study was that when competing groups are mixed together in close proximity, be they political, social, or religious, there will be violence if adequate social and governmental structures are not maintained. Just as loosing unionists against their secessionist neighbors created a level of personal violence for which the leadership on the border was not prepared, religious groups in Iraq and elsewhere must be restrained by common social and governmental structures to avoid a level of violence that is uncontrollable. The disagreements over slavery had gone on for many years, but maintained a peaceful veneer until war damaged the social and governmental structures that served to control the population. Similarities are evident in the violence raging in Iraq between Sunni and Shiite groups as the structures that kept these long-held animosities in check were dissolved.

24. Wright, p. 16.

25. *Louisville Daily Journal*, January 7, 1865.

26. *Louisville Daily Journal*, January 5, 1865.

27. Otho Miller to General Finnell, June 4, 1864, The Quartermaster and Adjutant General's Papers, Kentucky Military History Museum, Frankfort, KY.

28. *Louisville Daily Journal*, July 18, 1864.

29. *Louisville Daily Journal*, December 13, 1864.

30. *Louisville Daily Journal*, October 29, 1864.

31. *Louisville Daily Journal*, August 9, 1864.

32. Col. Thomas Campbell to General D.W. Lindsey. July 8, 1865, The Quartermaster and Adjutant General's Papers, Kentucky Military History Museum, Frankfort, KY.

33. These efforts to disrupt the economy of Border States is similar in many ways to the efforts by insurgents in Iraq to disrupt the flow of oil and the daily transactions of commerce, in order to incite terror and disorganize governmental systems. These passages reemphasize the importance of security to the economic climate of an area. If the government or authorities cannot provide adequate security for the progress of commerce, the population will question their legitimacy.

34. *Louisville Daily Journal*, November 19, 1864.

35. *Official Records*, Series 1, Volume 39, Part 2, p. 198.

36. *Louisville Daily Journal*, July 16, 1864.

37. *Louisville Daily Journal*, February 8, 1864.

38. John Jeffries to his friend William, February 13, 1864, Jeffrey Family Papers, Special Collections and Archives, University of Kentucky Libraries, Lexington, KY.

39. *Louisville Daily Journal*, October 19, 1864.

40. Herman Hattaway and Archer Jones, *How the North Won*, p. 250.

41. Hattaway and Jones, p. 356.

42. Hattaway and Jones, p. 357.

43. Hattaway and Jones, p. 263.

44. Hattaway and Jones, p. 721.

45. Hattaway and Jones, p. 356.

46. Gerald F. Linderman, *Embattled Courage*, pp. 196-199. The problems of retaliation are evident today in Iraq. The stress of continued combat and the pressures of dealing with a constant drumbeat of insurgent violence can be argued to have prompted random violence aimed at civilians who may or may not deserve to be singled out. This random violence can have negative effects on the relationship

between the populace and the government (or occupying force). The use of retaliation killings against insurgent forces can merely be a pretext for a spiral of violence from which the government (or occupying force) will gain little.

47. Shaler, p. 356.

48. *Louisville Daily Journal*, January 30, 1864.

49. *Louisville Daily Journal*, February 8, 1864.

50. *Louisville Daily Journal*, July 16, 1864.

51. Aloma Williams Dew, "Between the Hawk and the Buzzard: Owensboro during the Civil War," *The Register* 77(Winter 1979): 10.

52. These attempts to destabilize authority can be seen repeatedly today in Iraq and Afghanistan. By pointing out to the population that the government is not in control of the cities or countryside, insurgents prevent open support of the government and occasionally generate support for the insurgency.

53. *Official Records*, Series 1, Volume 39, Part 2, pp. 180-181.

54. *Louisville Daily Journal*, September 26, 1864.

55. Lewis and Richard Collins, *Annals of Kentucky*, vol. 1, (Covington, KY: Collins & Co., 1874), p. 130.

56. *Louisville Daily Journal*, July 29-30, 1864.

Chapter 6

Epilogue

The Civil War has long been a pinnacle of study for those interested in battles between grand and glorious armies. It has been called the last "gentlemen's war" and regarded as a test of chivalry. Books about the war, both scholarly and popular history, have been published on endless numbers of battles through the last 100 years. Unfortunately, most of these books have looked past the people who were not in uniform during the war. The men and women, who lived through the war at home, whether in the North or South, were all affected by the bloody conflict. Their story is yet to be told in adequate measure.

In the Border States, those unfortunate lands trapped between the adversaries, the war brought damage and destruction. These were the lands on which most of the war was fought and though the armies may have left them from time to time, the violence of war never did. Throughout the border, violence became a regular occurrence; before, during, and after the war. Kentucky, as a Border State, echoed many of the problems this nation had in general during the war. She was divided politically and socially along lines supporting North or South, with much of her populace supporting the Union while others believed in the justness of the Confederate cause. The brother-against-brother litany that fills Civil War literature is wholly true in the case of the Border States. Men from the same family often went in different directions and fought in different uniforms.

Unlike those states away from the border, the violence and fear in Kentucky, Kansas, or Missouri was not restricted to periods of organized combat between major armies. The men and women of the border had to deal with this violence and terror whether or not the main armies were anywhere near their state. For them the war was not a far-off battle in the valleys of Virginia, but a day-to-day happening in the streets of their hometowns, complete with pain and death. These people, and the war that so affected them, deserve to be studied because the history of America is, by definition, the history of her people.

The guerrillas who fought and died on the western border have long been dismissed as outlaws and bushwhackers. For this reason, legitimate scholars have not recognized their contribution to the history of the war; but does their legitimacy affect the importance of their contribution? The mere fact that these people "lived and fought," makes their contribution important. The men they killed are just as dead as if they were shot by members of the Stonewall Brigade or some equally famous unit. The fact that thousands of irregular warriors roamed the hills of Kentucky or Missouri, carrying out a shadow war against the Federal Government and its supporters cannot be argued. Their mere existence and their impact on the people of those states demand that their story be told.

These irregular soldiers might have been accorded more legitimacy by historians if they had operated under the command of Generals Nathan B. Forrest or John Hunt Morgan. The troops of these men, and other cavalry leaders, utilized much the same form of warfare as the guerrillas, and have been considered regular soldiers throughout the literature of the war. The facts show that Morgan was the father of guerrilla warfare in Kentucky. Exactly how many of the guerrillas learned their trade under his tutelage cannot be ascertained, but the list is impressive. Adam Johnson, Jacob Bennett, Colonel George Jessee, Sue Mundy, One-Armed Berry, Henry C. Magruder, and others served with Morgan before beginning their personal war in Kentucky. No other man can boast of a record like this. He believed in the "small war" and brought it to a new level of refinement.

The subject of legitimacy has taken up considerable space in this study. The dichotomy which has existed for years in the way that historians treated men like William Clarke Quantrill and John Mosby is well-represented in this study. In the large pool of irregulars who fought the fight in the west, there were groups that should be accorded differing degrees of legitimacy. Johnson and his troops were undeniably regularly enrolled soldiers of the Confederate Army. They were, however, treated as outlaws and murderers by the Union people of Kentucky and the historians who followed. They were thrown into the same category with men who had no identifiable connection with the Confederacy, and were not afforded the benefits or recognition that their status as prisoners of war should have gained them. The execution of members of the unit, without the benefit of trial, might well have been called a war crime if the South had been victorious. These Confederate soldiers played a large part in the Civil War history of Kentucky, but they have been relegated by scholars to the back pages of history. Quantrill and his followers in Missouri have received considerably more attention, but rarely in an objective evaluation. Their acts and the retaliation that they elicited have created a cult following around these men that often defies objectivity. Regardless of the bias found in the volumes on their war, each speaks to the same fact — these violent men lived on the border in very violent times. Their warfare and the responses by the Union forces had a pervasive effect on the population of the Border States in the Trans-Mississippi West.

Interestingly, the Union officials finally turned to their own version of these partisan rangers in an attempt to deal with the guerrilla problem. How did Captains Ed Terrell and James Bridgewater differ from Johnson and Bennett? They all operated separately from a main army, without the benefit of written orders for their specific actions. Both groups utilized the same method of horse resupply, but what was called theft when practiced by Johnson was termed *impressment* when it was done by Bridgewater. The joking remark in Kansas that a horse might be "out of Missouri by Jennison" was only a bit of levity, as many a horse in Kansas today can have its lineage traced to a stable in Missouri during the war. There was little difference between the tactics and actions of the Union and Confederate rangers, but there has been considerable difference in the way that history has treated them.

Other men, not part of the partisan rangers, also fought the war against the Union authorities. Though their legitimacy as southern soldiers can be questioned, their effects on the people of the border cannot. These war rebels and outlaws created an environment of fear and disorganization that forced the Federal and State authorities to take action to deal with them. Considerable time, money, and energy were expended by the authorities in their efforts to stop the actions of these small bands.

The delineation of outlaws versus war rebels is difficult, as they share many characteristics. The one possible factor that can be used to separate them is public support. In discussing this question over a century after the American Civil War, Che Guevara wrote that "...They [bandits] have all the characteristics of a guerrilla army, homogeneity, respect for their leader, valor, knowledge of the ground, and, often, even a good understanding of the tactics to be employed. The only thing missing is the support of the people; and, inevitably, these gangs are captured and exterminated by the public force."[1]

On the Civil War border, as in Che Guevara's Cuba, the guerrilla fighter required an infrastructure of support amongst the population. Without this support, the guerrillas would have been left without a safe place to go, and eventually would have been caught and punished. The fact that a support structure did exist, and that many guerrillas stayed active until the war's end, makes a statement in itself. If Che's model is accepted, it gives much greater credence to the war rebel's perception of themselves as Confederate soldiers.

What caused the growth of guerrilla warfare during the Civil War is a hard question to definitively answer. The mixing of people with different political and social leanings is always confusing, but during the Civil War the disagreements, which would have caused arguments at another time, brought charges of disloyalty and even death. In this environment of distrust, men chose to fight back against the enemies they perceived in their state. With the major armies gone, the best way to carry out the fight was the petty war. Capitalizing on this disorganization, the Confederate Government sent recruiters and cadre into Kentucky and Missouri to further stir up trouble for the Federal authorities. The imposition of martial law that followed, and the subsequent recruitment of black soldiers, served only to drive more Kentuckians into the service of these irregular bands. The Federal Government came to represent many of the things southern radicals had predicted years before. Free people do not easily submit to the restriction of their rights without just compensation, and the sacrifices that border residents were forced to endure at the hands of men like General E.A. Paine or General Ewing brought little or no respite from the guerrilla terror.

To deal with the growth of irregular warfare in America, we must refer to a modern proponent of guerrilla war, as Che questions; "...Why does the guerrilla fight? We must come to the inevitable conclusion that the guerrilla fighter is a social reformer, that he takes up arms responding to the angry protest of the people against their oppressors, and that he fights in order to change the social system..."[2] Though Che's words reflect the ideological flavor of his writings, his argument rings true. The guerrillas on the border were, in the main, fighting the Federal Government over political and social issues. Their violence was not intended to quench a bloodthirsty desire, but to preserve a social system that was being forcibly changed. Looking at the irregular war from this angle, these guerrillas fit well into a social-bandit scenario. Operating in an extra-legal manner, they strived for what they perceived as right and just against those whom they believed to be society's enemies.

Though accepting the possibility that Sue Mundy in Kentucky or Major John Thrailkill in Missouri might have been social-bandits is quite a departure from the prevailing wisdom, the evidence available can easily lend itself to Che Guevara's model of the guerrilla fighter. By accepting the war rebels in this light, the causes of the guerrilla war on the border become much more apparent to the historian.

Though the causes of the guerrilla war cannot be fully enumerated, the impacts from this petty war are apparent. The imposition of martial law and the drastic measures taken by Union commanders were openly based on the problems created in the state by these insurgent forces. Regardless of their legitimacy, these bands forced the Federal and, in the case of Texas, Confederate authorities to supersede the civil power and take actions that would later serve to alienate the populace from the administration. The military impact of this little war on the major conflict lies in the troops who were bled off from the field armies. Though not of major importance in the big picture, these irregular warriors dictated everything that the military authorities in the Trans-Mississippi and Kentucky did during 1864 and 1865. The actions of those authorities were consistently reactive to guerrilla actions, instead of conducting the proactive effort that was necessary.

The irregular war on the border, like irregular war anywhere, was accented by its psychological and social effects upon the people of the individual states. The residents of the border had to live with fear and uncertainty for nearly four years, based almost solely on the violence brought forth by the petty war. Additionally, this fear and uncertainty may well have caused the numbers of recruits these states provided to both armies to be diminished, as men hesitated to leave their families in such an unsafe environment.

Guerrilla wars can be waged independently or as part of a greater conflict. In Vietnam, the petty war was the main concern of the military, but in the Civil War the guerrillas represented only a sideshow. The study of this small war is an examination of a "Third War." Though the larger conflict raged to the south and the east, most border residents were far more concerned with what happened between Federal forces and guerrillas in the next county. People deal first with the closest threat, and the armies of Generals John B. Hood and Robert E. Lee were much farther removed from the Border than the troops of Johnson, Quantrill, or Charles R. Jennison.

Kentucky Unionists had little to fear from the Army of Tennessee, but their very lives were endangered daily by the likes of Mundy and Magruder. These men were realities in Kentucky, as other guerrillas were across the border region, and most of the people of the state had to deal with their terror in one way or another.

The guerrilla war on the border left a legacy for the months and years that followed. In Kentucky, lawless gangs of men continued to roam the hills for many months, causing disorganization and fear well after the war's end. These men learned their trade in wartime service, and whether they were connected to the Confederacy during the war or not, continued to practice that trade well after the Richmond Government ceased to exist. Kentucky was not alone in this legacy. The men who rode with Quantrill included names like Frank and Jesse James and the Younger Brothers; men who would make a reputation for themselves in the violent aftermath of the war. The life they led in Missouri after the war was an extension of that which they had grown used to during the war years. Linderman maintains that the irregular "was to soldierly combat what lice, fleas, and rats were to prisoner-of-war stockades, and to be dealt with as vermin."³ Again Professor Linderman's evaluation is very accurate, as these men would not receive the same kind of hero's recognition in the post-war years that could be expected by regular soldiers. Viewed as "wild beasts" by Union generals and other officials, many were left with little choice but to continue their old habits to the end.

The underlying theme of this study is the importance of violence, on whatever scale, upon the minds and lives of the people who lived through it. Terror and the fear for one's life have serious effects on society's organization and the way in which men deal with each other. The terror and violence, with which the people of South Vietnam and Cambodia endured decades ago and the people of Iraq and Afghanistan endure today, are brought home to us by the news media and our returning soldiers. This exposure to the ugly side of irregular war has served to awaken a new understanding of the importance of this petty war in many scholars, prompting an increased investigation into the phenomenon. One such scholar, Phillip Shaw Paludan, went to the heart of the question when he noted that this type of war "involves primary emotions that are less a part of a certain moment in history and more a part of the human personality."⁴ The study of irregular warfare is more than just an exercise in military history; it contains insights into the whys and hows of men and the way they deal with others. Though the study of combat is involved in the story, it is the residual fear that such random violence creates that has the greatest impact on society. On the border, that violence existed in the streets where children played and people traveled. Just as terrorist leaders have threatened to bring more violence to the streets of the United States, these Confederate soldiers brought fear and violence to the streets of the Border States. Though almost 150 years separates these events, the fear of physical violence and the emotional strain caused by irregular warfare is the same today as it was during the American Civil War. The American attack in Iraq during Desert Storm was a distant event to the American people, just as Gettysburg was to border residents, but the introduction of terrorism into this country in 2001 brought effects and impacts similar to those created by the irregular terror in the American Civil War.

To appreciate the mental effect that these threats and the operations of the guerrillas had on the border, the modern student has only to look around. Our world is currently afflicted with a form of irregular war on a global scale. Terrorism is the petty war, taken to a level of violence (or threatened violence) that exceeds the irregular warfare of the Civil War in both scale and impact. Though not located anywhere near the seat of the war, Kentuckians had to deal with the day-to-day realities that at anytime and in anyplace they could be brought to answer for their political allegiances. Civil authorities were unable to curb the depredations of the violent segment of the population, just as present day governments find themselves struggling to deal effectively with international terrorists. Americans today find themselves frustrated and frightened by this continuing threat, just as the residents of the border did 140-plus years ago.

As a professional soldier, this research has also raised the question of how modern military leaders can profit from knowledge of the irregular warfare during the American Civil War. While there is no magical answer in this knowledge, it is in searching to answer this question and to use historical context to inform military judgment that this study is closed with an examination of what might be learned.

First, no other lesson can be so clearly drawn from the study of guerrilla warfare on the border, and particularly in Missouri, than the importance of **quality intelligence** in the struggle with guerrillas. These irregular organizations had a natural network in the towns and countryside and only solid, timely intelligence allowed opposing forces the ability to effectively engage them. When that intelligence was faulty, often information inspired by an attempt to settle old scores amongst the population, anti-guerrilla operations was universal failures. This same problem is common in the historical literature of counterinsurgency warfare and the importance of intelligence is stressed in much of the present day writings of military scholars and leaders.

Second, a lesson that became clear in this study was that in unstable environments that include irregular violence, when competing groups are mixed together in close proximity, be they political, social, ethnic, or religious, **there will be violence if adequate social and governmental structures are not maintained**. Just as loosing unionists against their secessionist neighbors created a level of personal violence for which the leadership on the border was not prepared, religious groups in Iraq and elsewhere must be restrained by common social and governmental structures to avoid a level of violence that is uncontrollable. The disagreements over slavery had gone on for many years, but maintained a peaceful veneer until war damaged the social and governmental structures that served to control the population. Similarities are evident in the violence that raged in Iraq between Sunni, Shiite, and Kurdish groups as the structures that kept these long-held animosities in check were dissolved. It appears to be critical for military forces engaged in such an environment to do everything within their power to keep these social and governmental structures in place. Allowing a vacuum to be created, for even the shortest period of time, will open the door and potentially allow social and cultural disagreements to turn into violence.

Both of the last two lessons point to a third lesson — **the importance of understanding culture when dealing with a populace under pressure**. Conventional forces in the US Army did very little in the study of culture prior to Operation Iraqi Freedom. This military force did not see the importance of understanding the populace within which it operated, as it had long been focused on tank battles and air wars. When soldiers have to be placed on the ground in close proximity to the populace, it is of critical importance that they understand the people they are dealing with and their customs. The American tendency is to think the rest of the world is like us, but that is not true across the globe and it is easy to make mistakes that will cause strained relationships or violence by not paying adequate attention to their cultural norms. It is one thing to create conflict because a military leader understood what the response to a specific action would be and anticipated the reaction, but to damage vital relationships or bring on violence that was unnecessary due to a lack of knowledge of the populace is unprofessional and does not reflect a quality-risk assessment. In Civil War Kentucky, one such example was the decision to enlist black soldiers to police the Commonwealth. While the Union leadership knew that the response from Confederate sympathizers would be negative, and in all probability chose to take this path partly as a slap in the face to its enemies, it is apparent from the historical record that they badly underestimated how Unionists or those who were more moderate would react. The action did not have the positive consequences that the leadership expected and instead resulted in a violent response across the board in Kentucky.

Fourth, the problems created by the **authorities' inability to maintain security** for the people of the border areas served to fuel the guerrilla organizations and continually increase the pressure on the populace, government, and economy. Unable to feel safe in their own streets and homes, citizens turned away from the occupying Union forces and government; questioning where their loyalties should lie in the conflict raging around them. Aggressive measures taken by Union commanders often reaped few benefits, but contributed to the alienation of the more moderate forces in the Border State society. It was this moderate portion of society that was necessary to stabilize the Border States; and reprisal killings and draconian measures (such as the use of black soldiers to police Border States and unsuccessful martial law) served often to drive them, if not into the guerrilla camps, at least out of active support of the governing body. These same problems were evidenced in Iraq and point out the requirement in a counterinsurgency environment to provide for the security of the population as a method of slowing the insurgent movement. As the American Army was unable to provide for the security of the streets and homes of Iraqi citizens, the problems of the insurgency grew. Countless media sources lamented the fact that without the ability to consistently secure villages and towns in Iraq, the insurgent power in an area waited until American forces no longer posed a threat and then flowed back into virtual control of a town or province. Once Americans returned to their forward operating bases, the insurgents once again operated in the towns and villages. Only actions such as the stationing of troops in smaller outposts amongst the civilian population finally led to a consistently secure environment for Iraqi citizens and the reduction of insurgent violence. As martial law failed to provide security on the border, our efforts in Iraq initially failed to provide adequate security to the Iraqi population. Without this security, as was evidenced in all the Border States examined in this study, there is little chance to break the cycle of irregular violence and build a firm base for peaceful conditions.

Fifth, a recurring theme in irregular warfare environments is the problem created by the **brutality that is so often present**. The back and forth violence between General Burbridge and the Kentucky irregulars merely served to up the ante and led to the murder of unionists and irregulars alike in retaliation for previous violence. This eventually led to the execution of regularly enrolled Confederate partisan rangers by Union authorities without trial or due process. In Missouri, this violence spiraled until it was so out of control that at Centralia, William T. Anderson and George M. Todd's forces engaged in incomprehensible body mutilation. Through history, spiraling brutality has not led to solutions, but has led to even greater brutality and a breakdown in order and discipline in society and military forces. The problems of retaliation were evident in Iraq. The stress of continued combat and the pressures of dealing with a constant drumbeat of insurgent violence can be argued to have prompted random violence aimed at civilians who may or may not deserve to be singled out. The use of retaliation killings against insurgent forces can merely be a pretext for a spiral of violence from which the government (or occupying force) will gain little. The uncontrolled actions of a few US soldiers at Abu Ghraib probably did more to recruit young men to the insurgent cause than anything else during the war. Brutality of this nature is counter-productive in combating insurgency and only serves to worsen the environment that conventional forces face in trying to reduce the violence. Not only retaliation against irregular warriors must be considered, but the retaliation on the civilian populace for the actions of irregulars. Just as the retaliation by Union authorities in Kentucky against perceived southern sympathizers did little or nothing to combat the irregular violence, there is no evidence that such retaliation against more modern populations is any more effective. The determination of who is a "good guy" and who is a "bad guy" is so difficult in the fluid environment of irregular warfare, that conventional forces fighting against local irregulars run the risk of defeating their own cause by harming civilians either physically, emotionally, or economically. A heavy hand may feel good when responding to irregular violence, but if it is used in the wrong way against the wrong people it will only exacerbate the overall problem. This links back to the previous discussion on intelligence. The need to know where to apply the heavy hand to have the desired effect without alienating moderate parts of the population is a key competency in combating irregular forces.

Sixth, another lesson that modern leaders and soldiers can take from the experiences in the American Civil War revolves around **how leadership responds to insurgent warfare**. Military and civilian leaders have historically shown an inability to come to grips with the unique nature of irregular warfare and have tended to approach it with what Robert B. Asprey identified as the "arrogance of ignorance."[5] Because they do not take it seriously or do not view it as a legitimate form of warfare, they exhibit a tendency to inadequately plan to combat it or fail to recognize its existence at all. It has been argued that civilian leadership during the planning of Operation Iraqi Freedom did not fully comprehend the problems inherent in a potential insurgency after conventional combat ended. If this is the case, their thoughts were merely reflective of the historians mentioned earlier whose tendency is to slight or ignore irregular warfare because it is not neat and easily understandable. Press interviews with national leaders showed a denial when it came to the early stages of the Iraq insurgency. Because they did not understand it or granted it no place in the spectrum of warfare, they simply denied its existence and preferred to see just isolated instances of violence by individual criminals. Because of this arrogance of ignorance, the US leadership was slow in responding to the insurgency and it contributed to an environment where the momentum of irregular violence exceeded that which the ground forces could control.

Violence in any form is important for its psychological effects upon people. Though the size of the armies and the number of casualties make for good reading, and provide historians or statisticians with impressive numbers, they are often less important to a group of people than some smaller event. That insight is not limited to the study of the Civil War or Iraq or Afghanistan, as the conflict between the European-Americans and the North American Indians during the 1870s and 1880s contain many of these same attributes. It is important for the student of history to remember that larger events do not have to be more important to the understanding of people. Along the border that served to separate North from South from 1861 to 1865, this is particularly true and though the survey texts on the American Civil War make for good reading, the legacy of the region is not of great battles. It is a history of violent, unrelenting irregular war that destroyed families and communities in an attempt to win this internecine conflict.

Notes

1. Che Guevara, *Guerrilla Warfare*, (Lincoln, NE: University of Nebraska Press, 1985), p. 50.

2. Cuevara, p. 50.

3. Gerald F. Linderman, *Embattled Courage: The Experience of Combat in the American Civil War*, New York: The Free Press, 1987, p. 196.

4. Philip Shaw Paludan, *Victims: A True Story of the Civil War* (Knoxville, TN: The University of Tennessee Press, 1981), p. xv.

5. Robert B. Asprey, *War in the Shadows: The Guerrilla in History*, 2 vols. (Garden City, NY: Doubleday & Company, Inc., 1975), p. 165.

Glossary

abolitionist An individual who believes in the elimination of slavery.

Bluegrass State The nickname for the State of Kentucky.

Border Ruffians Pro-slavery activists from the State of Missouri, who in 1854 to 1860 crossed the border into Kansas to force the acceptance of slavery through violent acts.

bushwhacker Bushwhacking was a form of guerrilla warfare common during the American Civil War. It was particularly prevalent in rural areas where there were sharp divisions between those favoring the Union and Confederacy. The perpetrators of the attacks/raids during this time were called bushwhackers.

Cherokee East Members of the Eastern Band of the Cherokee Nation who did not participate in the "Trail of Tears" in 1838 to the Indian Territory (now known as the State of Oklahoma) and remained in their native lands of southeastern US (primarily in the State of North Carolina).

Cherokee West Members of the Cherokee Nation who were forcibly relocated to the Indian Territory (Oklahoma) in the 1830s under the provisions set forth by the US Government under the Indian Removal Act.

combatant One that is engaged in or ready to engage in combat.

Commonwealth A reference attached to some of the states (such as Kentucky or Virginia) of the United States.

depredation To lay waste, ravage, or plunder.

double-mindedness A concept by Danish philosopher, Soren Kierkegaard. A failure to exhibit goodness for its own sake, but instead make decisions or take action based on insincerity or fear of punishment.

guerrilla A member of an irregular, usually indigenous military or paramilitary unit operating in small bands in occupied territory to harass and undermine the enemy, as by surprise raids.

Haengerbande Loosely translated meaning "hanging bands." This was the name of a group of outlaws who rode the Texas hill country, hanging resident German settlers and stealing their property in the name of the Confederacy.

half-breed Anyone of mixed Native American and white European parentage.

highwayman A thief who preyed on travelers. This type of outlaw usually travelled and robbed by horse. Some robbed individually, but others operated in pairs or in small gangs.

impressment The act or policy of seizing people or property for public service or use.

Indian Territory A geographical region west of Arkansas with general borders that was initially set by the Indian Intercourse Act of 1834. This area was later declared the State of Oklahoma in 1907 and the designation "Indian Territory" ceased to exist.

irregulars Men and women who fought irregular warfare during the Civil War.

irregular warfare Favors indirect and asymmetric warfare approaches, though it may employ the full range of military and other capabilities, in order to erode an adversary's power, influence, and will. Frequently used to describe guerrilla warfare; essentially violent conflict between a formal military and an informal, poorly-equipped, but resilient opponent.

Jayhawker Pro-Union guerrilla fighters in Kansas using tactics similar to bushwhackers and border ruffians by conducting cross-border raids into the State of Missouri.

martial law	The imposition of military rule by military authorities over designated regions on an emergency basis (usually temporary) when order and security, and essential services, cannot function effectively.
noncombatant	An individual who does not actively engage in war as a military service member.
no-quarter	The term originates from an order by the commander of a victorious army that they "will not quarter (house)" captured enemy soldiers. Therefore, none can be taken prisoner and all enemy combatants must be killed.
partisan	A fervent, sometimes militant supporter or proponent of a party, cause, faction, person, or idea. A member of an organized body of fighters who attack or harass an enemy, especially within occupied territory; a guerrilla.
Red Legs	A member of a secret organization formed in Kansas in 1862 that engaged in guerrilla activities during the Civil War.
small war/petty war	Reference to the irregular warfare that was conducted in the Trans-Mississippi border states during the Civil War.
The Five Civilized Tribes	The five Native American nations — the Cherokee, Chickasaw, Choctaw, Creek, and Seminole — that were considered civilized by Anglo-European settlers during the colonial and early federal period because they adopted many of the colonists' customs and had generally good relations with their neighbors.
Trans-Mississippi	The geographic area west of the Mississippi River during the 19th century, consisting of the states of Arkansas, Louisiana, Missouri, Texas, and the Indian Territory (now known as Oklahoma).
Yankee	A term used by Confederate soldiers or sympathizers when referring to a Union soldier or citizen of the Northern United States during the Civil War.

Bibliography

Primary Sources

Austin, Texas. Barker Texas History Center. Banta and Cadwell Narrative.

Austin, Texas. Barker Texas History Center. Desmond Pulaski Hopkins Papers.

Austin, Texas. Barker Texas History Center. Jacob Kuechler Papers.

Frankfort, Kentucky. Kentucky Military History Museum. The Quartermaster and Adjutant General's papers.

Lexington, Kentucky. University of Kentucky Libraries. Special Collections and Archives. Herndon Family Papers.

Lexington, Kentucky. University of Kentucky Libraries. Special Collections and Archives. Thomas Henry Hines Papers.

Lexington, Kentucky. University of Kentucky Libraries. Special Collections and Archives. Gunn Family Papers.

Lexington, Kentucky. University of Kentucky Libraries. Special Collections and Archives. Jeffrey Family Papers.

Lexington, Kentucky. University of Kentucky Libraries. Special Collections and Archives. Means Family Papers.

Lexington, Kentucky. University of Kentucky Libraries. Special Collections and Archives. Moore Family Papers.

Lexington, Kentucky. University of Kentucky Libraries. Special Collections and Archives. Fountain and Roderick Perry Papers.

Lexington, Kentucky. University of Kentucky Libraries. Special Collections and Archives. George Dennison Prentice Letters.

Lexington, Kentucky. University of Kentucky Libraries. Special Collections and Archives. David Lewis Thornton Papers.

Norman, Oklahoma. University of Oklahoma. Western Historical Collection. Stephen Foreman Collection.

Norman, Oklahoma. University of Oklahoma. Western Historical Collection. A.M. Gibson Collection.

Norman, Oklahoma. University of Oklahoma. Western Historical Collection. John W. Morris Collection.

Norman, Oklahoma. University of Oklahoma. Western Historical Collection. William E. Connelly Collection.

Oklahoma City, Oklahoma. Oklahoma Historical Society. Oklahoma Indian Project.

Topeka, Kansas. Kansas State Historical Society. William E. Connelly Papers.

Tulsa, Oklahoma. The Thomas Gilcrease Institute of American History and Art. Diary of Hannah Hicks.

US War Department, *The War of Rebellion: A Compilation of the Official Records of the Union and Confederate Armies,* 128 vols, Washington, DC: Government Printing Office, 1880-1902.

Secondary Sources

Asprey, Robert B., *War in the Shadows: The Guerrilla in History,* 2 vols, Garden City, NY: Doubleday & Company, Inc., 1975.

Biggers, Don H., *German Pioneers in Texas*, Austin, TX: Eakin Publications, 1983.

Branda, Eldon Stephen, ed., *The Handbook of Texas: A Supplement,* Volume III, Austin, TX: The Texas State Historical Association, 1976.

Briggs, Richard A., *The Early History of West Point, Kentucky,* West Point, KY: By the Author, 1955.

Britton, Wiley, *The Civil War on the Border*, Two Volumes, New York: G.P. Putnam's Sons, 1899; Lawrence, KS: Kansas Heritage Press, 1994.

Britton, Wiley, *The Union Indian Brigade in the Civil War*. Ottawa, KS: Kansas Heritage Press, 1922.

Brophy, Patrick, *Bushwhackers of the Border: The Civil War Period in Western Missouri,* Nevada, MO: Vernon County Historical Society, 1980.

Brown, Dee Alexander, *The Bold Cavaliers: Morgan's 2nd Kentucky Cavalry Raiders,* New York: J.B. Lippincott Company, 1959.

Brownlee, Richard S., *Gray Ghosts of the Confederacy: Guerrilla Warfare in the West, 1861-1865,* Baton Rouge, LA: Louisiana State University Press, 1958, Louisiana Paperback Edition, 1984.

Castel, Albert, *William Clarke Quantrill: His Life and Times,* New York: Frederick Fell, Inc., 1962.

Castel, Albert, *A Frontier State at War: Kansas 1861-1865,* Lawrence, KS: Kansas Heritage Press, 1992.

Catton, Bruce, *Terrible Swift Sword,* Garden City, NY: Doubleday & Company, Inc., 1963.

Caudill, Harry M., *Night Comes to the Cumberlands: A Biography of a Depressed Area*, Boston: Little, Brown and Company, 1962.

Clark, Thomas D., *A History of Kentucky,* New York: Prentice-Hall, Inc., 1937.

Clausewitz, Karl von, *On War,* Baltimore: Penguin Books, 1968.

Clausewitz, Karl von, *On War*. London: Routledge & Kegan Paul, 1968.

Collins, Lewis and Richard H., *History of Kentucky*. 2 vols., Covington, KY: Collins & Co., 1874.

Connelly, Thomas Lawrence, *Autumn of Glory: The Army of Tennessee, 1862-1865*, Baton Rouge, LA: Louisiana State University Press, 1971.

Connelly, Thomas L., *Army of the Heartland: The Army of Tennessee, 1861-1862,* Baton Rouge, LA: Louisiana State University Press, 1967.

Connelly, William E., *Quantrill and the Border Wars,* Ottawa KS: Kansas Heritage Press, 1992.

Coulter, E. Merton, *The Civil War and Readjustment in Kentucky,* Chapel Hill, NC: The University of North Carolina Press, 1926; reprinted, Gloucester, MA: Peter Smith, 1966.

Craven, Avery, *The Growth of Southern Nationalism, 1848-1861,* Baton Rouge, LA: Louisiana State University Press, 1953.

Crawford, Samuel J., *Kansas in the Sixties,* Ottawa, KS: Kansas Heritage Press, 1994.

Dale, Edward E. & Litton, Gaston, *Cherokee Cavaliers: Forty Years of Cherokee History as Told in Correspondence of the Ridge-Watie-Boudinot Family,* Norman, OK: University of Oklahoma Press, 1996.

Davis, Jefferson, *The Rise and Fall of the Confederate Government*, Volume II, New York: De Capo Press, Inc., 1990.

Davis, William J., ed., *The Partisan Rangers of the Confederate Army,* Louisville, KY: Geo. G. Fetter Company, 1904; reprinted, Hartford, KY: McDowell Publications, 1979.

Dougan, Michael B., *Confederate Arkansas: The People and Policies of a Frontier State in Wartime,* University, AL: The University of Alabama Press, 1976.

Driver, Harold E., *Indians of North America,* 2d ed., Chicago: University of Chicago Press, 1969.

Duke, Basil W., *A History of Morgan's Cavalry*, Civil War Centennial Series, Edited by Cecil Fletcher Holland. Bloomington, IN: Indiana University Press, 1960.

Edwards, John N., *Noted Guerrillas or Warfare of the Border*, St. Louis, MO: J. W. Marsh, 1880.

Evans, Clement A., *Confederate Military History*, Volume IX, Atlanta: Confederate Publishing Company, 1899.

Fellman, Michael, *Inside War: The Guerrilla Conflict in Missouri During the American Civil War*, New York: Oxford University Press, 1989.

Goodrich, Thomas, *Black Flag: Guerrilla Warfare on the Western Border, 1861-1865,* Bloomington, IN: Indiana University Press, 1995.

Graham, Hugh Davis and Gurr, Ted Robert, *Violence in America: Historical and Comparative Perspectives,* 2 vols., A Report to the National Commission on the Causes and Prevention of Violence, Washington, DC: Government Printing Office, 1969.

Gray, Wood, *The Hidden Civil War: The Story of the Copperheads,* New York: The Viking Press, 1942.

Guevara, Che, *Guerrilla Warfare*, Lincoln, NE: University of Nebraska Press, 1985.

Halleck, Henry, *International Law or Rules Regulating the Intercourse of States in Peace and War*, New York: D. Van Nostrand, 1861.

Harrison, Lowell H., *The Civil War in Kentucky*, Lexington, KY: The University Press of Kentucky, 1975.

Hartigan, Richard Shelly, *Lieber's Code and the Law of War*, Chicago: Precedent Publishing, 1983.

Hattaway, Herman and Jones, Archer, *How the North Won: A Military History of the Civil War,* Urbana, IL: University of Illinois Press, 1983.

Horan, James D., *Confederate Agent: A Discovery in History*, New York: Crown Publishers, 1954.

Joes, Anthony James, *Guerrilla Conflict Before the Cold War*, Westport, CT: Praeger Publishers.

Jomini, Baron de, *The Art of War*, The West Point Military Library. Westport, CT: Greenwood Press, 1971.

Jomini, Baron de, *The Art of War,* Philadelphia: J.B. Lippincott, 1879.

Jones, Virgil Carrington, *Gray Ghosts and Rebel Raiders*, New York: Henry Holt & Co., 1956.

Keller, Allan, *Morgan's Raid,* New York: The Bobbs-Merrill Company, 1961.

Kinchen, Oscar A., *Confederate Operations in Canada and the North: A Little-Known Phase of the American Civil War,* North Quincy, MA: The Christopher Publishing House, 1970.

Kinchen, Oscar A., *Daredevils of the Confederate Army: The Story of the St. Alban's Raiders,* Boston: The Christopher Publishing House, 1959.

Kinchen, Oscar A., *General Bennett H. Young: Confederate Raider and a Man of Many Adventures,* West Hanover, MA: The Christopher Publishing House, 1981.

Laquer, Walter, *The Guerrilla Reader: A Historical Anthology,* Philadelphia: Temple University Press, 1977.

Laquer, Walter, *Guerrilla: A Historical and Critical Study,* Boston: Little, Brown and Company, 1976.

Lemke, W. J., ed., *The Robert Mecklin Letters,* Fayetteville, AR: Washington County Historical Society, 1955.

Leslie, Edward E., *The Devil Knows How to Ride: The True Story of William Clarke Quantrill and His Confederate Raiders,* New York: Random House, 1996.

Linderman, Gerald F., *Embattled Courage: The Experience of Combat in the American Civil War*. New York: The Free Press, 1987.

Lowenfels, Walter, *Walt Whitman's War*, New York: Alfred A. Knopf, 1960.

Mackey, Robert R., *The Uncivil War: Irregular Warfare in the Upper South, 1861-1865*, Norman: University of Oklahoma Press, 2004.

McCaslin, Richard B., *Tainted Breeze: The Great Hanging at Gainesville, Texas 1862*, Baton Rouge, LA: Louisiana State University Press, 1994.

McCorkle, John, *Three Years with Quantrill: A True Story Told by his Scout John McCorkle*, Norman, OK: University of Oklahoma Press, 1992.

McPherson, James M, *What They Fought For 1861-1865*, Baton Rouge, LA: Louisiana State University Press, 1994.

Millet, Alan R. and Maslowski, Peter, *For the Common Defense: A Military History of the United States Army*, New York: The Free Press, Inc., 1984.

Mountcastle, Clay, *Punitive War: Confederate Guerrillas and Union Reprisals*, Lawrence: University of Kansas Press, 2009.

Nichols, Bruce, *Guerrilla Warfare in Civil War Missouri, 1862*, Jefferson, NC: McFarland & Company, 2004.

Osanka, Franklin Mark, ed., *Modern Guerrilla Warfare: Fighting Communist Guerrilla Movements, 1941-1961*, New York: The Free Press, Inc., 1962.

Paludan, Phillip Shaw, *Victims: A True Story of the Civil War*, Knoxville, TN: The University of Tennessee Press, 1981.

Pickering, David and Falls, Judy, *Brush Men & Vigilantes: Civil War Dissent in Texas*, College Station: Texas A&M University Press, 2000.

Pioneers in God's Hills: A History of Fredericksburg and Gillespie County People and Events, Volume II, Fredericksburg, TX: Gillespie County Historical Society, 1974.

Sarkesian, Sam C., ed., *Revolutionary Guerrilla Warfare*, Chicago: Precedent Publishing, 1975.

Sensing, Thurman, *Champ Ferguson: Confederate Guerrilla*, Nashville, TN.: Vanderbilt University Press, 1942.

Shaler, Nathaniel S., *Kentucky: A Pioneer Commonwealth*, Boston: Houghton, Mifflin and Company, 1897.

Speed, Thomas, *The Union Cause in Kentucky, 1860-1865*, New York: G. P. Putnam's Sons, 1907

Sutherland, Daniel E., *A Savage Conflict: The Decisive Role of Guerrillas in the American Civil War*, Chapel Hill: The University of North Carolina Press, 2009.

Tapp, Hambleton and Klotter, James C., *Kentucky, Decades of Discord, 1865-1900*, Frankfort, KY: The Kentucky Historical Society, 1977.

Tarrant, E., *The Wild Riders of the First Kentucky Cavalry*, Louisville, KY: By the Author, 1894; reprinted, Lexington, KY: Henry Clay Press, 1969.

Watson, Thomas Shelby, *The Silent Riders*, Louisville, KY: Beechmont Press, 1971.

Williams, R. H. and Sansom, John W., *The Massacre on the Nueces River: The Story of a Civil War Tragedy*, Grand Prairie, TX: Frontier Times Publishing House, ca. 1911.

Wright, George C., *Life Behind a Veil: Blacks in Louisville, Kentucky, 1865-1930*, Baton Rouge, LA: Louisiana State University Press, 1985.

Young, Bennett H., *Confederate Wizards of the Saddle: Being Reminiscences and Observations of One Who Rode with Morgan*, Boston: Chapple Publishing Company, 1914; reprinted, Dayton, OH: Morningside Bookshop, 1979.

Secondary Works: Articles and Unpublished Papers

Alexander, Ronald Ray, "Central Kentucky During the Civil War, 1861-1865," Ph.D. Dissertation, University of Kentucky, 1976.

Barksdale, Ethelbert Courtland, "Semi-Regular and Irregular Warfare in the Civil War," Ph.D. Dissertation, University of Texas, 1941.

Barr, Alwyn, "Records of the Confederate Military Commission in San Antonio, July 2-October 10, 1862," *Southwestern Historical Quarterly* 70 (1966), 71 (1967), 73 (1969).

Belser, Thomas A. Jr., "Military Operations in Missouri and Arkansas, 1861-1865," Ph.D. Dissertation, Vanderbilt University, 1958.

Castel, Albert, "Order No. 11 and the Civil War on the Border," *Missouri Historical Review* 57 (1963).

Castel, Albert, "Quantrill's Missouri Bushwhackers in Kentucky," *The Filson Club History Quarterly* 38 (April 1964): 125-153.

Connelly, Thomas Lawrence, "Neo-Confederism or Power Vacuum: Post-War Kentucky Politics Reappraised," *The Register of the Kentucky Historical Society* 64 (October 1966): 257-269.

Copeland, James E., "Where Were the Kentucky Unionists and Secessionists?" *The Register of the Kentucky Historical Society* 71 (October 1973): 344-363.

De Falaise, Louis, "Gen. Stephen Gano Burbridge's Command in Kentucky," *The Register of the Kentucky Historical Society* 69 (April 1971): 101-127.

Dew, Aloma Williams, "Between the Hawk and the Buzzard: Owensboro During the Civil War," *The Register of the Kentucky Historical Society* 77 (Winter 1979): 1-14.

Doll, Howard D., "John Hunt Morgan and The Vidette," *The Filson Club History Quarterly* 47 (January 1973).

Gold, Gerald, "Gillespie County in the Civil War," *Junior Historian* 25 (January 1965).

Klotter, James C., "Feuds in Appalachia: An Overview," *The Filson Club History Quarterly* 56 (July 1982): 290-317.

Messmer, Charles, "Louisville During the Civil War," *The Filson Club History Quarterly* 52 (July 1978).

Meyer, Verdie, "Buergerkrieg Terror in Gillespie County," *Junior Historian* 22 (November 1961).

Smith, John David, "The Recruitment of Negro Soldiers in Kentucky, 1863-1865," *The Register of the Kentucky Historical Society* 72 (October 1974): 364-390.

Smyrl, Frank H., "Unionism, Abolitionism, and Vigilantism in Texas, 1856-1865," M.A. Thesis, University of Texas at Austin, 1961.

Tausch, Egon Richard, "Southern Sentiment Among the Texas Germans During the Civil War and Reconstruction," M.A. Thesis, University of Texas at Austin, 1965.

Valentine, L. L., "Sue Mundy of Kentucky," *The Register of the Kentucky Historical Society* 62 (July 1964): 175-205, (October 1964): 278-306.

Whitesell, Hunter B., "Military Operations in the Jackson Purchase Area of Kentucky," *The Register of the Kentucky Historical Society* 63 (April 1965): 141-167, (July 1965): 240-267, (October 1965): 323-348.

Newspapers

Ft. Smith New Era, 1865.

Louisville Daily Journal, 1863-1865.

APPENDIX A

General Orders No. 100

General Orders
No. 100

War Dept., Adjt. General's Office
Washington, April 24, 1863

The following "Instructions for the Government of Armies of the United States in the Field," prepared by Francis Lieber, LL.D., and revised by a board of officers, of which Major General E.A. Hitchcock is president, having been approved by the President of the United States, he commands that they be published for the information of all concerned.

By order of the Secretary of War:
E.D. Townsend
Assistant Adjutant-General

INSTRUCTIONS FOR THE GOVERNMENT OF ARMIES OF THE UNITED STATES IN THE FIELD.

Section I. Martial law – Military jurisdiction – Military necessity – Retaliation.

1. A place, district, or country occupied by an enemy stands, in consequence of the occupation, under the martial law of the invading or occupying army, whether any proclamation declaring martial law, or any public warning to the inhabitants, has been issued or not. Martial law is the immediate and direct effect and consequence of occupation or conquest.

    The presence of a hostile army proclaims its martial law.

2. Martial law does not cease during the hostile occupation, except by special proclamation, ordered by the commander-in-chief, or by special mention in the treaty of peace concluding the war, when the occupation of a place or territory continues beyond the conclusion of peace as one of the conditions of the same.

3. Martial law in a hostile country consists in the suspension by the occupying military authority of the criminal and civil law, and of the domestic administration and government in the occupied place or territory, and in the substitution of military rule and force for the same, as well as in the dictation of general laws, as far as military necessity requires this suspension, substitution, or dictation.

    The commander of the forces may proclaim that the administration of all civil and penal law shall continue either wholly or in part, as in times of peace, unless otherwise ordered by the military authority.

4. Martial law is simply military authority exercised in accordance with the laws and usages of war. Military oppression is not martial law; it is the abuse of the power which that law confers. As martial is executed by military force, it is incumbent upon those who administer it to be strictly guided by the principles of justice, honor, and humanity — virtues adorning a soldier even more than other men, for the very reason that he possesses the power of his arms against the unarmed.

5. Martial law should be less stringent in places and countries fully occupied and fairly conquered. Much greater severity may be exercised in places or regions where actual hostilities exist or are expected and must be prepared for. Its most complete sway is allowed — even in the commander's own country — when face to face with the enemy, because of the absolute necessities of the case, and of the paramount duty to defend the country against invasion.

To save the country is paramount to all other considerations.

6. All civil and penal law shall continue to take its usual course in the enemy's places and territories under martial law, unless interrupted or stopped by order of the occupying military power; but all the functions of the hostile government — legislative, executive, or administrative — whether of a general, provincial, or local character, cease under martial law, or continue only with the sanction, or, if deemed necessary, the participation of the occupier or invader.

7. Martial law extends to property, and to persons, whether they are subjects of the enemy or aliens to that government.

8. Consuls, among American and European nations, are not diplomatic agents. Nevertheless, their offices and persons will be subjected to martial law in cases of urgent necessity only; their property and business are not exempted. Any delinquency they commit against the established military rule may be punished as in the case of any other inhabitant, and such punishment furnishes no reasonable ground for international complaint.

9. The functions of ambassadors, ministers, or other diplomatic agents, accredited by neutral powers to the hostile government, cease, so far as regards the displaced government; but the conquering or occupying power usually recognizes them as temporarily accredited to itself.

10. Martial law affects chiefly the police and collection of public revenue and taxes, whether imposed by the expelled government or by the invader, and refers mainly to the support and efficiency of the Army, its safety, and the safety of its operations.

11. The law of war does not only disclaim all cruelty and bad faith concerning engagements concluded with the enemy during the war, but also the breaking of stipulations solemnly contracted by the belligerents in time of peace, and avowedly intended to remain in force in case of war between the contracting powers.

It disclaims all extortions and other transactions for individual gain; all acts of private revenge, or connivance at such acts.

Offenses to the contrary shall be severely punished, and especially so if committed by officers.

12. Whenever feasible, martial law is carried out in cases of individual offenders by military courts; but sentences of death shall be executed only with the approval of the chief executive, provided the urgency of the case does not require a speeder execution, and then only with the approval of the chief commander.

13. Military jurisdiction is of two kinds: First, that which is conferred and defined by statute; second, that which is derived from the common law of war. Military offenses under the statute law must be tried in the manner therein directed; but military offenses which do not come within the statute must be tried and punished under the common law of war. The character of the courts which exercise these jurisdictions depends upon the local laws of each particular country.

In the armies of the United States the first is exercised by courts-martial; while cases which do not come within the Rules and Articles of War, or the jurisdiction conferred by statute on courts-martial, are tried by military commissions.

14. Military necessity, as understood by modern civilized nations, consists in the necessity of those measures which are indispensable for securing the ends of the war, and which are lawful according to the modern law and usages of war.

15. Military necessity admits of all direct destruction of life or limb of armed enemies, and of other persons whose destruction is incidentally unavoidable in the armed contests of the war; it allows of the capturing of every armed enemy, and every enemy of importance to the hostile government, or of peculiar danger to the captor; it allows of all destruction of property, and obstruction of the ways and channels of traffic, travel, or communications, and of all withholding of sustenance or means of life from the enemy; of the appropriation of whatever an enemy's country affords necessary for the subsistence and safety of the Army, and of such deception as does not involve the breaking of good faith either positively pledged, regarding agreements entered into during the war, or supposed by the modern law of war to exist. Men who take up arms against one another in public war do not cease on this account to be moral beings, responsible to one another and to God.

16. Military necessity does not admit of cruelty — that is, the infliction of suffering for the sake of suffering or for revenge, nor of maiming or wounding except in fight, nor of torture to extort confessions. It does not admit of the use of poison in any way, nor of the wanton devastation of a district. It admits of deception, but disclaims acts of perfidy; and, in general, military necessity does not include any act of hostility which makes the return to peace unnecessarily difficult.

17. War is not carried on by arms alone. It is lawful to starve the hostile belligerent, armed or unarmed, so that it leads to the speedier subjection of the enemy.

18. When a commander of a besieged place expels the non-combatants, in order to lessen the number of those who consume his stock of provisions, it is lawful, though an extreme measure, to drive them back, so as to hasten on the surrender.

19. Commanders, whenever admissible, inform the enemy of their intention to bombard a place, so that the non-combatants, and especially the women and children, may be removed before the bombardment commences. But it is no infraction of the common law of war to omit thus to inform the enemy. Surprise may be a necessity.

20. Public war is a state of armed hostility between sovereign nations or governments. It is a law and requisite of civilized existence that men live in political, continuous societies, forming organized units, called states or nations, whose constituents bear, enjoy, and suffer, advance and retrograde together, in peace and in war.

21. The citizen or native of a hostile country is thus an enemy, as one of the constituents of the hostile state or nation, and as such is subjected to the hardships of the war.

22. Nevertheless, as civilization has advanced during the last centuries, so has likewise steadily advanced, especially in war on land, the distinction between the private individual belonging to a hostile country and the hostile country itself, with its men in arms. The principle has been more and more acknowledged that the unarmed citizen is to be spared in person, property, and honor as much as the exigencies of war will admit.

23. Private citizens are no longer murdered, enslaved, or carried off to distant parts, and the inoffensive individual is as little disturbed in his private relations as the commander of the hostile troops can afford to grant in the overruling demands of a vigorous war.

24. The almost universal rule in remote times was, and continues to be with barbarous armies, that the private individual of the hostile country is destined to suffer every privation of liberty and protection and every disruption of family ties. Protection was, and still is with uncivilized people, the exception.

25. In modern regular wars of the Europeans and their descendants in other portions of the globe, protection of the inoffensive citizen of the hostile country is the rule; privation and disturbance of private relations are the exceptions.

26. Commanding generals may cause the magistrates and civil officers of the hostile country to take the oath of temporary allegiance or an oath of fidelity to their own victorious government or rulers, and they may expel everyone who declines to do so. But whether they do so or not, the people and their civil officers owe strict obedience to them as long as they hold sway over the district or country, at the peril of their lives.

27. The law of war can no more wholly dispense with retaliation than can the law of nations, of which it is a branch. Yet civilized nations acknowledge retaliation as the sternest feature of war. A reckless enemy often leaves to his opponent no other means of securing himself against the repetition of barbarous outrage.

28. Retaliation will therefore never be resorted to as a measure of mere revenge, but only as a means of protective retribution, and moreover cautiously and unavoidably — that is to say, retaliation shall only be resorted to after careful inquiry into the real occurrence and the character of the misdeeds that may demand retribution.

Unjust or inconsiderate retaliation removes the belligerents farther and farther from the mitigating rules of regular war, and by rapid steps leads them nearer to the internecine wars of savages.

29. Modern times are distinguished from earlier ages by the existence at one and the same time of many nations and great governments related to one another in close intercourse.

Peace is their normal condition; war is the exception. The ultimate object of all modern war is a renewed state of peace.

The more vigorously wars are pursued the better it is for humanity. Sharp wars are brief.

30. Ever since the formation and coexistence of modern nations, and ever since wars have become great national wars, war has come to be acknowledged not to be its own end, but the means to obtain great ends of state, or to consist in defense against wrong; and no conventional restriction of the modes adopted to injure the enemy is any longer admitted; but the law of war imposes many limitations and restrictions on principles of justice, faith, and honor.

SECTION II. *Public and private property of the enemy – Protection of persons, and especially of women; of religion, the arts and sciences – Punishment of crimes against the inhabitants of hostile countries.*

31. A victorious army appropriates all public money, seizes all public movable property until further direction by its government, and sequesters for its own benefit or of that of its government all the revenues of real property belonging to the hostile government or nation. The title to such real property remains in abeyance during military occupation, and until the conquest is made complete.

32. A victorious army, by the martial power inherent in the same, may suspend, change, or abolish, as far as the martial power extends, the relations which arise from the services due, according to the existing laws of the invaded country, from one citizen, subject, or native of the same to another.

The commander of the army must leave it to the ultimate treaty of peace to settle the permanency of this change.

33. It is no longer considered lawful — on the contrary, it is held to be a serious breach of the law of war — to force the subjects of the enemy into the service of the victorious government, except the latter should proclaim, after a fair and complete conquest of the hostile country or district, that it is resolved to keep the country, district, or place permanently as its own and make it a portion of its own country.

34. As a general rule, the property belonging to churches, to hospitals, or other establishments of an exclusively charitable character, to establishments of education, or foundations for the promotion of knowledge, whether public schools, universities, academies of learning or observatories, museums of the fine arts, or of a scientific character — such property is not to be considered public property in the sense of paragraph 31; but it may be taxed or used when the public service may require it.

35. Classical works of art, libraries, scientific collections, or precious instruments, such as astronomical telescopes, as well as hospitals, must be secured against all avoidable injury, even when they are contained in fortified places whilst besieged or bombarded.

36. If such works of art, libraries, collections, or instruments belonging to a hostile nation or government, can be removed without injury, the ruler of the conquering state or nation may order them to be seized and removed for the benefit of the said nation. The ultimate ownership is to be settled by the ensuring treaty of peace.

In no case shall they be sold or given away, if captured by the armies of the United States, nor shall they ever be privately appropriated, or wantonly destroyed or injured.

37. The United States acknowledge and protect, in hostile countries occupied by them, religion and morality; strictly private property; the persons of the inhabitants, especially those of women; and the sacredness of domestic relations. Offenses to the contrary shall be rigorously punished.

This rule does not interfere with the right of the victorious invader to tax the people or their property, to levy forced loans, to billet soldiers, or to appropriate property, especially houses, lands, boats or ships, and the churches, for temporary and military uses.

38. Private property, unless forfeited by crimes or by offenses of the owner, can be seized only by way of military necessity, for the support or other benefit of the Army or of the United States.

If the owner has not fled, the commanding officer will cause receipts to be given, which may serve the spoliated owner to obtain indemnity.

39. The salaries of civil officers of the hostile government who remain in the invaded territory, and continue the work of their office, and can continue it according to the

circumstances arising out of the war — such as judges, administrative or political officers, officers of city or communal governments — are paid from the public revenue of the invaded territory until the military government has reason wholly or partially to discontinue it. Salaries or incomes connected with purely honorary titles are always stopped.

40. There exists no law or body of authoritative rules of action between hostile armies, except that branch of the law of nature and nations which is called the law and usages of war on land.

41. All municipal law of the ground on which the armies stand, or of the countries to which they belong, is silent and of no effect between armies in the field.

42. Slavery, complicating and confounding the ideas of property (that is, of a thing), and of personality (that is, of humanity), exists according to municipal or local law only. The law of nature and nations has never acknowledged it. The digest of the Roman law enacts the early dictum of the pagan jurist, that "so far as the law of nature is concerned, all men are equal." Fugitives escaping from a country in which they were slaves, villains, or serfs, into another country, have, for centuries past, been held free and acknowledged free by judicial decisions of European countries, even though the municipal law of the country in which the slave had taken refuge acknowledged slavery within its own dominion.

43. Therefore, in a war between the United States and a belligerent which admits of slavery, if a person held in bondage by that belligerent be captured by or come as a fugitive under the protection of the military forces of the United States, such person is immediately entitled to the rights and privileges of a freeman. To return such person into slavery would amount to enslaving a free person, and neither the United States nor any officer under their authority can enslave any human being. Moreover, a person so made free by the law of war is under the shield of the law of nations, and the former owner or State can have, by the law of postliminy, no belligerent lien or claim of service.

44. All wanton violence committed against persons in the invaded country, all destruction of property not commanded by the authorized officer, all robbery, all pillage or sacking, even after taking a place by main force, all rape, wounding, maiming, or killing of such inhabitants, are prohibited under the penalty of death, or such other severe punishment as may seem adequate for the gravity of the offense.

A soldier, officer, or private, in the act of committing such violence, and disobeying a superior ordering him to abstain from it, may be lawfully killed on the spot by such superior.

45. All captures and booty belong, according to the modern law of war, primarily to the government of the captor.

Prize money, whether on sea or land, can now only be claimed under local law.

46. Neither officers nor soldiers are allowed to make use of their position or power in the hostile country for private gain, not even for commercial transactions otherwise legitimate.

Offenses to the contrary committed by commissioned officers will be punished with cashiering or such other punishment as the nature of the offense may require; if by soldiers, they shall be punished according to the nature of the offense.

47. Crimes punishable by all penal codes, such as arson, murder, maiming, assaults, highway robbery, theft, burglary, fraud, forgery, and rape, if committed by an American soldier in a hostile country against its inhabitants, are not only punishable as at home, but in all cases in which death in not inflicted the severer punishment shall be preferred.

S<small>ECTION</small> *III. Deserters – Prisoners of war – Hostages – Booty on the battlefield.*

48. Deserters from the American Army, having entered the service of the enemy, suffer death if they fall again into the hands of the United States, whether by capture or being delivered up to the American Army; and if a deserter from the enemy, having taken service in the Army of the United States, is captured by the enemy, and punished by them with death or otherwise, it is not a breach against the law and usages of war, requiring redress or retaliation.

49. A prisoner of war is a public enemy armed or attached to the hostile army for active aid, who has fallen into the hands of the captor, either fighting or wounded, on the field or in the hospital, by individual surrender or by capitulation.

All soldiers, of whatever species of arms; all men who belong to the rising en masse of the hostile country; all those who are attached to the Army for its efficiency and promote directly the object of the war, except such as are hereinafter provided for; all disabled men or officers on the field or elsewhere, if captured; all enemies who have thrown away their arms and ask for quarter, are prisoners of war, and as such exposed to the inconveniences as well as entitled to the privileges of a prisoner of war.

50. Moreover, citizens who accompany an army for whatever purpose, such as sutlers, editors, or reporters of journals, or contractors, if captured, may be made prisoners of war and be detained as such.

The monarch and members of the hostile reigning family, male or female, the chief, and chief officers of the hostile government, its diplomatic agents, and all persons who are of particular and singular use and benefit to the hostile army or its government, are, if captured on belligerent ground, and if unprovided with a safe-conduct granted by the captor's government, prisoners of war.

51. If the people of that portion of an invaded country which is not yet occupied by the enemy, or of the whole country, at the approach of a hostile army, rise, under a duly authorized levy, en masse to resist the invader, they are now treated as public enemies, and, if captured, are prisoners of war.

52. No belligerent has the right to declare that he will treat every captured man in arms of a levy en masse as a brigand or bandit.

If, however, the people of a country, or any portion of the same, already occupied by an army, rise against it, they are violators of the laws of war and are not entitled to their protection.

53. The enemy's chaplains, officers of the medical staff, apothecaries, hospital nurses, and servants, if they fall into the hands of the American Army, are not prisoners of war, unless the commander has reasons to retain them. In this latter case, or if, at their own desire, they are allowed to remain with their captured companions, they are treated as prisoners of war and may be exchanged if the commander sees fit.

54. A hostage is a person accepted as a pledge for the fulfillment of an agreement concluded between belligerents during the war, or in consequence of a war. Hostages are rare in the present age.

55. If a hostage is accepted, he is treated like a prisoner of war, according to rank and condition, as circumstances may admit.

56. A prisoner of war is subject to no punishment for being a public enemy, nor is any revenge wreaked upon him by the intentional infliction of any suffering, or disgrace, by cruel imprisonment, want of food, by mutilation, death, or any other barbarity.

57. So soon as a man is armed by a sovereign government and takes the soldier's oath of fidelity he is a belligerent; his killing, wounding, or other warlike acts are no individual crimes or offenses. No belligerent has a right to declare that enemies of a certain class, color, or condition, when properly organized as soldiers, will not be treated by him as public enemies.

58. The law of nations knows of no distinction of color, and if an enemy of the United States should enslave and sell any captured persons of their Army, it would be a case for the severest retaliation, if not redressed upon complaint.

The United States cannot retaliate by enslavement; therefore death must be the retaliation for this crime against the law of nations.

59. A prisoner of war remains answerable for his crimes committed against the captor's army or people, committed before he was captured, and for which he has not been punished by his own authorities.

All prisoners of war are liable to the infliction of retaliatory measures.

60. It is against the usage of modern war to resolve, in hatred and revenge, to give no quarter. No body of troops has the right to declare that it will not give, and therefore will not expect, quarter; but a commander is permitted to direct his troops to give no quarter, in great straits, when his own salvation makes it impossible to cumber himself with prisoners.

61. Troops that give no quarter have no right to kill enemies already disabled on the ground, or prisoners captured by other troops.

62. All troops of the enemy known or discovered to give no quarter in general, or to any portion of the Army, receive none.

63. Troops who fight in the uniform of their enemies, without any plain, striking, and uniform mark of distinction of their own, can expect no quarter.

64. If American troops capture a train containing uniforms of the enemy, and the commander considers it advisable to distribute them for use among his men, some striking mark or sign must be adopted to distinguish the American soldier from the enemy.

65. The use of the enemy's national standard, flag, or other emblem of nationality, for the purpose of deceiving the enemy in battle, is an act of perfidy by which they lose all claim to the protection of the laws of war.

66. Quarter having been given to an enemy by American troops, under a misapprehension of his true character, he may, nevertheless, be ordered to suffer death if, within three days after the battle, it be discovered that he belongs to a corps which gives no quarter.

67. The law of nations allows every sovereign government to make war upon another sovereign State, and, therefore, admits of no rules or laws different from those of regular warfare, regarding the treatment of prisoners of war, although they may belong to the army of a government which the captor may consider as a wanton and unjust assailant.

68. Modern wars are not internecine wars, in which the killing of the enemy is the object. The destruction of the enemy in modern war, and, indeed, modern war itself, are means to obtain that object of the belligerent which lies beyond the war.

Unnecessary or revengeful destruction of life is not lawful.

69. Outposts, sentinels, or pickets are not to be fired upon, except to drive them in, or when a positive order, special or general, has been issued to that effect.

70. The use of poison in any manner, be it to poison wells, or food, or arms, is wholly excluded from modern warfare. He that uses it puts himself out of the pale of the law and usages of war.

71. Whoever intentionally inflicts additional wounds on an enemy already wholly disabled, or kills such an enemy, or who orders or encourages soldiers to do so, shall suffer death, if duly convicted, whether he belongs to the Army of the United States, or is an enemy captured after having committed his misdeed.

72. Money and other valuables on the person of a prisoner, such as watches or jewelry, as well as extra clothing, are regarded by the American Army as the private property of the

prisoner, and the appropriation of such valuables or money is considered dishonorable, and is prohibited.

Nevertheless, if large sums are found upon the persons of prisoners, or in their possession, they shall be taken from them, and the surplus, after providing for their own support, appropriated for the use of the Army, under the direction of the commander, unless otherwise ordered by the Government. Nor can prisoners claim, as private property, large sums found and captured in their train, although they have been placed in the private luggage of the prisoners.

73. All officers, when captured, must surrender their side-arms to the captor. They may be restored to the prisoner in marked cases, by the commander, to signalize admiration of his distinguished bravery, or approbation of his humane treatment of prisoners before his capture. The captured officer to whom they may be restored cannot wear them during captivity.

74. A prisoner of war, being a public enemy, is the prisoner of the Government and not of the captor. No ransom can be paid by a prisoner of war to his individual captor, or to any officer in command. The Government alone releases captives, according to rules prescribed by itself.

75. Prisoners of war are subject to confinement or imprisonment such as may be deemed necessary on account of safety, but they are to be subjected to no other intentional suffering or indignity. The confinement and mode of treating a prisoner may be varied during his captivity according to the demands of safety.

76. Prisoners of war shall be fed upon plain and wholesome food, whenever practicable, and treated with humanity.

They may be required to work for the benefit of the captor's government, according to their rank and condition.

77. A prisoner of war who escapes may be shot, or otherwise killed, in his flight; but neither death nor any other punishment shall be inflicted upon him simply for his attempt to escape, which the law of war does not consider a crime. Stricter means of security shall be used after an unsuccessful attempt at escape.

If, however, a conspiracy is discovered, the purpose of which is a united or general escape, the conspirators may be rigorously punished, even with death; and capital punishment may also be inflicted upon prisoners of war discovered to have plotted rebellion against the authorities of the captors, whether in union with fellow-prisoners or other persons.

78. If prisoners of war, having given no pledge nor made any promise on their honor, forcibly or otherwise escape, and are captured again in battle, after having rejoined their own army, they shall not be punished for their escape, but shall be treated as simple prisoners of war, although they will be subjected to stricter confinement.

79. Every captured wounded enemy shall be medically treated, according to the ability of the medical staff.

80. Honorable men, when captured, will abstain from giving to the enemy information concerning their own army, and the modern law of war permits no longer the use of any violence against prisoners in order to extort the desired information, or to punish them for having given false information.

Section IV. Partisans – Armed enemies not belonging to the hostile army – Scouts – Armed prowlers – War-rebels.

81. Partisans are soldiers armed and wearing the uniform of their army, but belonging to a corps which acts detached from the main body for the purpose of making inroads into the territory occupied by the enemy. If captured they are entitled to all the privileges of the prisoner of war.

82. Men, or squads of men, who commit hostilities, whether by fighting, or inroads for destruction or plunder, or by raids of any kind, without commission, without being part and portion of the organized hostile army, and without sharing continuously in the war, but who do so with intermitting returns to their homes and avocations, or with the occasional assumption of the semblance of peaceful pursuits, divesting themselves of the character or appearance of soldiers — such men, or squads of men, are not public enemies, and therefore, if captured, are not entitled to the privileges of prisoners of war, but shall be treated summarily as highway robbers or pirates.

83. Scouts or single soldiers, if disguised in the dress of the country, or in the uniform of the army hostile to their own, employed in obtaining information, if found within or lurking about the lines of the captor, are treated as spies, and suffer death.

84. Armed prowlers, by whatever names they may be called, or persons of the enemy's territory, who steal within the lines of the hostile army for the purpose of robbing, killing, or of destroying bridges, roads, or canals, or of robbing or destroying the mail, or of cutting the telegraph wires, are not entitled to the privileges of the prisoner of war.

85. War-rebels are persons within an occupied territory who rise in arms against the occupying or conquering army, or against the authorities established by the same. If captured, they may suffer death, whether they rise singly, in small or large bands, and whether called upon to do so by their own, but expelled, government or not. They are not prisoners of war; nor are they if discovered and secured before their conspiracy has matured to an actual rising or to armed violence.

SECTION V. *Safe-conduct – Spies – War-traitors – Captured messengers – Abuse of the flag of truce.*

86. All intercourse between the territories occupied by belligerent armies, whether by traffic, by letter, by travel, or in any other way, ceases. This is the general rule, to be observed without special proclamation.

Exceptions to this rule, whether by safe-conduct or permission to trade on a small or large scale, or by exchanging mails, or by travel from one territory into the other, can take place only according to agreement approved by the Government or by the highest military authority.

Contraventions of this rule are highly punishable.

87. Ambassadors, and all other diplomatic agents of neutral powers accredited to the enemy may receive safe-conducts through the territories occupied by the belligerents, unless there are military reasons to the contrary, and unless they may reach the place of their destination conveniently by another route. It implies no international affront if the safe-conduct is declined. Such passes are usually given by the supreme authority of the state and not by subordinate officers.

88. A spy is a person who secretly, in disguise or under false pretense, seeks information with the intention of communicating it to the enemy.

The spy is punishable with death by hanging by the neck, whether or not he succeed in obtaining the information or in conveying it to the enemy.

89. If a citizen of the United States obtains information in a legitimate manner and betrays it to the enemy, be he a military or civil officer, or a private citizen, he shall suffer death.

90. A traitor under the law of war, or a war-traitor, is a person in a place or district under martial law who, unauthorized by the military commander, gives information of any kind to the enemy, or holds intercourse with him.

91. The war-traitor is always severely punished. If his offense consists in betraying to the enemy anything concerning the condition, safety, operations, or plans of the troops holding or occupying the place or district, his punishment is death.

92. If the citizen or subject of a country or place invaded or conquered gives information to his own government, from which he is separated by the hostile army, or to the army of his government, he is a war-traitor, and death is the penalty of his offense.

93. All armies in the field stand in need of guides, and impress them if they cannot obtain them otherwise.

94. No person having been forced by the enemy to serve as guide is punishable for having done so.

95. If a citizen of a hostile and invaded district voluntarily serves as a guide to the enemy, or offers to do so, he is deemed a war-traitor and shall suffer death.

96. A citizen serving voluntarily as a guide against his own country commits treason, and will be dealt with according to the law of his country.

97. Guides, when it is clearly proved that they have misled intentionally, may be put to death.

98. All unauthorized or secret communication with the enemy is considered treasonable by the law of war.

Foreign residents in an invaded or occupied territory or foreign visitors in the same can claim no immunity from this law. They may communicate with foreign parts or with the inhabitants of the hostile country, so far as the military authority permits, but no further. Instant expulsion from the occupied territory would be the very least punishment for the infraction of this rule.

99. A messenger carrying written dispatches or verbal messages from one portion of the army or from a besieged place to another portion of the same army or its government, if armed, and in the uniform of his army, and if captured while doing so in the territory occupied by the enemy, is treated by the captor as a prisoner of war. If not in uniform nor a soldier, the circumstances connected with his capture must determine the disposition that shall be made of him,

100. A messenger or agent who attempts to steal through the territory occupied by the enemy to further in any manner the interests of the enemy, if captured, is not entitled to the privileges of the prisoner of war, and may be dealt with according to the circumstances of the case.

101. While deception in war is admitted as a just and necessary means of hostility, and is consistent with honorable warfare, the common law of war allows even capital punishment for clandestine or treacherous attempts to injure an enemy, because they are so dangerous, and it is so difficult to guard against them.

102. The law of war, like the criminal law regarding other offenses, makes no difference on account of the difference of sexes, concerning the spy, the war-traitor, or the war-rebel.

103. Spies, war-traitors, and war-rebels are not exchanged according to the common law of war. The exchange of such persons would require a special cartel, authorized by the Government, or, at a great distance from it, by the chief commander of the army in the field.

104. A successful spy or war-traitor, safely returned to his own army, and afterward captured as an enemy, is not subject to punishment for his acts as a spy or war-traitor, but he may be held in closer custody as a person individually dangerous.

Section VI. Exchange of prisoners – Flags of truce – Flags of protection.

105. Exchanges of prisoners take place — number for number — rank for rank — wounded for wounded — with added condition for added condition – such, for instance, as not to serve for a certain period.

106. In exchanging prisoners of war, such numbers of persons of inferior rank may be substituted as an equivalent for one of superior rank as may be agreed upon by cartel, which requires the sanction of the Government, or of the commander of the army in the field.

107. A prisoner of war is in honor bound truly to state to the captor his rank; and he is not to assume a lower rank than belongs to him, in order to cause a more advantageous exchange, nor a higher rank, for the purpose of obtaining better treatment.

Offenses to the contrary have been justly punished by the commanders of released prisoners, and may be good cause for refusing to release such prisoners.

108. The surplus number of prisoners of war remaining after an exchange has taken place is sometimes released either for the payment of a stipulated sum of money, or, in urgent cases, of provision, clothing, or other necessaries.

Such arrangement, however, requires the sanction of the highest authority.

109. The exchange of prisoners of war is an act of convenience to both belligerents. If no general cartel has been concluded, it cannot be demanded by either of them. No belligerent is obliged to exchange prisoners of war.

A cartel is voidable as soon as either party has violated it.

110. No exchange of prisoners shall be made except after complete capture, and after an accurate account of them, and a list of the captured officers, has been taken.

111. The bearer of flag of truce cannot insist upon being admitted. He must always be admitted with great caution. Unnecessary frequency is carefully to be avoided.

112. If the bearer of a flag of truce offer himself during an engagement, he can be admitted as a very rare exception only. It is no breach of good faith to retain such flag of truce, if admitted during the engagement. Firing is not required to cease on the appearance of a flag of truce in battle.

113. If the bearer of a flag of truce, presenting himself during an engagement, is killed or wounded, it furnishes no ground of complaint whatever.

114. If it be discovered, and fairly proved, that a flag of truce has been abused for surreptitiously obtaining military knowledge, the bearer of the flag thus abusing his sacred character is deemed a spy.

So sacred is the character of a flag of truce, and so necessary is its sacredness, that while its abuse is an especially heinous offense, great caution is requisite, on the other hand, in convicting the bearer of a flag of truce as a spy.

115. It is customary to designate by certain flags (usually yellow) the hospitals in places which are shelled, so that the besieging enemy may avoid firing on them. The same has been done in battles when hospitals are situated within the field of engagement.

116. Honorable belligerents often request that the hospitals within the territory of the enemy may be designated, so that they may be spared.

An honorable belligerent allows himself to be guided by flags or signals of protection as much as the contingencies and the necessities of the fight will permit.

117. It is justly considered an act of bad faith, of infamy or fiendishness, to deceive the enemy by flags of protection. Such act of bad faith may be good cause for refusing to respect such flags.

118. The besieging belligerent has sometimes requested the besieged to designate the buildings containing collections of works of art, scientific museums, astronomical observatories, or precious libraries, so that their destruction may be avoided as much as possible.

SECTION VII. *The parole.*

119. Prisoners of war may be released from captivity by exchange, and, under certain circumstances, also by parole.

120. The term parole designates the pledge of individual good faith and honor to do, or to omit doing, certain acts after he who gives his parole shall have been dismissed, wholly or partially, from the power of the captor.

121. The pledge of the parole is always an individual, but not a private act.

122. The parole applies chiefly to prisoners of war whom the captor allows to return to their country, or to live in greater freedom within the captor's country or territory, on conditions stated in the parole.

123. Release of prisoners of war by exchange is the general rule; release by parole is the exception.

124. Breaking the parole is punished with death when the person breaking the parole is captured again.

Accurate lists, therefore, of the paroled persons must be kept by the belligerents.

125. When paroles are given and received there must be an exchange of two written documents, in which the name and rank of the paroled individuals are accurately and truthfully stated.

126. Commissioned officers only are allowed to give their parole, and they can give it only with the permission of their superior, as long as a superior in rank is within reach.

127. No non-commissioned officer or private can give his parole except through an officer. Individual paroles not given through an officer are not only void, but subject the individuals giving them to the punishment of death as deserters. The only admissible exception is where individuals, properly separated from their commands, have suffered long confinement without the possibility of being paroled through an officer.

128. No paroling on the battle-field; no paroling of entire bodies of troops after a battle; and no dismissal of large numbers of prisoners, with a general declaration that they are paroled, is permitted, or of any value.

129. In capitulations for the surrender of strong places or fortified camps the commanding officer, in cases of urgent necessity, may agree that the troops under his command shall not fight again during the war unless exchanged.

130. The usual pledge given in the parole is not to serve during the existing war unless exchanged.

This pledge refers only to the active service in the field against the paroling belligerent or his allies actively engaged in the same war. These cases of breaking the parole are patent acts, and can be visited with the punishment of death; but the pledge does not refer to internal service, such as recruiting or drilling the recruits, fortifying places not besieged, quelling civil commotions, fighting against belligerents unconnected with the paroling belligerents, or to civil or diplomatic service for which the paroled officer may be employed.

131. If the government does not approve of the parole, the paroled officer must return into captivity, and should the enemy refuse to receive him he is free of his parole.

132. A belligerent government may declare, by a general order, whether it will allow paroling and on what conditions it will allow it. Such order is communicated to the enemy.

133. No prisoner of war can be forced by the hostile government to parole himself, and no government is obliged to parole prisoners of war or to parole all captured officers, if it paroles any. As the pledging of the parole is an individual act, so is paroling, on the other hand, an act of choice on the part of the belligerent.

134. The commander of an occupying army may require of the civil officers of the enemy, and of its citizens, any pledge he may consider necessary for the safety or security of his army, and upon their failure to give it he may arrest, confine, or detain them.

SECTION VIII. *Armistice – Capitulation.*

135. An armistice is the cessation of active hostilities for a period agreed between belligerents. It must be agreed upon in writing and duly ratified by the highest authorities of the contending parties.

136. If an armistice be declared without conditions it extends no further than to require a total cessation of hostilities along the front of both belligerents.

If conditions be agreed upon, they should be clearly expressed, and must be rigidly adhered to by both parties. If either party violates any express condition, the armistice may be declared null and void by the other.

137. An armistice may be general, and valid for all points and lines of the belligerents; or special — that is, referring to certain troops or certain localities only.

An armistice may be concluded for a definite period of time; or for an indefinite time, during which either belligerent may resume hostilities on giving the notice agreed upon to the other.

138. The motives which induce the one or the other belligerent to conclude an armistice, whether it be expected to be preliminary to a treaty of peace, or to prepare during the armistice for a more vigorous prosecution of the war, does in no way affect the character of the armistice itself.

139. An armistice is binding upon the belligerents from the day of the agreed commencement; but the officers of the armies are responsible from the day only when they receive official information of its existence.

140. Commanding officers have the right to conclude armistices binding on the district over which their command extends, but such armistice is subject to the ratification of the superior authority, and ceases so soon as it is made known to the enemy that the armistice is not ratified, even if a certain time for the elapsing between giving the notice of cessation and the resumption of hostilities should have been stipulated for.

141. It is incumbent upon the contracting parties of an armistice to stipulate what intercourse of persons or traffic between the inhabitants of the territories occupied by the hostile armies shall be allowed, if any.

If nothing is stipulated the intercourse remains suspended, as during actual hostilities.

142. An armistice is not a partial or a temporary peace; it is only the suspension of military operations to the extent agreed upon by the parties.

143. When an armistice is concluded between a fortified place and the army besieging it, it is agreed by all the authorities on this subject that the besieger must cease all extension, perfection, or advance of his attacking works as much so as from attacks by main force.

But as there is a difference of opinion among martial jurists whether the besieged have a right to repair breaches or to erect new works of defense within the place during an armistice, this point should be determined by express agreement between the parties.

144. So soon as a capitulation is signed the capitulator has no right to demolish, destroy, or injure the works, arms, stores, or ammunition in his possession, during the time which elapses between the signing and the execution of capitulation, unless otherwise stipulated in the same.

145. When an armistice is clearly broken by one of the parties the other party is released from all obligation to observe it.

146. Prisoners taken in the act of breaking an armistice must be treated as prisoners of war, the officer alone being responsible who gives the order for such a violation of an armistice. The highest authority of the belligerent aggrieved may demand redress for the infraction of an armistice.

147. Belligerents sometimes conclude an armistice while their plenipotentiaries are met to discuss the conditions of a treaty of peace; but plenipotentiaries may meet without a preliminary armistice; in the latter case the war is carried on without any abatement.

Section IX. Assassination.

148. The law of war does not allow proclaiming either an individual belonging to the hostile army, or a citizen, or a subject of the hostile government an outlaw, who may be slain without trial by any captor, any more than the modern law of peace allows such international outlawry; on the contrary, it abhors such outrage. The sternest retaliation should follow the murder committed in consequence of such proclamation, made by whatever authority. Civilized nations look with horror upon offers of rewards for the assassination of enemies as relapses into barbarism.

Section X. Insurrection – Civil war – Rebellion.

149. Insurrection is the rising of people in arms against their government, or a portion of it, or against one or more of its laws, or against an officer or officers of the government. It may be confined to mere armed resistance, or it may have greater ends in view.

150. Civil war is war between two or more portions of a country or state, each contending for the mastery of the whole, and each claiming to be the legitimate government. The term is

also sometimes applied to war of rebellion, when the rebellious provinces or portions of the state are contiguous to those containing the seat of government.

151.   The term rebellion is applied to an insurrection of large extent, and is usually a war between the legitimate government of a country and portions of provinces of the same who seek to throw off their allegiance to it and set up a government of their own.

152.   When humanity induces the adoption of the rules of regular war toward rebels, whether the adoption is partial or entire, it does in no way whatever imply a partial or complete acknowledgment of their government, if they have set up one, or of them, as an independent or sovereign power. Neutrals have no right to make the adoption of the rules of war by the assailed government toward rebels the ground of their own acknowledgment of the revolted people as an independent power.

153.   Treating captured rebels as prisoners of war, exchanging them, concluding of cartels, capitulations, or other warlike agreements with them; addressing officers of a rebel army by the rank they may have in the same; accepting flags of truce; or, on the other hand, proclaiming martial law in their territory, or levying war taxes or forced loans, or doing any other act sanctioned or demanded by the law and usages of public war between sovereign belligerents, neither proves nor establishes an acknowledgment of the rebellious people, or of the government which they may have erected, as a public or sovereign power. Nor does the adoption of the rules of war toward rebels imply an engagement with them extending beyond the limits of these rules. It is victory in the field that ends the strife and settles the future relations between the contending parties.

154.   Treating in the field the rebellious enemy according to the law and usages of war has never prevented the legitimate government from trying the leaders of the rebellion or chief rebels for high treason, and from treating them accordingly, unless they are included in a general amnesty.

155.   All enemies in regular war are divided into two general classes — that is to say, into combatants and non-combatants, or unarmed citizens of the hostile government.

The military commander of the legitimate government, in a war of rebellion, distinguishes between the loyal citizen in the revolted portion of the country and the disloyal citizen. The disloyal citizens may further be classified into those citizens known to sympathize with the rebellion without positively aiding it, and those who, without taking up arms, give positive aid and comfort to the rebellious enemy without being bodily forced thereto.

156.   Common justice and plain expediency require that the military commander protect the manifestly loyal citizens in revolted territories against the hardships of the war as much as the common misfortune of all war admits.

The commander will throw the burden of the war, as much as lies within his power, on the disloyal citizens, of the revolted portion or province, subjecting them to a stricter police than the non-combatant enemies have to suffer in regular war; and if he deems it appropriate, or if his government demands of him that every citizen shall, by an oath of allegiance, or by some other manifest act, declare his fidelity to the legitimate government, he may expel, transfer, imprison, or fine the revolted citizens who refuse to pledge themselves anew as citizens obedient to the law and loyal to the government.

Whether it is expedient to do so, and whether reliance can be placed upon such oaths, the commander or his government have the right to decide.

157. Armed or unarmed resistance by citizens of the United States against the lawful movements of their troops is levying war against the United States, and is therefore treason.*

*Official Records, Series III, Volume 3, pp. 148-164.

APPENDIX B

General Orders No. 11

General Orders
No. 11

Headquarters, District of the Border
Kansas City, Mo., August 25, 1863

I.   All persons living in Jackson, Cass, and Bates Counties, Missouri, and in that part of Vernon included in this district, except those living within 1 mile of the limits of Independence, Hickman Mills, Pleasant Hill, and Harrisonville, and except those in that part of Kaw Township, Jackson County, north of Brush Creek and west of the Big Blue, are hereby ordered to remove from their present places of residence within fifteen days from the date hereof. Those who, within that time, establish their loyalty to the satisfaction of the commanding officer of the military station nearest their present places of residence will receive from him certificates stating the fact of their loyalty, and the names of the witnesses by whom it can be shown. All who receive such certificates will be permitted to remove to any military station in this district, or to any part of the State of Kansas, except the counties on the eastern border of the State. All other shall remove out of this district. Officers commanding companies and detachments serving in the counties named will see that this paragraph is promptly obeyed.

II.   All grain and hay in the field or under shelter in the district from which the inhabitants are required to remove within reach of military stations after the 9th day of September next will be taken to such stations and turned over to the proper officers there, and report of amount so turned over made to district headquarters, specifying the names of all loyal owners and the amount of such produce taken from them. All grain and hay found in such district after the 9th day of September next not convenient to such stations will be destroyed.

III.   The provisions of General Orders, No. 10, from these headquarters will be at once vigorously executed by officers commanding in the parts of the district and at the stations not subject to the operation of Paragraph I of this order, and especially in the towns of Independence, Westport, and Kansas City.

IV.   Paragraph III, General Orders, No. 10, is revoked as to all who have borne arms against the Government in this district since the 21st day of August, 1863.*

By Order of Brigadier-General Ewing:

H. HANNAHS,
Acting Assistant Adjutant-General

---

* *Official Records*, Series I, Volume 22, Part II, p. 473.

APPENDIX C

General Orders No. 59

General Orders
No. 595th

Headquarters, District of Kentucky and
Division, 23d Army Corps
Lexington, Ky., July 16, 1864

  The rapid increase in this district of lawless bands of armed men engaged in interrupting railroad and telegraphic communications, plundering and murdering peaceful Union citizens, destroying the mails, &c., calls for the adoption of stringent measures on the part of the military authorities for their suppression. Therefore, all guerrillas, armed prowlers, by whatever name they may be known, and rebel sympathizers are hereby admonished that in future stern retaliatory measures will be adopted and strictly enforced, whenever the lives or property of peaceful citizens are jeopardized by the lawless acts of such men. Rebel sympathizers living within five miles of any scene of outrage committed by armed men, not recognized as public enemies by the rules and usages of war, will be arrested and sent beyond the limits of the United States, in accordance with instructions from the major-general commanding the Military Division of the Mississippi. So much of the property of rebel sympathizers as may be necessary to indemnify the Government of loyal citizens for losses incurred by the acts of such lawless men will be seized and appropriated for this purpose. Whenever an unarmed Union citizen is murdered four guerrillas will be selected from the prisoners in the hands of the military authorities and publicly shot to death in the most convenient place near the scene of outrage.*

By command of Bvt. Maj. Gen. S. G. Burbridge:

J. BATES DICKSON,
Captain and Assistant Adjutant-General

*Official Records, Series I, Volume 39, Part II, p. 174.

www.ingramcontent.com/pod-product-compliance
Lightning Source LLC
Chambersburg PA
CBHW050501110426
42742CB00018B/3326